BUSINESS TRAVEL
SUCCESS

How to
Reduce *Stress*,
Be More
Productive &
Travel with
Confidence

CAROL MARGOLIS

NEW YORK

BUSINESS TRAVEL **SUCCESS**

How to Reduce *Stress*, Be More *Productive* & Travel with *Confidence*

by **CAROL MARGOLIS**

ISBN 978-1-61448-129-4 Paperback
ISBN 9781614481300 eBook
Library of Congress Control Number: 2011937112

Published by:
MORGAN JAMES PUBLISHING
The Entrepreneurial Publisher
5 Penn Plaza, 23rd Floor
New York City, New York 10001
(212) 655-5470 Office
(516) 908-4496 Fax
www.MorganJamesPublishing.com

Cover Design by:
Rachel Lopez
www.r2cdesign.com

Interior Design by:
Bonnie Bushman
bonnie_bushman@optimum.net

In an effort to support local communities, raise awareness and funds, Morgan James Publishing donates a percentage of all book sales for the life of each book to Habitat for Humanity Peninsula and Greater Williamsburg.

Habitat for Humanity®
Peninsula and
Greater Williamsburg
Building Partner

Get involved today, visit
www.MorganJamesBuilds.com.

TABLE OF CONTENTS

ACKNOWLEDGEMENTS

Thank you to the thousands of travelers I have spoken with over the years, expressing challenges of being away from family, frustration with travel delays and ever-changing rules, and the never-ending search for a better way. You are the reason I started putting pen to paper to share my years of travel experience. I hope I can have a small impact on your Business Travel Success. To you I express my deepest gratitude.

To my many clients who gave me the opportunity to travel and see the world, thank you for seeing the value in my work and for continuing to bring me into your companies and onto your stage. I am honored by the trust you have placed in me.

To my colleagues and friends around the world, thank you for experiencing so many adventures together and for taking time from your busy lives to share your time when my travels land me in your part of the world.

To my editor, Athena Sargent, my vocabulary is not good enough to shower you with the proper superlatives. You peeked over my shoulder and fixed the frequent grammatical errors with precision. And you did so much more, serving as the first reader and offering many wonderful comments from the perspective of a traveler. The readers benefit from your insight, thoughts, and ideas. Your patience was exceeded only by your talent. I am eternally grateful.

• • • • •

My greatest thanks and heartfelt love go to my family.

To my Mom, for your endless love and concern as I flit around the planet. Your belief in my work, and sharing it with travelers you meet in your journeys, means the world to me. I love seeing you in a first class seat as no one deserves it more than you!

To my husband, Bruce … words can never express my gratitude and my love for you. It is such a joy to explore this great planet with you, and equally wonderful to spend time at home together. Your contributions to my inspiration and knowledge, your 100% support of everything I do, and standing side-by-side with me in this great life we share fills my heart with overflowing love.

To my children, David, Jenn and Michael, thank you for understanding my work and its requisite travel demands. Today you are all strong, independent adults with great values in spite of me not being there for all your school events and homework assignments. It warms my heart to see my love of travel within all of you.

To my dog, Toby, who for almost fifteen years always greets me with a wagging tail when I return home. I pray I see your excited eyes greeting me at the front door for years to come.

While I feel extremely privileged and fortunate to travel the world, my family will always be the reason I can't wait to return home.

FOREWORD

You may know me as the originator of the ***Chicken Soup for the Soul*** series, the author of ***The Success Principles***[TM], or you may have seen me in the movie, The Secret. You may not know me as a business traveler. And yet, I am most definitely that.

Over the past 30 years, I have traveled for business throughout the world. In the beginning days of the ***Chicken Soup for the Soul*** series, I was signing books in seemingly every town, large and small, throughout America.

I would pack my car full of books, drive to the next town, stay in a modest (also known as "low budget") motel room far away from my family, sign books in one or more local bookstores, pack up the car and start it all over again the next day. I did this for months on end in an endeavor to reach the masses with this series.

Fast forward to today with more than 500 million books sold: I speak to groups throughout the world on creating peak performance for entrepreneurs, corporate leaders, managers, sales professionals, corporate employees, and educators. I also host several events each year where people travel from all over the globe to be a part of my Breakthrough to Success series workshops.

I sit in the same airports as you, deal with the same flight delays, have challenges with eating healthy and exercising while on the road, balance being productive with jet lag, and struggle with family and staff communication when I'm half-way around the world.

When Carol shared some of her pearls of travel wisdom with me and the audience at one of my events, I realized that it required only a few simple solutions to alleviate many travel challenges. Even though I consider myself an experienced traveler, I learned several new travel tips from Carol that benefit not only me but my family as well.

In addition to quickly resolving many travel irritations, the tips and advice that Carol offers in *Business Travel Success* are extremely valuable to the people attending my seminars and events. My staff spends countless hours addressing travel-related questions prior to and during the events. Now they have a reference source.

I wonder how many more people might have attended if the issues of taking care of family, pets and home were addressed with the advice contained in this book, providing comfort and security to those leaving home for several days.

Just as important as the tactical travel advice offered in this book is the spirit of travel that Carol has. She lives by my principle of the E+R=O (EVENT + RESPONSE = OUTCOME) formula and invites you to do the same.

The Event can be anything such as nasty weather, delayed flight, noisy hotel neighbor, or your partner's behavior. In other words, anything and everything that is out of your control and may trigger you emotionally. It is our Response to the events of our travels that determines our outcomes, and over this we have 100% control.

Rather than stomp up to a gate agent and demand an answer to, "Do You Know Who I Am?" to get a desired response, I instead take advantage of the extra time offered by a flight delay to make a few phone calls, catch up on my reading or get to know someone who is waiting alongside me. I may arrive later than intended but I arrive with less stress and feel good about how I turned what is typically called "a travel nightmare" by others into an outcome that has been productive.

One such outcome that is etched in my mind forever is the response I witnessed by a fellow delayed passenger. Upon the announcement by the gate agent of a lengthy flight delay, this passenger went to the nearest airport store and came back with an armful of bottled water. He started passing these bottles out to fellow delayed passengers.

I looked at him and thought, "What a great way to turn a frustrating and stressful situation into magic." Sullen and unhappy faces instantly turned cheerful and smiling. Grumbling turned into positive conversation. It was an amazing outcome to watch.

I'm not suggesting that you replicate this act of kindness on your next flight delay (though it isn't such a bad idea) but that you consider your response and the possible outcomes that can arise as travel events unfold. A small shift in perspective can result in less stress and true enjoyment in your travels.

When dealing with any of the myriad travel nuisances, Carol, like me, knows that her response can turn an unexpected event into a positive outcome. This book is full of realistic responses – and often laced with humor – addressing concerns such as travel stress, easier packing, traveling safer, being on the road alone, communicating with family and friends, and maintaining trust in your relationships from across the miles.

Business Travel Success is the bible for business travelers, even if you only do one business trip a year. This book certainly will make you more knowledgeable, confident, and productive when you travel. While it is a wealth of information for all travelers, the book is also an invaluable resource for corporate travel departments, meeting planners, and those who manage business travelers.

A book like this would have been very helpful when I began my business travel many years ago. Nevertheless, I still was amazed at how much I learned from this book even after 30 years of traveling.

With the help of this book and the tips and strategies that Carol shares, I'm convinced you will achieve Business Travel Success!

—**Jack Canfield**
Co-author, *Chicken Soup for the Soul®* and *The Success Principles*[TM]

INTRODUCTION

"**R**eally, you fly to work?"

      I am asked this question frequently. The answer is yes, and there are a surprising number of other business travelers joining me each week.

To most people, the first thought that comes to mind thinking about those who fly to work are pilots and flight attendants. After all, this is how they make their livings.

But there is a whole business world out there joining them.

It is estimated that perhaps 50 million Americans travel each year for business. Indeed, the number was nearly 44 million back in 1998.[1] With business becoming more mobile and global, the numbers of business travelers are only increasing. Some travel every day, some a few times a week, some perhaps once a week, maybe once a month, or possibly once or twice a year.

According to a study by Oxford Economics, U.S. companies spent $246 billion for travel in 2008, responsible for 2.3 million jobs. Moreover, business travel was a key element in professional development (66%), job performance (58%), and morale (56%).[2]

Digging deeper into the Oxford study, their research is quite telling. For example, their measurements indicated that each dollar invested in business travel was responsible for an average of $12.50 in higher revenue and $3.80 in profits. The study warned, however, that severely reducing business travel would require three years of profits to recover.

Adding more data, the U.S. Bureau of Transportation Statistics reports that we make over 405 million business trips each year.[3] While most are relatively short distances (under 250 miles), that still leave many millions that are greater than 1,000 miles.

So who are these people? They might be consultants or salespeople, engineers or designers, marketers or product buyers, auditors or executives. They might be employees attending business meetings or conferences, or they might be artists who travel around to different shows and exhibitions.

For that matter, the list also includes many who work for the government directly or indirectly such as contractors, even member of Congress and their staffs. And the list certainly includes Federal Air Marshals.

And many who travel for business don't fly. For various reasons, they may travel by car or train but what all these people have in common is they travel for business. In any given week, tens of thousands of people earn their livings by traveling regularly in their occupations while tens of millions travel at least infrequently for business each year.

My husband explains it to people this way...

> On Monday morning, I put on my suit and drive downtown to work. On Monday morning, Carol puts on her suit, drives to the airport, and flies to work.

See, at first glance there really is no difference. After all, both of us are working.

But of course, there really is a big difference. Monday evening my husband returns home after working. For my Monday evening, I am in a hotel somewhere. This is where the challenges begin.

So why don't business people just use a telephone or email to communicate instead of traveling to some destination? Well, they do – and frequently.

There are many ways to communicate: Email, phone calls, Facebook, Twitter, Skype, etc. But have you ever tried a handshake over the phone? Connecting with others is more than just trying to communicate with them. Real connections happen only face-to-face.

Clearly in-person meetings are the preferred method. A recent study by *Harvard Business Review* confirmed the preference for direct contact meetings, noting that 79% believe it to be the most effective way to meet new contacts and 89% believe it is essential for closing deals.[4]

There are many benefits to reaching out and literally touching someone. Only by working with others directly can you apply the benefits of body language, the ability to use your other senses, and, as a British Airways ad says, an opportunity to have a "real foot in the door."

Connecting directly with suppliers, customers, and clients brings many rewards. For example, it is easier to present new ideas when working directly with someone. Much can be accomplished over a meal away from the business environment. Face-to-face contact in the business world increases the opportunity to build lasting relationships.

While business travel may be essential for success, that doesn't mean it is always pleasant. In 2009, Wakefield Research (wakefieldresearch.com) offered some insight into the road warrior family in a survey commissioned by Logitech.[5] We learned, for example, that nearly 3 of every 4 significant others left behind expressed concern about being left home alone. Almost 4 out of 5 worry about their spouse or mate when traveling for business.

These concerns include matters of health, personal relationships, and safety. Some argue that it is most difficult for the significant other left at home while the partner is traveling. I have lived on both sides and know that each can be challenging.

Often with nothing more than minor adjustments, business travel can not only be successful, but actually quite enjoyable. A study by the National Business Travel Association (now known as the Global Business Travel Association) noted that 62% of business travelers add at least some leisure time to one or more business trips each year. In addition, two-thirds of them include family members.[6]

As a business road warrior for the past 25 years, I am convinced part of the problem with business travel is lack of knowledge and preparation for living the life of a road warrior. I well recall trying to learn about not only the travel aspects but how to deal with matters of family, safety, and other concerns when traveling.

I learned a lot by trial and error. Eventually I learned some tips and shortcuts – many of them the hard way – but there was no single source to make this travel easier. Oh, if I only knew in the beginning what I know now.

No longer do you need to do this alone. Here I am giving you what I wish someone had given to me. Everything in this book is based on personal knowledge and experience and includes some of the best I can offer to business travelers.

This book is devoted to helping those who travel for business, and their families. All this information is relevant for anyone who may attend a conference related to their work or profession only once a year, just as it is for those who feel like they "live on the road."

Nevertheless, some travel considerations are different depending on whether you are attending a relatively brief business event or are a weekly road warrior like me. Business travel is broken down into four primary groups:

- Employees of business and government who travel, generally company paid excursions that are reimbursed (though perhaps subject to certain limitations)
- Client-reimbursed travel, which also might be subject to certain limitations
- Employees who attend business events occasionally but perhaps pay for the travel and events themselves
- Self-employed and small business owners who are required to pay for their own non-reimbursed travel expenses

For those working for firms, it is very important to know your corporate travel policies. To make it easy, I will refer to *corporations* or *firms* throughout the book but it applies equally to governments, non-profits, and all other organizations that have travel departments.

If you are new to travel, determine if your firm has an internal travel office or a recommended travel agent. Also, there may be certain constraints. If you are flying, for example, you may be required to use certain airlines or fly only the shortest or least expensive routes.

Another consideration is hotel restrictions. In some cases, corporations have travel agreements with certain chains that require you to stay at one of their contract hotels. Another possibility is a rule that you stay within a certain distance of your destination.

The same applies to car rentals. Some firms have contract arrangements that dictate which car rental companies may be used or the type of car you may rent.

This list could go on but I hope you get the idea that every company you work for may have travel policies and you need to know them fully. It would be sad if you learned them the hard and expensive way. Failure to follow their rules may result in your having to pay for these expenses out of your own pocket.

On one hand you have many more travel options if you are self-employed or otherwise don't have any travel restrictions imposed by others. On the other hand, you also may be more budget conscious. This is discussed throughout the book.

Regardless of which category applies to you, this book is loaded with tips and strategies to help reduce stress, be more productive, and travel with confidence. The book also addresses the concerns of those whom you leave behind when stepping out the door. By the end of this book, you will be a successful business traveler.

You may notice that some things are mentioned twice in this book. While they may appear redundant, there are a few reasons for this:

- Some items are appropriate in more than one section of the book
- Some are important enough to be said twice
- Some readers will not read the entire book
- Some may want to re-read those areas that apply to them before they travel.

Business travel certainly is challenging at times but reading this book, you will find that the travel is far from torture. Indeed, it can be downright fun if not outright funny. Though the primary purpose of this book is to educate, there are also many lighthearted stories.

Throughout the book are tales and anecdotes that happen when people travel. And yes, many of them are my personal stories. You might relate to some of these, and realize that others could have just as easily happened to you.

There are numerous references to various travel providers and products throughout the book. None of those mentioned should be seen as endorsement for any program or product. They are cited for example only.

I wish this book could include every tip and strategy I have learned over the years but *that* book would be well over a thousand pages. It was difficult to limit the size but as is, this book includes some of the best of what I have learned over the past 25 years.

To learn even more travel tips and strategies, please visit my websites:

http://www.BusinessTravelSuccess.com: Learn about our Business Travel Success seminars and more.

http://www.SmartWomenTravelers.com: Includes copious articles and videos dealing with ways to travel safer, smarter and with more enjoyment. Includes an online community for travelers and recommended travel products.

http://www.PearlsofTravelWisdom.com: My blog which offers helpful tips and my musings as I travel the world.

Here's to your Business Travel Success!

1

BUSINESS TRAVEL:
FROM ONLY ONCE A YEAR
TO TRAVELING EVERY WEEK

It's Saturday afternoon and I'm getting my nails done. Next to me is a woman who is crying . . . body shaking, tears running down her cheeks. Her manicurist is desperately trying to keep her client's hands steady as she applies the polish. The woman was frantic about a business trip she was leaving for the next day.

When I heard "business trip," I had to listen in. She had never left her 8-year-old son before and was worried about what might happen to him while she was gone. The child's dad (her husband) was going to be with the boy during this 3-day trip.

I could have rolled my eyes and said, "Get over it. It's only three days and he will be with his father!" but I didn't, because I understood. I know how much planning went into leaving my kids each week that I traveled and I know how much my heart wanted to be with the children instead of spending time in some far away city or town.

Business travel presents unique challenges to mind and body, requiring adaptation unlike anything else. For some travelers, it is seen as a necessary evil while others see it as opportunity, even excitement.

There is no broad brush to describe or define the business traveler, in part because of the wide array of frequency of travel. Some people hit the road only once or twice a year, usually for meetings or conferences. Others soar through the friendly skies a bit more often, attending seminars or workshops throughout the year.

Still others are away from home once a month, while other business travelers are gone every week. Some of these road warrior travelers move along to multiple destinations every week, staying at each only a night or two, while others stay at a particular location for a couple of weeks before moving on to another.

No uniformity here when it comes to frequency but there is still a common denominator: Traveling for business purposes.

Challenges for Small Businesses

Many business travelers do not work for large corporations, non-profits, or government. Instead they are part of the small business and self-employed arena. Thus it is no surprise that when these individuals need to travel for business, it may create additional hardships. Even if this is an online business, an owner who needs to commit time to traveling can't very well operate the business at the same time.

Some small businesses might be challenged because there are no other employees to handle certain tasks. For others, it might mean hiring temporary workers or even closing up a shop.

If this sounds like you, creating a travel policy is a must. Begin by thinking about what you are responsible for in the business. In other words, identify specifically what tasks you perform. I suggest writing them down so you can see them clearly.

For each of these tasks, write down who will be responsible for them in your absence. Who can help out when you are not available? The first choice usually is other employees. Next would be hiring temporary help but don't automatically exclude friends, relatives, or anyone else you trust.

Some businesses have "friendly competition" where someone who knows your industry could watch your business while you are away. Sometimes an employee at one company will temporarily work for another. You might find more opportunities by contacting your professional trade association.

Also think about designating someone to handle very important matters such as signing checks. A tip here, it would be a good idea to have this person bonded before allowing them access to your business funds.

When the travel policy list is complete, assign the tasks to employees and other trusted individuals as necessary. Voila, you are ready to hit the road!

As the owner of a small business – and a very frequent traveler – I can appreciate all these challenges. But think about what I just said. I figured out how to run a business while traveling nearly every week by doing exactly what I suggested above. I give you the tools so you can, too!

It can be done if you are willing to commit the time. The best part about having this travel policy is it also can be used for any reason you are absent or unavailable for work, such as an illness or vacation.

Single Purpose Business Travel

We begin with those who travel very infrequently for business. By definition, this would be someone who travels occasionally, no more than a few times a year.

Business travelers in this category may be meeting at a company's headquarters or company retreat at a resort. Members of this group also may attend an occasional convention, workshop, or seminar.

Many readers are probably thinking this is the easiest type of business travel. After all, it refers to someone who maybe travels only once or twice a year for business. Actually, this type of traveling is more difficult because the lack of frequency means a far greater chance for travel-related errors to arise.

While this portion of the chapter is devoted to helping those who travel infrequently, much of the content relates to others who also attend business group functions that often last up to a few days.

GENERAL TIPS

The business purpose often affects the travel plans. For example:

- Are you attending a 1-day meeting or is it a multiple-day conference?
- Do you have choices for your airline and/or hotel or are they pre-selected?
- Do you need a car rental? If so, check with the group organizers to see if they have a deal with certain companies. If not, use a travel agent or let your own fingers do the walking on the internet.
- Are meals included for this event? If not, where do you plan to eat, what are the meal times, and who pays for the meals?
- Are you reimbursed for expenses? If so, do you need to keep track of all expenses or are you traveling on a per diem (rate set by the day)?

In some instances, it is a combination. For example, you may need receipts for airfare and hotels but other expenses, such as meals and tips, may have a daily rate. The point here is to find out about your company's policies before you travel.

Some business travelers pay all their own expenses. Perhaps they are self-employed or maybe just attending an occasional conference in their area of interest. In other words, no one will reimburse you for your costs.

Conference Airfares

As for airfares, it is somewhat rare to get "corporate" rates. Nevertheless, I have attended conferences where the organizers have worked out discounts with certain airlines.

Generally, you want to take advantage of those airline deals even if the discount is only 10% or so. After all, it's your money. Before you book your airline tickets, however, consider this:

- Are the airlines offering discounts flying out of your airport? If not, it may mean a "code share" trip or flight booked with a different airline, which might mean a longer connecting flight if one is available at all. Indeed, a code share flight may cost more.

- What is the possible impact on your airline status (see Chapter 13 on Loyalty Programs)? This means that if you stay with one airline or its partners, you will achieve elite status with that airline much faster, but the lower airfare may be with another airline. You may have to decide if the discount is worth more than the miles that will get you closer to elite status with one airline.

- Can you find a less expensive flight – not to mention a nonstop flight – by working with a different airline altogether?

Conference Hotels

Hotels nearly always offer group rates for those attending conferences, depending on the size of the group and the number of rooms that will be used. Sometimes hotels may offer this discount only if the organizers guarantee a certain number of room rentals.

Just because a hotel offers a group rate doesn't mean it is the least expensive rate. I have seen instances where a hotel's group rate was actually higher than the rate offered to the general public.

However, there is one important difference: This highly discounted rate to the public may be non-refundable (ask if you're not sure). In other words, perhaps you don't make this trip or for whatever reason, don't need or use this hotel room. Well, you paid for it up front and the fee is non-refundable.

Some see this as an expensive gamble. Obviously the further away the actual event date, the greater the likelihood that something in your personal life could interfere with your ability to actually use these accommodations. There is a potential for big losses against savings that may be comparatively nominal.

On the other hand, some say it is worth the risk as long as you hedge this by buying travel insurance. My response: Any potential savings from the non-refundable rate is long gone after you add in the cost of the travel insurance.

Sometimes there are accommodations available in the same geographical area for less money. Smaller hotels/motels don't have the overhead of conference and meeting rooms plus other facilities that increase their operating costs.

TIP: Using Google Maps (maps.google.com), find the hotel where the conference is being held. Then type in "search nearby" for a listing of other hotels and their distances from the main hotel. Check for lower rates or better amenities at these nearby hotels.

Staying Where the Action Is

If it costs more, why stay at a location where a meeting is taking place? Two reasons come to mind: convenience and camaraderie. In my experience after attending hundreds of conferences/seminars/workshops over the years, I prefer to be as close to the main location as possible.

Some events include exhibit halls where you pick up samples, books, videos, or other items. If you have a room at the main location, it is easy to drop off those things in your room. If you stay elsewhere, it means carrying everything with you unless you have a rental car. This can become a real burden.

As for the camaraderie, it can't be beat at the host hotel. Many times after a meeting or seminar ends, attendees get together for dinner, discussions, or simply networking. Staying at another location means adding travel time between the two, sometimes an hour or more, which could mean arriving late or leaving early.

And don't forget, even if hotels offer group rates, the space is not unlimited. A certain number of rooms are available at that rate, but once they are gone, you either stay at that location paying a higher regular rate – if rooms are still even available – or stay elsewhere.

If you are sure there is another location nearby where the cost is less, feel free to make your reservation there but also do it as soon as possible. After all, if you are thinking like this, so are other people.

It is probably obvious but I will say it anyway: The larger the group event, the more important it is to make your travel arrangements early. I have failed to do this on occasion and paid dearly by needing to stay in a hotel miles away from an event. Yes, the accommodations were less expensive but when I added back the car rental or taxi cost, the end result was actually more.

Dress for the Occasion

What do you wear to a business event? The answer is... it depends.

I have been to some events where people wear shorts and t-shirts. Other events, people dress in business suits. At most meetings, the clothing is somewhere in the middle. Check with the event coordinator to find out about appropriate clothing for your event, though a business casual wardrobe is likely to be appropriate for the majority of events.

Nevertheless, there are some dressing tips worth mentioning:

- On your feet and walking most of the day? Wear comfortable shoes. You will appreciate this at the end of the day.

- Wear wrinkle-free clothing. Many or perhaps most hotels today offer an in-room clothes iron but really, is the purpose of your trip to unpack your clothing and break out the ironing board? Yeah, there may be some touching up of clothing but you certainly don't want to waste an evening ironing either.

As a coordinator of events in the past, I can tell you the single greatest complaint is that a meeting room is either too hot or too cold. There is definitely no way to make everyone happy about the room temperature.

- The best way to deal with this is to dress in layers. This means packing things like a lightweight shirt or blouse along with perhaps a sweater, jacket, or a shawl. You may need none of the outerwear or you may need all of it. However, this will ensure that you will always be able to get comfortable as the room temperature fluctuates during the day or evening.

- Check the weather forecast before leaving for those times when you'll be outdoors. No, it is not perfect and yes, they are sometimes downright wrong, but they are always your best chance to avoid over-packing. You probably could pick up an emergency sweatshirt or shawl at the hotel gift store but do you really want to take a chance, plus have more to pack when you return home and an unexpected expense?

Other Considerations

Here are some good general tips about traveling to conferences or similar events...

- Always either turn off your cellphone or at least set it to vibrate. Virtually all phones today are capable of that. One of the most irritating things while listening to a great speaker is hearing someone's cellphone ring. It has a way of bringing even a large room full of people to a halt.

- If you are the type of person who needs to go out of the room frequently, sit at the end of a row, preferably in the back of the room. The more you can make your exit without disturbing others, the better.

- Store somewhere in your mind that if you are in a different time zone, it is more difficult to arrange contact with work and loved ones back home. Before you leave for your trip, create a contact schedule that works for everyone.

Perhaps the most depressing part of attending business events like this is, well, it's for business. Finding time to "see the city" is often rare, if at all. Okay, I suppose that often applies to business travel generally, but we're talking about leaving home only for a business event here.

I have been to dozens of cities where I fly in, go to the hotel, attend the business event, return to the airport and fly away. For one event at a resort in Key Biscayne, I was there for four days and never saw the beach, even though the resort is on an island.

Some years ago, I was leading a seminar on the big island in Hawaii. I planned on hitting the beach on the day after the seminar. The weather, which had been perfect while I was teaching indoors for two days, turned to dark rain clouds on my beach day. My plans were all washed out. This happens sometimes.

When traveling to new locations, many travelers prefer to include time for sightseeing and learning about the local culture and customs. Consider adding a bit more time to the front or back end of the trip if possible. In many cases, hotels will honor a group rate for a few days before or after a business event, but of course, check out other accommodations as well.

Oh, That Budget Thing

Like others, I enjoy daydreaming about traveling to exotic locations so I understand how a budget can easily ruin the excitement. Sorry to include this in the beginning of the book, but you want to be realistic from the start.

When you look at the list of primary types of business travelers, it is easy to assume that those with the greatest budget constraints are the self-employed or the small business travelers. Yes, this is sometimes true, but then there are the exceptions.

For example, most business and government employees are often required to book their travel through their in-house or pre-arranged travel department. These travelers may face such constraints as a limited list of airline carriers or hotel choices.

Moreover, some travelers are limited by daily rates or per diem spending, meaning their budgets are limited to a certain amount per day for items that may include food or even overnight accommodations. In other words, any expenses beyond these predetermined amounts are typically paid for by the employee.

Obviously the greater your travel budget, the more options you have. But even if your budget is tight, there are many tips here to help stretch your travel dollars.

Booking Your Travel

When traveling for business, you usually do not have a choice about destination. You go where you are assigned, perhaps where your clients are located or simply to a specific destination for a meeting or conference. Regardless of where your travels take you, someone needs to arrange that travel.

Many companies today, including some government agencies, have their own corporate travel departments. It is not unusual for employees of these companies to book all their business travel through them.

Alternatively, some organizations allow employees to arrange their travel through alternative sources but may require travel department approval. Also note that if you are seeking client-reimbursed expenses, it is not uncommon for clients to require use of their travel companies and policies and perhaps get pre-approval on the itinerary. The point here is that there is no one universal system. Know the corporate/government policies thoroughly before any travel is arranged.

As for airline flight arrangements, note that many commercial travel agents no longer offer this service. Of the ones that do, most charge a fee. The reason is airlines stopped paying commissions to travel agents years ago.

Nevertheless, don't discount using agents altogether. They still have exceptional contacts in the travel industry and know a great deal about how to arrange flights, especially difficult connections.

Travel agents can quickly scan airlines for deals and promotions. Not only can they find you the least expensive flights but also the best connections. For example, you might not be aware that one flight will cost a bit less but may require a much longer layover. Agents can give you these alternatives quickly.

Most importantly, when you utilize the services of a travel agent you will have an ally to help you in the event of a travel disruption or need to reschedule.

Some business travelers prefer to arrange all their own travel. Generally they are more experienced travelers who are familiar with the many facets of travel and, of course, are not constrained by any company or client policies.

If you want to schedule your own flight plans, simply go to the airline website. Don't know which airlines fly to your destination? Try one of the many online travel sites such as Travelocity, Orbitz, Kayak or Skyscanner.

All airlines today offer an opportunity to book flights directly with them. The online process is very straightforward: Put in your travel dates and destination, they will give you a list of available flights.

 TIP: If your travel dates are flexible by a day or more, check the flights for other days. Tuesdays and Saturdays are typically less expensive than flying on Mondays and Sundays.

Sometimes airlines offer discount codes for business travel. This might mean a stipulation to use only certain airlines and it might be limited to only certain travel. Of course, it also might require booking only through a corporate or government site.

Sometimes these codes are used for all business flying; sometimes it is a unique code for a special event. If the latter, it is usually noted on the website of the organization sponsoring the event.

Caution! Do not book a flight unless you are certain of the dates and times. Once the flight is reserved, some airlines will charge you a change fee in addition to any change in airfare. Depending on the type of ticket you buy, some will allow up to 24 hours after booking for cancelling a ticket without charge, while other tickets, usually the more expensive ones, are fully refundable. Check and double-check everything before you make a commitment.

Travel Agent – Use or Not?

When I was considering the use of a travel agent for my own travels, I kept vacillating between "I can do it myself so fast" and "My time is better spent generating revenue."

To help me make my decision (and help you at the same time), I asked myself these questions and then searched out the answers.

Q: **Why in these days of online booking of everything should I use the services of a travel consultant?**

A: Online booking of travel may be the best way to go if you have a simple flight to book with no long list of special needs. Most importantly, you know what you're doing. When you add complexity with connections or different airlines, those with more knowledge and experience can be very helpful.

For example, a travel consultant may make more sense when an itinerary includes multiple stops. Also, if you have special needs (allergic to peanuts, pets, people, etc.), then a travel consultant can help ensure that your seats and/or flights are suitable for you.

If you are traveling internationally and concerned about connecting flights, tight connections, passport or health requirements, go to the expert on your team.

Q: **What can a travel consultant really do that I can't do myself?**

A: Besides what is mentioned above, they can also:

- Scout out lower prices than you may be able to find.
- Help with recommendations and prices on cruise bookings and most other forms of travel packages (guided tours, all-inclusive resorts, safaris, etc.) based on your personal needs and desires.
- Keep you in the know about luggage fees, luggage limits, TSA, travel rules in other countries, best times to travel based on weather, and more.
- Help resolve travel issues (cancelled flights, oversold hotels) and complex travel itineraries.

They do all this with personal service and expert knowledge.

Q: What do travel consultants charge to use their services?

A: The fees depend on the consultant. While some of the more luxury agencies have higher fees, the average fee is affordable. Some travel consultants may drop the fee or offer a discount once you have finalized your trip with them. Plus, you can always ask consultants upfront what their fees are and decide for yourself if it's worth it.

Your time is valuable, too. After considering the value of the hours spent searching for your own travel needs, travel consultant fees may seem very reasonable.

Q: What are the requirements for a travel consultant to become part of my "team of experts"?

A: Just a few minor requirements to fulfill:

1. They recognize who you are when you call. You don't want an agency where it is necessary to speak with someone different each time.

2. They know your preferences and type of travel.

3. They know the 1,000 places you want to see before you die, know where you have already been, and call you when they see a great deal to a place you desire to visit.

4. They book your cruises, hotels, and flights.

5. They provide recommendations for places to see, things to do, restaurants, etc., because they have already been there!

6. If they are not an expert in a certain area, such as finding a house to rent in the Greek Islands, they will find someone who is.

7. They offer reasonable fees and perhaps throw in a freebie now and then because you use their services so much.

Tipping

In the U.S., it is customary to tip many travel service providers. However, there is no universal agreement as to proper amounts.

Those who receive tips usually include taxi drivers, the outside skycaps who handle your luggage at the airport, and people who work in restaurants. The most frequent location for tipping is usually at hotels. There you have help with your luggage, valet parking, housekeeping, room service, concierge services, but may also include things like spa services, maybe even pool or daycare services.

For skycaps and those who handle luggage in a hotel, it is not uncommon for them to receive around $1-2 per bag, perhaps more if the luggage is large or heavy or there is something special about their services.

Valet parking attendants tell me they usually receive a couple dollars for cars they park or retrieve. I am sure some guests tip more while others pay less.

Tipping for housekeepers is the subject of debate for a couple of reasons. First, there is the matter of how much and then there is the question of timing.

Tips for cleaning a room usually range from $2-10 per day depending on how many people are using the room, how messy it is, etc. Some believe a tip in the $5-20 range is appropriate for the more expensive hotels and resorts. Regardless, better tips almost always result in better service.

As for the timing, I am one who tips the housekeeping staff daily. Others prefer to tip at the beginning of a stay (to encourage good service) or at the end of a stay (to offer thanks for good service). There is no right or wrong here but I tip daily because it is possible and very common that the services may be provided by different people each day.

Hotel room service is also difficult. Some hotels add a room service charge or delivery fee into the bill, usually in the 10-15% range but it can be as much as 20%. There is a lot of debate over whether this charge goes directly to the person who provides the service or whether the hotel simply keeps it as an additional fee.

Some hotels claim that the fee is split. In other words, the person who actually provides the service gets some but not all of the additional charge. How much each gets varies among hotels.

Many of the room service wait staff tell me that they get none of the delivery fee. If you are curious about this, ask a hotel manager to explain their procedure (I have found that most front desk personnel really do not know the rules).

Often the highest tip is reserved for the hotel concierge services. Generally, if you are only asking directions, no tip is expected. However, one of the reasons hotels offer a concierge service is because these are the people most familiar with requests made by guests and more importantly, they know how to get them taken care of for you.

If you want to know the best restaurants for a certain type of food, need help with procuring business services, or would like assistance in securing event tickets, usually this is in the $5-20 range, depending on service. This may be in addition to a service charge if they secure tickets to events for you.

Note: Some hotels complicate the tipping calculations by adding service charges to the room automatically. Usually it is around 10-20% daily and may be called a resort or administrative fee. Whatever it is called, the result is the same: You have an additional amount to pay every day.

If a daily fee is added to your room rate, does that cover all tipping? Generally no, at least not that I have ever seen. Tips are all in addition to the hotel's daily fee.

Just what do these daily resort fees cover? They may include internet charges, a daily newspaper delivered to your door, in-room coffee, a shoe shine, use of the hotel gym, and other various services. Ask at your hotel, and ask if you can have this removed if you use none of these included services. I have never been successful in getting them removed, but it's always worth a try! My mother and her sisters (in their 70's and 80's) actually had their resort fee waived in Las Vegas after they said "Do we look like we work out in the fitness center, get online or need our shoes shined?"

Given that so many in travel services depend on your generosity for their livelihoods, here's a suggestion: Always carry small bills with you. They are great for tips, you don't have to worry about whether a larger bill can be changed, and some places will not accept credit or debit cards. I usually start each week with twenty $1 bills.

One of my favorite tips on tipping comes from CBS travel guru Peter Greenberg. He carries around $2 bills and offers a couple good reasons for doing this.

The recipients are surprised because, frankly, no one gives them $2 bills. That alone is enough to make him stand out and be remembered. And because what he does is so unusual, Greenberg says he receives even better service than most.

The idea is very clever, though I admit to not trying it out yet. If this appeals to you, $2 bills are available at most banks.

2

PACKING

I spent years working on a system of traveling with only one carry-on size bag. If I showed you the bag I used in my early years as a business traveler (nicknamed the "Double Heavy" because one airline marked it with two Heavy tags), you would never trust my advice on packing only one carry-on bag. But that was eons ago when I was just a novice traveler. Oh, what I have learned since then!

When I begin talking at speaking engagements about packing for trips, the first thing I usually hear from the audience is, "Ugh!" Honest, this could be a book all by itself.

I understand, even more so as a woman. It seems almost like instinct to want to pack everything we own for a business trip. Obviously that is quite impractical. No, make that impossible. It is no surprise that *The Top 7 Tips for Packing Your Suitcase* is the most popular article on my Smart Women Travelers website.

If you are one of the few lucky ones who has an unlimited budget for travel and can take all your clothing and personal effects, this chapter is not for you. I do not personally know these people but I suppose rock stars and the like hire managers to take care of things like packing.

If you are a rock star, Welcome! My name is Carol. Have we met before?

You Wanna Pack WHAT?

Of course it is not always possible to travel without large bags. Sometimes they are necessary for longer trips; sometimes they are required for bulky clothing or extra items. Business travelers doing sales demos often need all kinds of accessories on the road.

Sometimes you just gotta pack the huge item that you have carried around on every trip since you were a baby.

There was even a survey done in 2010 that showed as many as one in every four grown men might just have a teddy bear tucked away in their suitcase to remind them of home.[7]

If you drive for business travel, feel free to pack your entire closet if you like. Load up the trunk and back seat of the car with whatever makes you happy and go on to the next chapter unless you want to learn some packing strategies.

Speaking of driving, many times my sewing machine would be in the trunk of the car on a driving trip because sewing is one of my hobbies. It was easy to bring this along when I drove . . . not so easy to carry through an airport.

If you use other methods of transportation, there are limits to what you can travel with. For ease, I am going to use the airlines as the standard rule for packing. Feel free to adjust these tips to your mode.

Flying is easily the most difficult because of baggage limits and fees for checked luggage. Currently, many (but not all) airlines charge fees for luggage that must be checked. However, because limits change periodically, check out each carrier's rules before you leave.

General Packing Tips

Let's begin with some general tips that apply to all travelers, no matter what your mode of transportation.

First, prepare a travel checklist of items you need to include. Even if you travel every week, it is easy to forget something in the heat of packing.

Your checklist might include items such as specific toiletries, medications, eyeglasses or sunglasses, and digital items such as phone, camera, GPS, or laptop. Obviously it would include the type of clothing you plan to pack.

A nice checklist tip is to include a section for the numbers of days you will be away and how many of these days are business vs. pleasure. This helps to determine the number of outfits for each that you need to pack.

A simple way to try to remember all your very important items is to count how many of them you are supposed to pack. Keeping that number in mind or writing it down, check to see that the number matches your total. This is not as efficient as a checklist but still works as a helpful reminder when you are packing for your return home.

Before beginning your journey, find out what may be available from your accommodations provider. Most, of course, provide linens and bath items including certain toiletries. Many today provide use of a hair dryer and clothes iron and some even include bathrobes and/or slippers.

Here are some more general packing tips:

- To the extent possible, take only permanent press clothing. Anything else and you might be ironing or running up a dry cleaning bill.

- Learn to mix and match your clothing. Here's an example: Select two shirts/blouses and two pairs of slacks or pants. Including what you are wearing, you just came up with nine combinations of clothing, enough for more than a week of travel! Create a new look each day with belts, scarves and jewelry for women, different ties for men.

- If you are mixing colors – like black or gray with brown – look for a reversible belt with black and brown. This saves packing an additional one.

- Layers are always important when traveling. Of course you don't want to pack a bulky coat unless absolutely necessary. Instead, pack your lighter layers and wear heavier items such as a sweater or coat.

- If flying, wear your heaviest clothing on the plane and remember to load up the pockets, too. Once you are on the plane, the heavy coat can either go in the overhead storage bin (if there is room) or be used as a blanket or even a pillow.

- Traveling with someone else and checking bags? In each person's bag, place half your clothing and half from the other person. That way if one checked bag gets delayed or lost, the other bag will keep both of you in clean clothes for a few days or more.

- Always check the weather before you go. Websites like CNN.com or Weather.com offer 5- and 10-day forecasts. They are not perfect but good enough to make clothing adjustments based on their projections. This is also helpful information regarding whether to pack an umbrella.

  When I arrive at the airport in Orlando in winter, I can easily spot those who didn't check the weather. They come out of the jetway ready to embark on their Disney vacation wearing shorts and flip-flops – in January when a cold front of 32 degrees has blown in. Their first stop: anywhere they can buy a sweatshirt!

- Keep two sets of all toiletries, one each for home and luggage. One stays in your travel bag permanently, coming out only when necessary for refilling or replacing. This way you only need to remember to pack the bag, not the individual items.

- Pack travel-size items such as toiletries in 3.4 ounce (100 ml) or smaller sizes so they meet the requirements of airport security. Unless you are planning a very long trip, there is no need to pack large size containers of toothpaste, deodorant, or hair spray. The travel-size equivalents are easily good for a week or more and save precious space in your luggage.

SUBSTITUTION TIPS FOR TOILETRIES

- Use packets of sugar (brown or white) to mix in with your facial cleanser to replicate a facial scrub.

- Mix in similar packets of sugar into your body lotion for a body scrub.

- Instead of using hair conditioner while in the shower, run a dime-sized amount of conditioner through your towel-dried hair.

- Buy a small bottle of spritz hair spray and refill from your full-size bottle when back at home to save money.

- Shampoo, conditioner, or a good lather of soap fill in for shaving cream.

- Baking soda can substitute for both toothpaste and deodorant, so bring along a small amount. For the toothpaste, dip your toothbrush into a small container of baking soda and brush. For deodorant, sprinkle a little baking soda onto a damp wash cloth and apply it to your underarms or dust it on dry. It'll keep you fresh throughout the day since baking soda absorbs perspiration and neutralizes odors.

- To prevent leaking of liquids, leave space at the top of the bottles for expansion during flight. Keep the containers in a tightly sealed, quart-sized bag so that no leakage spills onto your clothes. Also, keep an extra quart-sized bag tucked into your luggage in case your original bag decides to rip or not seal.

- Save on space by packing fewer garments and using laundry facilities while you are traveling. This works well for trips that last a week or longer. Instead of packing so much clothing, consider packing a couple of small, airtight bags filled with detergent and dryer sheets. Make each bag pre-measured for one load.

It is rare that I will do laundry on a 7-day trip but if I do, it will likely be on the 3rd or 4th day if necessary. If the trip is for a couple of weeks, laundry is usually done around the halfway point and each week thereafter for longer trips. I have quite a few business trips that last more than 30 days where this works out well. Most importantly, I can do all this with only a carry-on bag.

There are some business travelers who insist on carrying fresh clothing for each day of their trip. This is fine. Just note that you need to pack more and may be checking your bag because of it.

- Some business clothing, of course, requires dry cleaning. For extended trips, seek out a nearby dry cleaner. Most hotels offer this service as well, often with one-day service, but of course they may be more expensive than the shop around the corner.

- Never pack anything that will break your heart if it is lost or stolen. The first thing that comes to mind is jewelry, though it may also be something like an expensive camera.

  Whatever the item, it is never worth your valuable travel time worrying about it. For other valuable items, make sure they are insured. They might or might not be covered by your homeowner's insurance so check with your insurance carrier.

Regardless of transportation mode, place your name, itinerary and phone number *inside* your travel bags. Some people include their address. Note I said inside the bag, not on the outside. Include the address of your destination as well.

Placing that information on the outside of your bags tells the world not only that your home may be vacant but also the address of the empty home if you included that information. That is the last thing you want to do when leaving your home with no one to watch over it.

- For checked bags especially, consider sewing your contact info into the lining. Why? Well, it might seem like a stretch but it actually happened that thieves stole hundreds of bags from an airport and threw away everything that would have identified the owners.

It only takes a few minutes to add the peace of mind that if your bag is stolen, your information will remain with the bag. I know it is an unusual situation, but as I have said hundreds of times in my travels, stranger things than this can happen.

When I asked an agent from a major baggage claim office what the number one issue was with lost luggage, she said it was bags with no names. She said they search inside the bag for a name, even looking for prescription pill bottles, but often come up empty. Reduce the chance of your bag going to the land of lost bags by always ensuring your name is on the inside <u>and</u> outside of the bag.

TIP: Keep a photo of your bag in your mobile phone. In the event you have to file a claim on your bag, it's very easy to describe it if you have a photo.

Your Bag: Check It or Carry it On?

Whenever possible, avoid checking a bag when flying. There are lots of reasons, including:

- Far too much luggage never makes it to their destinations or is at least delayed, sometimes for days. Even if the luggage does arrive with the flight, there can be damage and sometimes even theft from the bags.

- If you are fortunate and your bags are not delayed in some other city, there is still the wait at the baggage carousel, usually 20 minutes or more. Even with special priority tags, I have waited over 40 minutes. All of this wait time is valuable time lost.

- Flights are often delayed or otherwise changed. Your bags may well be on their way to the proper destination but that does you little good if you are stuck in the airport or at a hotel overnight before resuming your flight.

- All airlines impose strict limits on coverage. Bottom line, never – yes, that's _N-E-V-E-R_ – place valuables, medications, or electronics in any checked bag. If an airline insists you check a bag, remove these items first.

If your carry-on is too large or there is insufficient space in an airplane, the bag will be checked. If it is an otherwise qualified carry-on because of its size, generally it is gate checked for free if there is insufficient space in the overhead compartments.

I have been bag-less overnight on a few occasions. One time I checked my bag in Boston after a multi-week New England fall vacation because I had both vacation and business clothes with me. The airline cancelled my flight due to mechanical issues and there were no further flights that day.

Even though the baggage was in the cargo hold of the plane that was sitting at the gate, the airline refused to return them to the passengers. I headed to my hotel bag-less with no clothing, no hair brush, no makeup, nothing. I was happy to find a hotel robe in the closet, until I opened up the robe to put it on and saw stains from the robe's previous occupant. Eeeww!

I really missed my own clothes that night. Two lessons learned here: If you do check a bag, at least bring a change of clothes in your carry-on AND always check that the hotel robe is clean!

Many travelers are selecting another option for luggage: Shipping their bags to the destination. UPS and FedEx offer this service but there are also luggage delivery companies that will pick up your luggage at home and deliver it directly to your destination accommodations.

Needless to say, this can be quite expensive. The costs to ship the boxes are at least as much as what the airlines charge – usually more – but some people love the convenience and knowledge that their belongings will arrive on time at their destination with less likelihood of damage.

Sometimes these services are necessary anyway. For example, it is common if you are working a trade show booth where many items need to be shipped ahead of time. Some companies have no problem adding your luggage to the pick-up list.

This works well for getting your luggage back home, too. More travelers today put their clothing in a box at the end of a trip and have it shipped home. It is nice to return home with lighter bags and no dirty clothing. Of course, you need to consider the shipping cost but there are some benefits to this, especially if you have been doing a lot of shopping!

I have shipped dirty clothes home after completing a marathon or other activity where some of my clothes are no longer needed (and I really don't want to smell them any longer!).

Another inventive traveler has clothing shipped directly to the dry cleaner back home. That's a great time saver, and the clothing is ready for pick-up when you get home.

Yet another traveler prefers sending clothing or other items back to a local UPS/FedEx office with a request to hold until pick-up. That achieves the same thing. For that matter, I suppose you could mail the package to your post office if you have a box there.

Why not just send the package back to your home? Because the package may arrive before you do and may sit outside until you arrive home. That's a great way to broadcast to everyone, including burglars, that no one is at home.

What Is the Best Way to Pack?

If I had a penny for every time someone asked me this question, I'd be flying in my own private jet!

There are numerous methods of packing with pros and cons to each. I have tried all of them, switching around depending on need and the mood at the moment. There is the following:

- Rolling Method
- Folding Method
- Bundle Wrapping Method
- Cube or Bag Methods
- Pack in the Sequence of Use Method
- Just-Throw-It-All-In Method
- Or a combination of the above

Searching for the first three methods online, you will find lots written on them as well as many videos. The other names are just my terms for what I see and hear about, as well as what I do sometimes.

Rolling Method

Some travelers insist that the best way to pack is to roll up clothing. Others prefer folding. I find rolling works very well with small items and synthetic fabric garments. Examples include slacks, skirts, sports shirts, jeans, t-shirts and workout clothes. It doesn't work as well with jackets and certain blouses.

Generally, rolling clothing takes up less room but be aware, even permanent press items sometimes need to be ironed. Nevertheless, the space savings can make up for that little inconvenience, and chances are if clothing is not rolled, you will be doing at least a little touch-up ironing anyway.

About half of my suitcase has rolled-up clothes.

Folding Method

In some cases, folding is the best. For example, most cotton clothing does not roll well. Well, it does, but you will be ironing when you reach your destination. Rolled up cotton can leave many visible creases.

Instead of folding each item individually like they are in your dresser drawers, fold multiple items together. This gives each item some cushion where they are folded, making it less likely to crease or wrinkle in the folds.

For example, take two or more slacks and lay half of one pair on top of the other. Fold the one on the bottom across the pair on the top. Then take the other and fold it on the top.

If you have a combination of clothing, use a combination of methods! Place your folded cotton and other clothing in the center of your luggage and surround it with those items that are easily rolled.

Some examples include underwear, socks, t-shirts, etc. The rolled items can fill out the bag and minimize your luggage needs. Don't forget to fill your shoes with clothing or other items so no space is unused.

Bundle Method

I think of this as the "hobo" method. I picture myself holding a pole over my shoulder with a bundle of clothes all tied up in a red kerchief.

Basically, the bundle method is a way to make one big square bundle out of all of your clothes. It cushions each item so no big creases result.

This method offers some practicality when unpacking your luggage all at once, not so practical if you need one item that happens to be stuck deep in the center of the bundle. If this description doesn't make much sense to you, refer to the **Business Travel Success Ultimate Travel Resource** for links to online videos for the how-to of bundling.

Bags or Cubes

Many travelers swear by packing cubes, square or rectangular mesh-type bags (or even the plastic bags that your bedroom sheets came in). They are great for organizing clothing into separate compartments.

There are large size cubes for slacks and jeans with smaller sizes for shirts, t-shirts, underwear and socks. If your dresser drawers are all neatly lined up, these organizational cubes may be to your liking, especially for keeping together smaller items that tend to go helter-skelter, like underwear and socks.

Other packers prefer the plastic compression-style bags, the most famous being the Space Bag. After the garments are placed inside, either a vacuum or a method of rolling is used to take out all the air from the bag.

Because most travelers do not have a vacuum at their destination, this might be impractical. However, the style where you can roll out the air may be prefect for you. Think big Ziploc bag that you close and squish out the air.

These bags can be great for multi-week travels where maximizing the inside space in your luggage is important. By taking the air out of the bag, it minimizes the unused space in the luggage.

Pack in the Sequence of Use Method

For those who travel to a new location every day or two, your suitcase is probably never fully unpacked. You may want to roll or fold items in the sequence that you'll be wearing them, making it easy to pull out just what you need.

Just-Throw-It-All-In Method

I suppose this also could be called the I-Don't-Care-As-Long-As-It-Gets-In-The-Bag method. For those who just don't care what clothing looks like at their destination, this is perfect. It is also a trip-saver for those who failed to pack the night before or overslept in the morning.

Actually it is not uncommon for business travelers to use this method when returning home. Since everything needs to be cleaned when the trip is finished, do you really care how wrinkled everything is?

Other Packing Tips

Some travelers suggest taking older clothing that you actually leave at your destination. This used to be a favorite for those traveling to Europe with blue jeans. Years ago they could be sold for much more than what you paid for them. Today, think in terms of donating such clothing if you are inclined to leave it behind.

Think ahead to souvenirs and clothing items you may pick up during your travels. Leave extra space for them before you begin your journey.

Use Ziploc plastic bags for any items that could leak or possibly break in transit (hair spray, hair mousse and perfume are the items that I've had major accidents with in a checked bag).

Use dry cleaner bags over your business clothes to keep a few more wrinkles away – and also keep them protected from any leaking liquids.

Do not overpack your bag. If your luggage gets selected for inspection, airport security screeners may have a difficult time closing your luggage. Items may be lost, damaged or end up with extra wrinkles. On the other hand, fill your bag sufficiently so that your clothes don't shift during transit; this keeps them more organized.

If checking a bag is necessary, keep it unlocked. If your bag is selected for screening, airport personnel will break the locks to get inside. Skip the locks to avoid any damage to your luggage and instead use plastic cable ties, twist ties or a small key ring.

What about TSA-approved locks? They are a great idea in theory and actually do work - sometimes. You have a combination or key lock and TSA has a standard entry system to open up the lock even without having your code or key.

My experience has been one of *now you see it, now you don't*. Each time I have used a TSA-approved lock (after spending money to buy it), my luggage comes off the conveyor belt minus the lock. I think someone in the airport must be collecting them as souvenirs.

An inexpensive alternative that works pretty well are twist ties. Carry a few extras in your bag for that time when one comes up missing.

When Is a Good Time to Pack?

The best time to pack for a trip can be any time before your travels begin, but there are some practical reasons to complete as much as possible the day or evening before the trip. This is especially true for trips that begin early in the morning. The last thing you want to think about before leaving is remembering if everything is packed. Instead, use those last moments to go through your checklist.

This system works just as well when leaving the destination city. Pack as much as you can the day or evening before you leave. Clean out as many drawers as possible beforehand. Why? Because most items left behind by travelers are usually found in drawers and closets.

If you only need one day's clothing before leaving, place it on a chair instead of in a drawer. That way you can be sure the drawers are cleaned out and of course, there is little chance you will go outside without wearing that clothing sitting on the chair!

Luggage and Laptop Bags

Business travelers typically have multiple bags and decide which to use based on business needs for the trip and the length of stay. There are so many types and styles of luggage, but that's a good thing because there is something to satisfy everyone's individual needs. Here are some of the variations.

We'll start with the **laptop bag**. They might be shoulder style, rolling case, or backpack. These bags are easy to find in nylon or leather as well as in hardcover cases. Leather bags tend to be more expensive, sometimes much more so.

The type that fits on your shoulder is very practical and easy to maneuver. However, the disadvantage is that it might be heavy, and carrying it for extended lengths of time may be something of a chore.

Different features set the various laptop bags apart. Here are a few things to look for:

- Pockets. They are very useful for business travelers. Look for at least two exterior pockets, one in the front and one in the back. Each pocket serves a specific purpose. For example, the front pocket may be used for boarding passes while the rear pocket is good for holding business receipts.

- Separate sections inside the bag. These are great for magazines or a notepad as well as accessibility to pens, business cards, eyeglasses, keys, snacks, etc., and to small accessories such as flash drives and extra batteries.

- Strong bag strap. Some straps are thin and feel awkward on the shoulder. Look for one with a thick strap that is comfortable, preferably with adjustable padding that fits nicely across the shoulder. Also check out the connections between the strap and the bag. They should be strong and secure.

- Separate padded compartment for a laptop or similar electronics such as a tablet. The padding should be thick and the inside straps made of something secure, like Velcro. Bonus points if the compartment is removable and has handles.

Rolling style laptop bags have a few advantages. They take the weight off the shoulder and they roll. Also, many of them are larger than shoulder bags. That means an option to pack more in them. A few bags offer a separate section for clothing, possibly a great one-bag alternative if your trip is only one or maybe two nights.

However, these bags are disadvantageous when lifted. Since they are larger – and have heavier components, including wheels – they can become quite heavy, perhaps 20 lbs. or more. If you have to carry these bags up and down steps or lift the bag over your head to put it in the plane's overhead bin, the stress can be noticeable quickly.

There is a third style of laptop bag becoming more common among some business travelers – the backpack. Many of them include compartments for laptop computers or other electronic devices, and some include a section for clothing.

There are some shoulder bags that can convert to a backpack style. They have an additional strap often hidden in the underside. When weight and balance are considerations, this might be a good alternative.

The next piece of luggage is the **carry-on bag**. There are many sizes and styles but they are generally sized to comply with airline regulations. That is, these bags are no more than 22" tall. Some have two wheels while a few of the newer models have four or eight wheels, called "spinner" bags.

TIP: "Spinner" bags are great for navigating into a non-luggage-friendly airport bathroom stall. Slide the bag in sideways and you'll actually be able to close the door without feeling like you need to stand on the toilet to do so!

Some travelers prefer a smaller carry-on bag, say around 18". This is a great choice as long as your packing needs are somewhat minimal. Others like the additional room in a 20-21" bag. The latter is a good choice for a couple of reasons.

First, it meets nearly all of my airline carry-on needs. Second, sometimes the 22" bags are too large for airline overhead compartments. Here's why:

- Older style aircraft where the depth may be a bit shy of 22". Of course, some planes, such as regional jets, have very minimal overhead space so those bags nearly always need to be gate-checked anyway.

- Manufacturer variance. Some do not include the height to the top of the handle in the overall length measurement (for example, some bags claim to be 22" but in fact are more like 23-24"). These bags often will be just a bit too long to get in many overheads. Putting the bag in sideways is an option, though there may not be sufficient available width in the overhead bin. The result is the bag has to be gate-checked, frustrating at best and possibly causing you to miss a connecting flight at worst.

Like bags for laptops, the carry-ons are available in either nylon or leather but there are more color choices. However, you need to be careful with leather here.

Because the material is more sensitive, leather is subject to greater potential wear and tear. If the bag needs to be checked, the possibility of bag damage is increased.

Look for features in a carry-on bag similar to that in a laptop bag. For example, three exterior pockets are very helpful. However, some manufacturers use the exterior space on the rear of the bag for handles. You give up an exterior pocket to gain space inside the bag.

The front pockets should include a smaller one for items such as sunglasses or boarding passes, while the larger pocket is ideal for items such as an umbrella, clothing, or a smaller fold-up tote bag. Sometimes it is perfect for a laptop. If a rear pocket is available, it is ideal for things like magazines and business receipts.

 TIP: Do not place your car or house keys in a pocket of a checked bag. What if your bag is delayed or lost upon your return home?

If your choice is a nylon bag, there are many variations in quality. For a better, stronger bag, look for one with a high thread count that is water-resistant.

The wheels are often the first thing to fail on a rolling carry-on bag. Sometimes it is because of the construction of the wheel, sometimes because of the way it is secured to the bottom of the bag. Look for excellent construction and balance with waterproof inline skate wheels.

If you plan to travel more than once or twice a year, consider staying away from many of the inexpensive bag sets. Their wheels (and zippers) may have you cursing by the end of your first trip.

TIP: Looking carefully at carry-on bags, you will notice that most have a side handle on either the left or right side. This is an issue of belated thought to many business travelers who use one hand to grab the top handle and the other to grip the side handle when lifting the bag into an overhead bin. Make sure your side grip is on the correct side for your needs. .

Weight is another consideration. There is a difference of more than 2 lbs. between the heaviest and the lightest. Since most use similar outer material (though quality varies), the difference is primarily in the construction and handle. Some use steel, others use aluminum, and there may be some using carbon fiber. If weight is important to you, check out a number of bags before settling on a choice.

Another great feature seen in many carry-on bags is that they are expandable. Most have an additional zipper that inflates the inside depth of the bag, often eliminating the need for a larger bag. However, this nice feature may be a downside if you are flying.

The general limit to carry-on bag thickness is 8-9". When the zipper is used to inflate the size of the bag inside, it is very possible you may exceed this limit, even if the length is within the guidelines. For that matter, it is possible to exceed the limit on any bag where a front pocket is so stuffed that the size exceeds 10". That's not to say this is not a handy feature. I have used it many times and it has kept me from needing a larger bag. However, if the bag is too thick to fit into the overhead compartment for airline travel – or if it's too heavy to lift into the overhead – then the bag needs to be checked.

There is a newer style of carry-on bag that is gaining popularity. It is a hard-side style often made of polypropylene, making it very lightweight. These are wonderful bags but they typically have no exterior pockets. Because of the practicality of exterior pockets, that's a dealbreaker for some.

The insides of carry-on bags vary widely among manufacturers. Some include a small pocket or two while others may include a removable garment attachment. With so many styles, it is impossible to cover everything here. It's best for you to check them out yourself and see which meets your individual needs.

Next is the **large bag**. They begin at 24" but some are larger than 30". While I have gotten by with a 20" carry-on for business trips longer than a month, there are times when it is necessary to travel with a larger bag.

For example, a business trip may include a leisure portion that requires totally different types of clothing. Also, a large bag may be necessary for heavier clothing or bringing home souvenirs.

The larger bags are essentially similar to carry-on bags except, of course, they are larger. The criteria for quality is the same as for carry-ons. Look for good construction, exterior pockets, handle on the correct side, quality wheels, etc.

But the larger bags have some advantages because, well, they are larger. Some include pockets for shoes or other items, there are more mesh pockets inside, and removable garment attachments are common.

Most travelers want to avoid checked bags, especially if flying, because of the fees. However, if it is necessary to travel with a larger bag, better to have one that is really large. It costs less to pay the airlines for one large bag than for two smaller ones.

 TIP: Check the quantity and weight limits for bags with each airline. The quantity may be two or three while the weight limit is generally about 40-70 lbs. per bag. This varies depending on airline, destination, and flight specific weight limit rules.

Another option for travelers is a luggage cover. There are a few manufacturers who offer covers that fit over bags to keep them clean and supposedly undamaged. I have not used them myself but for those who are concerned about exterior damage to a bag, this is something worth looking into further.

While I typically fly to work for business, I realize not everyone else does. For those who drive for business travel, larger bags may well suit your needs. Most fit easily in the trunk of a car and of course, you can pack much more.

It is very easy to overpack and get carried away here. Remember, you still need to get the luggage inside once you reach your destination. Moreover, some accommodations do not provide elevator service. Pack what you like but don't forget that you may still have to carry everything you are packing.

Luggage Tags

No one ever expects to lose or misplace their luggage, but the more you travel, the more likely it will happen at some point. *I am knocking on wood as I write this as I've had my bags delayed on multiple occasions but never lost.* Luggage tags can be a lifesaver in these cases. Of course, tags won't help if a bag is stolen, but if you leave a bag on a train or aircraft, the tags tell the finder how to contact you.

Some travelers use the luggage tags sitting on the airline check-in desk – those little paper tags you quickly fill out at the last minute when you realize your bag has no tag on it. While these are better than no tag at all, they can easily come off the first time in use. At a minimum, fill out a second tag with your info and tuck it inside your luggage.

Most travelers simply use the tags that came with the bag when purchased. They typically provide a place to enter your name, address, and maybe a phone number. Most of the tags attach to the bag with a strap but some of the better bags include a slot on the outside of the bag that keeps the information from being viewed by everyone else.

Straps have a few downsides. They are known to either tear off or be taken off. I can't give any reason why someone would remove them but it is a frequent complaint from airline passengers that when they retrieve their checked bags, the tags are missing. Even a leather strap may become shredded after being checked several times.

In any case, tags are most secure on a bag using a metal ring-style attachment instead of a strap. Most any kind of small ring works well. Assuming your luggage tag has a pre-punched hole on one end, slide the tag into the ring, then attach the ring to the end of the handle where it is thin.

If you use the tags provided with the bags, consider not including your address. Alternatively, if you want to use an address, use that of your business. You might not want others to know your address, much less that you are traveling.

Another option: If you are a member of a frequent flyer program, include your airline and member number on the tag. It can be traced through the airline to find your personal information such as name, address, phone number.

If you have elite status with an airline, they may supply you with status tags. The better ones have no names, instead using barcodes with your personal information that can be read only by the airlines. These are nice in that none of your personal information is available to anyone else, including your name. Anyone who finds your bag can simply turn it in to the airline. When the tag is scanned, they know how to contact you.

Many travelers prefer using a business card as a luggage tag. If the bag is misplaced, there is sufficient information for the finder to locate you without providing too much personal information.

Some luggage grips include a space on the inside where you can add personal information. This is nice because it is out of sight, and if you select a unique color for the luggage grip, it is easy to spot.

In all cases, include the necessary contact information inside the bag as well. This is very important if the exterior tag is missing or perhaps illegible. Business cards are great to keep inside all bags but at the very least, make sure there is sufficient contact information inside in the event it happens to you.

A few years ago, my mother and her sisters were traveling to Europe for a cruise. Their luggage, all checked, did not arrive as planned nor did it arrive before the cruise took off – or on the first few stops of the cruise.

Their bags finally arrived halfway through the cruise. While they were sick of washing out their one set of clothes each night, they were happy that they had placed the cruise itinerary inside each of their bags. The airline was able to track down the ship and have their bags delivered to them, and they were happy to finally wear something different each day!

Packing for Women

Ask 100 women what their biggest packing challenge is and 99 will say it is shoes, shoes, shoes! (The remaining one woman must have been snoozing when the question was asked.)

Let's go through several packing tips for non-shoe items and see if we can leave ample room in your bag for your must-have footwear.

It took me several years to really get suitcase packing down to a science but I continue trying out smaller containers or new tricks in my quest for constant and never-ending improvement.

Here are some tips that may work for you:

1. Decide on a color scheme for your trip. Pack slacks and skirts that you can wear twice, rotating them during the week (for example, black slacks or skirt worn on Mon/Wed; gray pants worn on Tues/Thurs) with varying colored tops, blouses and jackets, scarves or belts. Reversible skirts are also great because they can be worn twice with different tops for an entirely new look.

2. Camisoles are great for under jackets and take up almost no space at all in your luggage. They are a great look under an opened blouse on one day (wear the blouse buttoned on another day). Camis are also very easy to wash out in a hotel sink.

3. A shirt worn under a sweater or jacket on one day may be worn alone on another day and is also great for switching from business clothes to casual clothes.

4. Select a few pieces of jewelry that can be interchanged with the above clothes, giving a different look each day. Have a small jewelry pouch to keep things together and prevent tangling or use snack-size plastic bags for each item. I put only costume

jewelry in my bag so that if I do end up checking it, I am not worried about my valuable jewelry disappearing.

TIP: Leave the larger, metallic jewelry items or belts for a non-flight day, otherwise you'll spend valuable time removing them when going through the security lines..

- *More tips:* Here are a few ideas for keeping necklaces from being a tangled mess in your bag:
- Get yourself a few straws (McDonald's has nice, fat straws), cut them to a little less than half the length of the necklace chain. Drop one end of the chain through the straw and clasp the chain shut.
- Flatten an empty toilet paper tube and hang several necklaces in each one, clasping the chains shut.
- Use the tiny Ziploc bags that extra buttons come in when you buy clothes. They're great for holding a thin necklace or a pair of earrings.

5. Toss a shawl into your laptop tote instead of your luggage. It'll keep you warm if the plane feels cool and it's a great item to dress up your outfit in the evening. Like skirts, there are reversible shawls that do double-duty for new looks.

6. If your luggage does not have a fold-out section for you to lay out your clothes, then roll or fold up your items as discussed earlier.

7. Create a permanent travel bag of makeup items — small kabuki brushes, neutral colors of eye shadows that can match virtually any clothing, a powder blusher, a couple of neutral lipsticks and mineral makeup (a great non-liquid makeup). This small bag of non-liquids can just stay in your bag for future travels. And it's small enough to toss into your laptop tote in case your checked bag goes astray and you end up spending a night in a hotel room with no luggage.

TIP: I love the "bonus time" at cosmetic counters for picking up very small sizes of facial products, eye colors, blushes and mascara as well as small carrying cases. Plus it's fun to try new products!

8. Place a family photo (in a plastic frame, not glass) or a recent greeting card into your bag for displaying on your hotel room nightstand. This requires little luggage space but really enhances your hotel experience by making you feel connected with home.

9. Follow the Substitution Tips for Toiletries from earlier in this chapter to further scale down on the items you pack.

Okay, how are you doing on shoe space now? Hopefully much better since you reduced the amount of clothing, cut down on liquids and makeup, brought only the jewelry that you're going to wear and moved your shawl over to your laptop tote.

So how many shoes do you bring? If you go with a color scheme of one or two colors that work well together, the shoes on your feet on the day you travel may be all you need.

Heresy, you say!

All right, toss in shoes for working out as well as flip-flops for walking around your hotel room (and showering in them, as many travelers do). Add a pair of sandals – either dressier for evenings or casual for weekend wear -- and you should be all set.

If a lot of walking will be required, for instance at a convention, focus on comfort and have two pairs of shoes that can be rotated every other day.

Make the best use of shoes, stuffing small items (maybe your jewelry in the snack-size plastic bags or socks or hose) into them. Use shoe bags or hotel shower caps to cover the shoes. This way the dirty soles never come in contact with clean clothing.

Packing for Men

Men have unique packing concerns as well. Unlike women, men often need to travel with bulkier clothing, like suits, and their shoes are larger. While suits can be folded, they almost always need at least some pressing upon arrival. Dress shirts also do not lend themselves well to rolling up. It can be done, but expect them to need touching up as well.

For those men who can travel with permanent press clothing, it is much easier and often eliminates the need for a large bag. Many clothing items can be rolled while others can be folded neatly.

If your business travel requires non-permanent press items such as suits or dress shirts, you may want to consider something like a garment bag. These bags are designed to allow travelers to place items in the bag while limiting wrinkles.

Garment bags are often capable of fitting a few suits along with casual shirts and slacks. Rather than folding up the clothing, the items are placed in the bag on hangers and generally maintain their shape very well.

Some men simply prefer the ease of garment bags even if they travel only with shirts and slacks. If they are packed well, there is minimal wrinkling, and the clothing can be hung up immediately at the destination.

There are some airline-size carry-on bags that include garment attachments. These are fine if you have only a couple of suits or a few shirts. However, there may not be sufficient space for additional clothing because of the bulk.

There are some men who are okay with folding their suits. You can easily find a few videos online showing the proper way to fold a suit and place it in a carry-on bag with a minimum of wrinkling.

Note that larger garment bags might need to be checked as baggage if you are flying. Some of the smaller, non-wheel garment bags might qualify as carry-ons, but the larger bags, especially if they have wheels, are usually too large for an overhead compartment, not to mention they can be quite heavy.

Just how much can you get into a qualifying airline carry-on bag? That depends, of course, on the type of clothing you need. If the clothing is permanent press, it is possible to easily pack a week's worth in a carry-on bag.

Like women, men will fill their bags quickly if they pack too many shoes. For some, three pairs of shoes are necessary but that takes up a lot of space. Of course, you can minimize that by filling your shoes with anything possible such as socks, underwear, maybe rolled belts and ties.

Men would do well to pack similar to women. That is, color coordinate your outfits. For example, you may have a few shirts that can be worn with a pair of slacks. Changing the slacks to another color gives you an entirely different outfit.

My husband created his own travel system. If he needs 2 or 3 suits, he usually wears one and packs the others in a carry-on bag. If he needs more suits, he uses a rolling garment bag. With or without suits, it is generally easy to pack a week's worth of clothing in a carry-on bag.

For longer trips where a larger bag must be checked, he does one other thing. He always packs toiletries and a change of clothing in his carry-on bag. This is much appreciated foresight when a flight is canceled and he is in a city overnight while his luggage is held captive at the airport.

Like many other business travelers, my husband has multiple travel bags, depending on need. For luggage, he prefers a 21" carry-on whenever possible. His bag includes a garment attachment, and for trips up to a week or so, this is usually the only bag he needs. Because of the small size, it is perfect in the event of problems such as a canceled flight or a change in itinerary.

When a separate laptop bag is necessary, he uses either a rolling laptop case, shoulder laptop bag, or a backpack. No preference here; just depends on destination and purpose of the trip.

For longer business trips, he usually replaces a carry-on with a large garment bag. For long, casual trips, it might be a 26" bag. The large bag is handy on some overseas trips where only one carry-on is allowed since it has extra space for souvenirs.

Where do we store all these bags, you ask? One spare bedroom's closet is filled with our various luggage options, and many bags do fit inside another. We also keep our travel accessories in this same location.

Conferences, Meetings, Seminars, etc.

There are a few things you want to remember to pack when traveling for business purposes. The first thing is always bring business cards. Lots of them.

Regardless of whether the event is for a brief meeting or a multi-day convention, always have enough cards on hand. Whatever you think you might need, double the amount. This is one of those things where it is better to have too many than not enough.

I typically fly to business events but even when I drive, there is always a stack of business cards with me. I give them out to many people besides those I am meeting. These include airline and hotel personnel as well as seatmates on a plane. Some flight attendants remember me simply because of the logo on my Smart Women Travelers, Inc. business card.

The purpose of the business trip will dictate what you need to bring but here are a few additional things to think about:

- Meeting rooms are either too hot or too cold so pack layers of clothing to minimize this problem. Something lightweight plus a sweater, shawl, or jacket will do in most cases.

- Full tablet of paper for taking notes. This is extremely helpful for meetings and seminars, less helpful for conventions where most of the time is spent walking around. Nevertheless, there are times even at conventions when it is necessary to write things down. The benefit of using a tablet of paper is that it keeps all your notes in one place.

- Sufficient number of pens and perhaps a few different-colored highlighters, as well as colored pens. A calculator is another handy tool.

- Digital audio recorder. Some events allow personal recordings of meetings and seminars. I still take notes to highlight certain comments but it is helpful to have a full backup to review after the event.

- Small travel video recorder. This is used mostly for conventions for recording a product demonstration. In other words, there are times when video says a lot more than audio.

For all events, check with the event coordinator or the individual who is speaking before doing any audio or video recording to ensure it is permissible. It is their show so their rules will apply.

Your mobile device may replace a few items listed above and reduce your packing needs. Be sure to have your device fully charged before heading into the event. Meeting rooms and convention centers often drain the battery life of a smartphone quickly.

- Foldable bag for trade shows. For those who collect brochures and pamphlets at trade shows or some conferences, the bag holds lots of material in one place and helps keep information organized. If you are unable to carry the bag on your return trip home, consider either checking it as luggage or shipping it home.

- Power adapters for your equipment. That could mean cords for your phone, computer, camera, recorder, etc. It makes for a painful trip when you watch the re-chargeable batteries die one at a time.

- Extra batteries. Most small electronic appliances use either AA or AAA batteries. Whether replaceable or rechargeable batteries, always pack a few extra.

- Extension cord. This can be used for a laptop computer or other small electronic device where your battery may die long before the event ends.

While a little more expensive than a standard extension cord, there are a few "travel size" extension cords on the market. They are lightweight and extremely compact. The one I use is less than 5" long and includes 3 outlets.

This means you can plug electrical items into one convenient location instead of getting on your knees under a desk or unplugging a lamp. A benefit – or downside, depending on how you look at it – is that the cord is very short. Great for travel, maybe not so great for sharing with others.

If you have an extension cord, others will appreciate it if you let them use one of the connections for their devices on your cord. It is a nice way to help other attendees and make new friends.

Note that most meeting rooms do not have nearly enough power outlets. Some rooms have addressed this by including outlets in the floors or even in the tabletops, but they are the exception.

When outlets are available, they are most often along the walls. That means getting a seat nearby so you will have a power source.

Be very careful with power or extension cords. If you are in a high traffic area where people need to step over your cord, do everything possible to minimize risk to them and your power source. No one wins if they are injured tripping over a cord or if they pull the cord to the point that it drags your device off the table.

If you are a presenter or exhibitor, there are many additional things to pack. Every person has different needs, but some things that come to mind are 3x5 cards, notes, your own microphone, laser pointer, duct tape, handouts, PowerPoint presentation, computer, and flash drive.

Of course, your own needs might be very different. But then, you probably already have a list of items if you are used to doing this.

If you don't, make your own checklist for items that you certainly do not want to forget. Oh, and put that list in writing so you can review it every time you travel. Some of those items you forget could turn out to be very expensive mistakes.

3

GETTING TO WORK

"*L*adies and gentlemen, please raise your tray tables and seat backs, and buckle your seat belts... we'll be taking off shortly.*"

I try to oblige but the right half of my seat belt is missing! Oh no, where is this other half? I reach down, around and back, there is no right side of my belt. Besides wondering who would walk off a plane with half a seat belt, the flight was necessarily delayed awaiting a replacement.

Maintenance finally shows up with half a belt (did it get nabbed from a nearby plane so that another unsuspecting passenger will soon be experiencing my dilemma?). After matching it to its left side partner, we finally take off.

Many people drive to work for business travel. Others, of course, fly. Some take a train or bus (local and commuter). Whatever your method of transportation, we have you covered.

Driving to Work

One frequently asked question: Is it better to drive or fly? Of course, you also could substitute train or bus but the question is valid.

My personal limit in the car is about 2-3 hours. If I can drive to my business location in that amount of time, I will do it. Anything more, I usually look for alternative transportation.

If traveling on your own dime for business, you may want to stretch that travel time out a bit. Remember, there is a reason the IRS currently uses 55.5 cents a mile (as of this writing and subject to change) as an estimate for substitute costs.

41

Besides gasoline, the IRS allowance covers other costs such as maintenance and repairs. (There is another tax option to use a percentage of the use of your vehicle for tax purposes. Check with your tax advisor and see which works best for you.)

Some, out of need or preference, use their cars frequently for business travel. Indeed, some travelers seem to literally live out of their cars, traveling from city to city.

There are many advantages to driving for business. Here are a few of them:

- Possibly the least expensive transportation alternative;
- Option to stop driving when you choose;
- Avoid time and aggravation dealing with airport parking, long walks with luggage, long lines inside airports, airport security lines, etc.;
- Ability to travel with as much luggage as you like; and
- No annoying seat neighbors.

Then there is the one big disadvantage of driving: The need to stay awake and alert, which means the time cannot be used for working, reading, or taking a nap.

Safety is always at the top of the list when driving. Make sure everything in your car is working properly. Periodically check the tire pressure (including the spare tire) and fluid levels.

Create a checklist of items you may need during your travels. This list might include:

- Roadside emergency kit
- Basic tools
- First aid kit
- Jumper cables
- Flashlight and flares
- Blanket

Another item for the checklist might be a GPS unit. Also, don't forget car adapters you might need such as for a GPS, phone, or computer. When driving in the winter, your checklist might include items such as a snow/ice brush, bag of salt, and perhaps a small shovel.

Clicking on the Night Train

At the beginning of the last century, travel by train was king. Then a couple of guys in Kitty Hawk got an airplane to fly and the rest, as they say, is history.

Well, not totally. U.S. train service is certainly lacking compared to Europe but Amtrak offers over 500 stations in 46 states, making it a popular transportation method for many business travelers.

Consider these statistics: During the period May 2007-08, Amtrak reported a 15% increase in ridership for long-distance routes and a 14% increase in shorter routes. While their numbers dipped during the recession, the 2010 traveler statistics showed strong support once again for train travel.[8]

Trains also offer many benefits over flying. Here are some...

- No long airport security lines and restrictive regulations.

- Baggage is more likely to reach its destination.

- You can expect more legroom and the aisles are wider.

- Time and cost savings. For many travelers, airports are often located outside of cities, whereas train stations are often found in downtown locations. This saves the time and cost of renting a car or hiring a taxi.

- Getting through train stations generally takes less time than going through airports. Airports usually require more time to park, longer walks to get to the gate, and certainly more time getting through security.

- Comfort factor. Trains still offer sleeping berths, while flying generally offers nothing better than lie-flat seats, but those routes are very infrequent and expensive.

Easily the most popular train route for business travelers is Amtrak's service up the eastern corridor of the U.S. Throw in free Wi-Fi and this is a winning combination for those who are served in this area.

But will the train be less expensive than flying? Like everything else, that depends. Airlines periodically offer discounts on certain routes so at any particular moment, the answer may be yes or no. Nevertheless, train service should be considered, at the very least for relatively short haul routes lasting up to a few hours.

Hop on the Bus, Gus

More business travelers are opting for bus service. While some use a bus for local transportation, we will look here at using bus service for business travel.

Agreed, bus transportation has a seedy image, and few can imagine getting on a bus for business travel. Fact is, more are doing it, partly because the buses are much improved, the costs are often substantially lower than the alternatives, and there is the convenience factor.

Greyhound has been increasing legroom in their buses and offering free Wi-Fi. Newer services, such as BoltBus (a Greyhound joint venture) and RedCoach, also promise power outlets along with Wi-Fi and more comfort.

Is bus service a viable alternative? Seems to be, at least for relatively short rides, say a few hours or less. When you consider flying as an alternative and factor in the time for getting to the airport, checking in, going through security, and the typically long walk to the gate, taking a bus becomes a real possibility.

Also, there is the advantage of Wi-Fi from the moment you leave, not having to wait until an aircraft reaches 10,000 feet. For those who fly in coach seats, another benefit of riding a bus is larger seats with more legroom. And of course, the cost is substantially less, an important element if you work for a small firm or are traveling on your own dime.

Another benefit: You can use your cellphone for the entire trip. Of course, that might not always be considered a benefit since it is possible that 40 other passengers will all be talking at the same time.

RedCoach, for example, claims that 12% of their passengers are traveling for business. As expected, the company believes that number will only grow in time.

Yeah, I know what you're thinking: You know how to get to the airport but have no idea where the bus station is in town. Most of the bus terminals are located in downtown areas but they do not offer long-term parking. Sensing that this is an issue, some bus lines offer a pickup service at off-site airport parking lots.

A couple routes that come to mind where busing is a viable alternative would be the Orlando-Tampa and Washington, DC-Philadelphia areas. Boston-New York and Chicago-Milwaukee are other possibilities, too.

Longer trips to consider might be Orlando-Miami, Washington DC-New York or even DC-Boston. The latter two are not only popular shuttle flights but also very popular Amtrak routes.

If time is a more important factor than money, airline travel will almost always win out. However, if you are more flexible on time, and cost is a major consideration, traveling by bus may be an excellent alternative for business travel.

Flying to Work

It is difficult for most business travelers to imagine but until airline deregulation, airfares were quite expensive compared to today. That was a different era. Back then, most people wore suits and ties when flying and relatively few families could afford airline travel.

Deregulation changed all that for the foreseeable future. Today most people and families can easily travel across a state or even the entire U.S. for a nominal cost.

Flying is a wonderful mode of transportation to get you from one place to another. Unfortunately, it is also the most stressful for many people because of more rules, the highest security requirements, the easiest chance for error, and the most complaints. Indeed, this topic could be a book by itself.

If you are flying to a business meeting, always check the weather first. It is quite common to check the weather at your own airport and even the one you are flying to but the real problems may be in between.

Let's say your flight is San Diego to Minneapolis. While the weather may be okay in both cities, what you really want to know is the weather in the city where the plane was before it arrived in San Diego for your flight.

Put simply, if your airplane is delayed getting to San Diego, there's a good chance it will be late departing to your destination city. Sometimes airlines will provide this information, sometimes they won't. Best to be proactive and find out as much as you can on your own.

In some cases, it is possible to switch to another flight if you determine that your original flight may be delayed. Always look at other possibilities and options before you head out.

Getting to the Airport

Some business travelers have pre-arranged transportation to the airport. This may be a friend or family member, taxi, limousine, perhaps even a bus.

The best part about these services is the door-to-door treatment. This is a big help for a few reasons. First, you have help with your baggage. Second, you can leave a little later because you don't have to deal with parking. Third, someone else is doing the driving, freeing up your time to do whatever you like.

If you are driving yourself, parking at the airport is almost always an option. It offers convenience and frequently includes covered parking. Many airports today have parking lots that connect to the airport, making it easier to travel from the lot to inside the terminal without having to go outside, so you're at least covered for the entire walk.

However, on-site airport parking may be expensive for some, especially for longer trips. Most airports offer off-site parking that is less expensive. These services typically use shuttles to get passengers to the airports.

Note that while these off-site lots may be less expensive than parking at an airport, they still can be quite expensive, especially if you have to leave your car for more than a few days. Also, some of them may require reservations, especially at peak travel times.

Like airport parking, most off-site lots are open 24 hours a day. That means if your flight is unusually late arriving, it takes no more than a phone call to have the shuttle arrive at the airport to pick you up.

There are actually websites to help you locate off-site parking lots near your airport. See the *Business Travel Success Ultimate Travel Resource* for a few such sites.

Here's another parking possibility that works in some areas: Some hotels offer "park and fly" packages. For booking one or two nights at a hotel, some will let you park there for free. Many are located near airports and include shuttle service to and from the airport.

There are still some hotels near the airport that will let you make a reservation for only one night. Yes, you have to pay for a night to be a registered guest but if the parking is free there, the cost for one hotel night may be less than parking elsewhere for an extended stay.

Always check with the specific hotel property first before doing this. Note I said check with the hotel, not a reservation phone number. It is very important to contact the individual hotel to get their permission.

Some hotels are well aware that travelers do this. In my experience, most don't seem to mind unless it is their busy season. Definitely get their approval first because you don't want to return late at night after a long week away and find that your car has been towed. However, even if you can leave your car there, note that the shuttle buses usually do not run all day long. Again you need to check with each hotel but I often see the shuttle service stopping around 10 pm. If your flight doesn't arrive until 11 pm – or perhaps your flight leaves before 6 am – you may have to pay for a taxi to get to the airport or hotel.

Some cities offer subway or light rail service to the airport. This can be an economical compromise that works well but, of course, there are some disadvantages. Depending on how much luggage you have, are you okay traveling from your home to the airport lugging your bags with you?

The distance from these services to the airport may be another consideration. In some cities, they go right into the airport; for others it may be a mile or more away. You always want to know the hours of operation ahead of time. Again, will this service be available if your flight leaves early in the morning or arrives late at night?

This is a good place to remind you that if you use off-site parking or any other service to get to and from the airport, always have their phone number handy. Since delays are very common when flying, you always want to have the phone numbers of all your service providers.

 TIP: With your mobile phone's camera, take a photo of the aisle name or number where you parked your car. Or, if given a ticket with a parking spot number, snap a photo of that. This can save time and anxiety when returning home.

What's This "Code Share" Thing?

Some airlines offer non-stop flights while other will get you to a destination by working with what is called "code share" agreements.

Code share is an agreement between airlines where one makes arrangements with another to help you get to your destination. You book the flight with the one airline but – *and this is a very important but* – that airline might not be the one that really controls your flight.

An example here will help. Let's say you book a flight with United Airlines but it requires you to fly to an airport and change planes before reaching your destination. Since United doesn't fly between your host airport and your destination, they use one of their "partners" to fly part of the way.

In this example, let's say that USAir has a flight from your host airport to another airport, and United can fly you from the interim airport to your final destination.

USAir is now your OPERATING carrier even though you booked the ticket with United. Moreover, it is USAir's baggage policies that apply to you, not United's, even though you booked the flight through them.

This is very important: Even though you booked your flight through United, it is still considered a USAir flight because they are the first segment (sometimes referred to as a leg) of your trip. That means when you arrive at your host airport, you may have to *check in at USAir, not United*. On the return flight, you would check in at United since they would be the first carrier.

Don't forget: In the example above, just remember to go to the USAir gate if necessary for your outbound flight, not United.

Confused? Yeah, I hear you. I fly most every week and have never understood this strange system but it seems to make sense to them.

Here's a real life example before the Delta/Northwest merger. I booked a certain flight on Delta. My husband booked the identical flight through Northwest. Both of us had the same flight number because we were on the same flight.

Nevertheless, we couldn't sit together on the plane. Why? Because we booked our tickets through "different" airlines even though the two airlines were merging. Even Delta and Northwest personnel were baffled by this but neither one could change our seats.

Arriving at the Airport

Most airlines say to arrive about 90 minutes before a domestic flight, generally meaning flights within the United States. For international flights, it is best to arrive 2-3 hours beforehand because of additional check-in requirements.

In my experience, that is usually a pretty good estimate if you don't have to check any bags and don't run into other unexpected delays. For larger airports, 2 hours may be more realistic. Remember, the airlines often try to begin boarding flights 30-45 minutes before the actual takeoff time of domestic flights (1 hour or more for international flights).

If you are checking any baggage, it is best to allow at least 15-30 minutes more, even longer if you arrive at a particularly busy time like Monday mornings at most airports, and you don't have "status" (discussed in Chapter 13) with your chosen airline.

However, here's something to consider that may get you to leave your home a little earlier...

No matter how much time an airline suggests arriving at the airport before a flight, add time to it. Things they never factor in for that drive from your home to the airport include road construction, traffic accidents, stops for coffee or gasoline, parking lot delays, shuttle buses, etc.

If you meet the necessary criteria and don't have any bags to check, it is easy. Virtually all airlines allow online check-in, usually 24 hours before a flight. That means you can go directly to the gate with your carry-on luggage as long as you have your boarding pass with you. Well, not quite *directly* since you still have to deal with the security lines, discussed later in this chapter.

Uh Oh, I'm Gonna Be Late

What if you are running late? Don't panic. Or panic just a little but don't get carried away. It won't help you or anyone else. Here's a little insider secret. Shhh, don't tell anyone.

Airlines have been known to hold up a plane departure for certain elite status flyers or dignitaries. I'm not talking about an hour here, but if that passenger is running a few minutes late, the boarding doors may remain open a bit longer.

Of course, these "special" travelers slink into first class so no one gets to see who they are but you know it is a passenger delay issue when the door closes right behind them.

There are times when an airplane is held up due to late arriving connecting passengers. For you this may be an originating flight but for someone else, it is just another connection. If the passengers' first flight is late, the airline may try to accommodate them even if it means holding the connecting plane for a few minutes.

Why the accommodations? Because if the airlines do not do this, they need to find seats for these passengers on other flights. That has become increasingly difficult as airlines are operating with very tight capacity. This becomes the lesser of two evils.

The higher the number of passengers who are arriving on an inbound flight that is connecting with your flight, the greater the chance that your flight will wait for them, but only briefly.

For everyone else, an airline may use something called a *"flat tire rule."* This is a discretionary policy where each carrier may – that's *may* – allow you to get on the next flight without penalty. Well, at least if your excuse is good enough.

However, this rule normally won't extend beyond a couple of hours past your original flight departure. That means you absolutely need to contact the airline as soon as possible and review your options.

Actually, I need to qualify this a bit. Airlines will try to put you on the next flight if seats are available. If the plane is full, all they can offer you is standby service.

Flying standby means you are put on a list and if there are available seats on the next flight, you might get on the plane. However, be aware that there may be many people ahead of you on that list. This means you may spend hours in an airport – maybe even overnight or more— waiting for the next flight. Obviously airlines won't guarantee you a seat unless you pay for it. To put this in cold and harsh terms, you are left hoping someone else has the misfortune to miss their flight just so you can be on it.

Certain circumstances make this more difficult. For example, the more people in your party, the less likely there will be seats. As planes are more likely to be full today, it is much easier to find a single seat to a destination than two or three, much less four.

Because air traffic is much higher during holiday and other peak periods, it may be impossible to get you on another flight that day. Adding to your insecurity, poor weather conditions may delay or cancel flights, meaning there might be a backlog of a couple of days for seats trying to get to your destination.

There can be yet another constraint. If you chose a destination that has limited flights to that city, you just may be out of luck if there are no later flights that day. This is one reason you may want to consider flying out on the first available flight of the day to any destination.

Alas, the best you can do here is contact the airline, be as polite as possible – maybe even apologetic – and see what the carrier will offer you. Sadly, they are in the driver's seat in this situation, not you.

Here's a last ditch effort possibility: No one wants to lose money but if the airline insists you have to pay a change fee plus a higher rate for the seat just to get on a later flight, consider looking at another airline that is going to the same destination.

Why would they charge a higher rate for the same flight? There are two reasons. First, tickets are often more expensive if purchased just before a flight because they know these passengers have few, if any, options.

Second, airlines charge more because they can. This is even truer if they know there are no other carriers going to that destination on the same day. And believe me, all of them know the others' routes. Put another way, you either fly on this airline paying whatever they charge or you don't fly at all.

I am not suggesting you bail on the first carrier, just keep your options open. If another airline can get you to your destination faster and the cost will be the same or less than the original airline, it might be worth it to you.

Elsewhere I mention that it is always a good idea to have your flight information as well as the airline's phone number stored in your cellphone. Here's one of those situations where it will come in very handy.

Note: If you must buy a ticket at the counter, be prepared to pay yet another fee. Some airlines charge an additional fee simply because the flight was booked at the counter or via a phone call, not online or maybe using one of their kiosks.

I know -- this is just one more thing that makes passengers go, "Grrrrr!" It is not well publicized and may not apply to all airlines. I have heard of fees in the $20-30 range for counter ticket purchases but have not yet experienced it.

Checked Baggage

Before selecting an airline, find out about their baggage policy. Many airlines charge a fee to check bags. As of this printing, only a few do not, at least for the first bag. Since these rules can change frequently, it is always a good idea to check with each airline before booking a flight.

Most airlines have a search box on their websites. Type in "baggage fees" and you will most likely be taken to the page that contains their baggage policy.

While it is easier if you never need to check a bag with an airline, there are many reasons why it may be necessary. If so, consider the following:

- Never – yes, that's *never* – put medications or any valuable items in your checked luggage. There are far too many bags disappearing today. It is never worth the chance that yours may be one of them, and you can be sure every airline will challenge your claim that there were any valuables in your bag.

- Keep a copy of your itinerary in your checked bag. In the event the baggage gets lost or misplaced, this information will help the airline get the luggage back to you quicker.

- Have at least a name and phone number inside the bag, preferably a cellphone number so someone can contact you immediately if necessary. If you want to include an address, make it your office address. For many reasons mentioned, you don't want to announce to the world that you are out of town, especially if your home is empty.

- Always use the airline's online check-in if possible. Besides being faster, some airlines are now charging fees if you wait to check in at the ticket counter with your bags.

- Regardless of whether you check in online or at the ticket counter, you still need to stand in their lines to get your bags checked. Be advised, these lines can be quite long at times. The wait can easily be 30 minutes or more.

- For some airlines, there is the curbside check-in option. That is, you drop off your bags right at the check-in facility at the curb. There may be a fee for this, and a gratuity is also expected for the porter helping you with your bags, but the lines are often shorter.

- Nevertheless, there is a check-in time limit outside, usually around 45-60 minutes before a flight. If you are running late for check-in, ask first before standing in their line.

- Note also that airlines have weight limits. Each bag, for example, may have a limit of 50 lbs. If your luggage is over their weight limit, expect yet another charge for your bag.

For just this reason, it is always a good idea to weigh your bag before you leave home. Yes I know, easy to say but hard to do. I have tried a couple of methods to do this with my home scale but I always come up with a lower weight than the airline scales (the same thing happens with the scale at my doctor's office!).

There are plenty of portable luggage scales available, and some newer bags even come with built-in scales. Note that portable scales can add 2-8 oz. of weight to your bag.

Are the airline scales accurate? Well, let's say it is possible that the ticket counter scales may give different results.

 A POSSIBLE COST-SAVINGS TIP: If your luggage is only a little over the limit, ask the ticket agent to weigh it again on one of their other scales. Who knows, maybe the way the bag was placed on the scale or even the scale itself may give a different result. As long as you stay under the excess baggage limit, you really don't care.

One last thing: The only locks you can put on a bag are those that are TSA approved. If any other lock is used, the folks scanning your checked bag may break it open. I saw the results on the face of a foreign tourist who had brand new luggage destroyed by a baggage checker because the locks were not approved. Don't let it happen to you.

Speaking of foreign – know that the master key system used by TSA in the U.S. for the approved locks is not used by all countries. It's best not to use TSA locks when traveling internationally, or you may end up with damaged luggage.

Oh Yeah, Those TSA Rules

This is one reason this chapter is so large. The rules are not all that difficult to follow but only if you already know them. For those who don't know the frequently changing rules, it is like walking through a mine field.

First, a paragraph explaining about the **Transportation Security Administration**, often just called TSA. They are the division of Homeland Security charged with keeping our airlines and airways safe.

Let's begin with a relatively new rule known as the **Secure Flight Initiative** (SFI). This requires that the name on an airline ticket matches the name on the identification used to pass through security at the airport. In addition, airlines and travel agencies need to record your date of birth and gender, which likewise must agree with your identification.

This rule created some problems before it was implemented. It seems there are a substantial number of U.S. citizens who use nicknames. For example, a man might be known as Mike but his passport says his name is Michael. And then there is Liz, whose driver's license says that her name is Elizabeth.

Middle names compound this problem. Some people use them, others simply use their middle initial or perhaps leave it out altogether.

The TSA rule is straightforward, albeit frustrating: The name on the boarding pass must be *identical* to the picture identification. There have been very vocal requests – even demands – that TSA exercise common sense when looking at names. Just be aware, any differences may delay your boarding.

Airport Security Lines

Security lines can be challenging, especially at peak travel times. As you get closer to your flight time, each minute can feel like five. At some airports, you can whisk through in maybe 10 minutes. At others, the wait can be closer to an hour.

The lines always move faster when everyone knows the rules. Unfortunately, most travelers are infrequent fliers and simply don't know what to do.

I compare this to what we strangely call "rush hour" traffic, one of the grossest misnomers we have in our language. Very simply, you cannot go any faster than the slowest person in front of you.

Yes, it would be wonderful if everyone knew all the rules and what to remove before walking through the TSA lines but alas, all I can do is inform you, not them.

Some airports have separate lines for "experts" and families. In theory, this is helpful because families tend to need more time. In practice, however, such line distinction is worthless without TSA enforcement. Also available at some airports is a separate TSA line for an airline's elite passengers.

To get through the TSA lines as quickly as possible, follow these rules:

- Remove everything in your pockets (except for boarding pass and ID) *before getting in line* and place them in your carry-on bag or coat pocket. This includes your cellphone, probably the most common thing forgotten.

- Wear slip-on shoes. Since shoes have to be removed before going through the scanner, it is always easier and faster on both sides of the machine if your shoes simply slip on and off.
  Note: As of this writing, TSA is actively searching for vendors to provide shoe scanning devices that pick up either explosives or any type of weapon, so the rules may change.

- Remove coats, jackets, shoes, belts, and anything metallic like loose change or big necklaces. Put paper money in a secure jacket pocket.

- Computers and some other electronics must be removed from your bag and placed in bins separately. If you are using a check-point friendly bag, just open up the bag to have the side with the laptop lay flat against the security belt – no need to remove the laptop from this type of bag.

- Attach a bright label to the top of your laptop so it is easier to see once it's inside the dull gray bin of airport security. A piece of pink or neon green duct tape works well and does not rip off easily (yes, duct tape comes in many colors now!).

- Follow the 3-1-1 rule on liquids. See tsa.gov/311 for specifics.
  This last tip is the shortest and yet can cause the most delays in a security line, especially when someone tries to reason with TSA that their almost empty but full-size tube of toothpaste is not holding more than 3.4 ounces. Note: The traveler will always lose this argument.

Can gifts be brought through the security line?

Yes, as long as they are not wrapped prior to your flight and are not liquid items weighing more than 3.4 ounces. TSA usually will either ask you to remove the wrapping or they will do it themselves. If something is wrapped, they may want to see it.

Why do they need to see the gift wrapped item since it already went through their scanner? I don't know, maybe because they are always looking for good gift ideas. Actually, I have heard that the reason is due to some of the metallic-looking wrapping paper. This may apply to only certain types of wrapping papers, but be safe and leave the wrapping for when you arrive at your destination.

If you want to keep the gift wrapped, another option is to ship it ahead. Note, however, if this gift has a high value and you desire insurance, the shipper also may insist on inspecting it first. There goes the wrapping paper again.

If you are traveling with a snow globe of any size (even less than 3.4 ounces), your bag must be checked or you will forego your snow globe in the security line. These are not allowed as carry-on items at all.

What about paperless boarding passes?

More airlines are going to an optional paperless boarding pass. Instead of printing it out from your computer, the boarding pass is in your device (smartphone or tablet, for example).

When you reach the first TSA security point, show them your regular ID (driver's license or passport) along with the boarding information on your mobile device. I have used this method many times and so far, it has worked *most* of the time.

On the other hand, it is disastrous when it fails. You must take all your belongings, exit the TSA line, return to the ticket area to obtain a printed boarding pass, and then get back in line. The worst part, though, is starting at the end of the line again, unless an agent is kind enough to tell you to come back up to the front of the line.

If you're lucky, there would still be enough time to catch your flight. Key word here is *lucky*. At the very least, most people would probably roll into panic mode. After all, you just added perhaps a minimum of 15 minutes to the time required to get to your gate. In a busy airport environment, it can be 30 minutes or more.

Of course, you can always create a safety net by also printing out a version of your boarding pass but that kind of defeats the purpose of the electronic version, doesn't it?

TIPS for success with a mobile boarding pass:

- Have the boarding pass displayed on your mobile device <u>before</u> you reach the security agent. If the internet connection is questionable, it may not be possible to display the boarding pass quickly.

- Once you have the boarding pass displayed, use the camera on your mobile device to take a photo of it. Alternatively, just use a screen capture. This way, if the internet isn't working when you reach the agent, the photo of the boarding pass is ready for display. (This is also a great idea for keeping proof that you boarded a flight, in case the miles are not posted to your mileage account at the end of a flight.)

Lost or forgotten ID?

You'll feel your heart skip a few beats when you realize at the airport that you forgot or lost your ID. I agree that this is a bad time to realize it but don't go postal, TSA has seen it before.

BEST TIP FOR THIS: Make sure you have a photocopy of your ID in your carry-on bag. No carry-on bag? Then keep the information in your purse or wallet.

Which ID do you need? Photocopies of both your driver's license and passport if you have them. If you have neither, then copy whatever ID you do use, e.g., military or state ID or permanent resident card.

TIP: Use the camera in your cellphone to take a photo of your ID papers. Try to make sure the numbers are as clear as possible. As an alternative, copy those identification numbers into your phone just as you would a phone contact. Password-protect either the photo or the document with apps available for your mobile device to keep your information secure.

Either way, it is important to be able to prove you are who you say you are. Yes, you can expect a delay but if you are early enough, you might not miss your flight.

What If Your ID Has Expired?

TSA should accept your driver's licenses at the checkpoint for 12 months after they expire, according to a senior advisor in the Transportation Security Administration. Some officers might not say anything to you about the expired license, while others might make a comment if it's nearing the expiration date. I recommend you always have something else with you just in case an officer asks to see another form of valid ID.

Remember Your Stuff!

Always check the machine belt where your items come through the scanner. TSA claims that there are actually thousands of computers and cellphones left behind by passengers. I have seen it a few times myself. I have even seen the full bins of miscellaneous items that TSA has collected throughout the day. And I wonder how much money they have accumulated in any given day. Have you ever looked underneath the belts and seen all the coins lying there?

To avoid this problem, place your items on the TSA conveyor belt in this order:

- Carry-on bag(s)
- Laptop or other computer
- Coats, belts, and other items
- Shoes

Why this order? You want to ensure you don't forget anything on the other side of the belt. Your bag, the largest item, will be first and few people ever forget them. You want your computer in the middle because you surely will wait for your shoes. Funny, it is very rare for people to walk off without their shoes but they leave their laptops all the time, especially if it is the last item placed on the belt.

Most people do this the other way around. Once they have their shoes on, they forget the trailing items like phones, keys, and computers. Of course, you won't forget the small items because you were smart enough to place them in the pockets of your coat or jacket, right?

I created this little ditty to help me remember all my things:

Remember to collect my purse, laptop, liquids and shoes,
Or else I'll be letting out a curse and feeling the blues.

Here's another idea: remember the first letter of each item: PLLS = purse, laptop, liquids, shoes (Guys: Substitute wallet for purse and you'll have WLLS).

I admit it sounds dumb but if you can come up with an acronym or ditty to use, your chances of leaving something behind go way down.

Seat Neighbors and Etiquette

Unless you are traveling with a friend or family member, it is most likely that the person sitting next to you is a stranger. You don't know them, they don't know you, and strange things can happen at 36,000 feet.

There are thousands of reported stories about bad seat neighbors. Some passengers want to talk endlessly while you want to read a book or sleep. Some are so large they need to put up the middle seat arms just to get seated.

Then there are some passengers who drink way too much while others fall asleep on you. I've had all these types of neighbors. Knock on wood: the drinkers haven't gotten sick on me yet.

One of the most common complaints is crying babies. I have been on flights where a baby begins crying as soon as the doors are closed and continues almost nonstop until the plane reaches the destination gate. As a mother, I am sensitive to this problem but I have to admit, as a passenger on the plane trying to work or sleep, a crying baby – no, make that a wailing baby – certainly tries even my patience.

The types of problems that cause ire are endless but the bottom line is you are squeezed into a tube – in a seat only about 17" wide – with other passengers for the duration of the flight. If there are issues, definitely ask the flight attendant if other seats are available but don't expect a positive response.

My suggestion: lead by kindness and example. Remember, most passengers fly very infrequently, maybe only once or twice a year. Perhaps your generous behavior will be picked up by others.

I have yet to meet a person who likes to use an airplane bathroom. Out of necessity, we trudge to the back of the plane, waiting our turn to squeeze into the tiniest of bathrooms. We do our business, and then come out smelling like blue Saniflush.

On a recent trip, the door said "Unoccupied," so I gave the door a hard push to open it up. Imagine my surprise when a gentleman was standing there with his back to me, still doing his business, with no reaction at all when I bombarded his space.

When he finished, he walked right by me as if nothing had happened. What do you do in these circumstances... look him in the eye, look down at the floor, what?

My turn now, so I squeezed into the bathroom, closed the door, and then noticed that the so-called "gentleman" I had walked in on had peed all over the seat. GROSS! I made a fast exit and waited for another available bathroom.

I appreciate how difficult it is to be tolerant of others, especially strangers, but maybe because of traveling so much, I believe in good travel karma. Think about the following:

- If the person next to you insists on conversation and you don't want it, simply pull out a book or magazine and begin reading, or sit back and close your eyes. Other options: Put on a pair of eyeshades or stick some headphones in your ears. This is usually enough to quiet anyone.

- Alternatively, learn how to say, in a few foreign languages, "I don't speak English." This might work but remember, it is possible they are fluent in the language you selected. Then they will never keep quiet.

- The food you bring on an aircraft may be your favorite but to others it may downright stink. Whenever possible, consume your food prior to boarding or bring something fairly odorless.

- Invest in a pair of noise-canceling headphones. They minimize contact with noisy neighbors and drown out those unwanted sounds.

- Recline your seatback only enough to be comfortable. After all, you know how difficult it is when the person in front of you just has to put their seat back as far as it will go.

- If you must cough or sneeze, always cover your mouth and nose (even if this is by sneezing into the crook of your arm). This is important because it's the easiest way to pass along germs on a plane. See the Health and Fitness chapter for much more on germs.

- It should go without saying but bathe before heading to the airport. It is very difficult to deal with odors when you are trapped in a small seat of a plane for hours. In case you end up next to a stinky seatmate, consider carrying a tiny bottle or sachet of lavender or peppermint to help deal with the offensive odor. Or ask a flight attendant for a bag of coffee to open up and place in your seat back pocket to help with odor absorption.

If you notice the obnoxious odor before the flight has taken off, let a flight attendant know immediately. There are actions they can take while the door is still open. In fact, most airlines have a clause in their "Conditions of Carriage" policies that gives them the right to deny boarding to someone who is really stinky.

I learned this *after* my episode with Mr. Poopy Pants (an adult, not a baby) aboard one of my flights.

- Don't kick or pull on the seat in front of you. If you have children who are doing this, stop them. This is really annoying to the entire row in front of you since the seats are connected. Everyone feels the kicking.

- Speaking of connected seats, if your legs are restless and constantly in movement bouncing up and down, think about how this feels to your seatmates in the connected row. Instead, walk around (once the seat belt light is off) to manage the restlessness.

- Always use the overhead compartment above your own seat or maybe a row behind it. Using the compartments many rows in front of you means those seat passengers are forced to store their items much further back, slowing down their exit from the plane as well as that of everyone else.

- Know thy arm-rest etiquette. For travelers in the middle seat between two strangers, the general rule is that the middle seat passenger gets both armrests. The window seat has an armrest, as does the aisle seat. If the middle seat person's arm is encroaching into your seat, gently push back.

- It's also ok to gently push back if a tall person next to you sits with his knees out wide and is invading your leg space. Same with a head that leans on your shoulder. I've had several times where someone falls asleep and their head droops to my shoulder. If you're not comfortable pushing back their head, get up and take a walk. When their head bounces lower, they almost always wake up and sit upright once again.

If you have a difficult neighbor, mention it to the flight attendant as soon as possible. Sometimes they can locate another seat for you. I have seen a passenger moved up to first class, no doubt because the request was made kindly, not angrily.

Finally, you can always file a complaint with the airline. I would not expect a refund simply because you had to deal with a difficult seatmate but if you detail the problems, it is possible the airline will issue some kind of credit or extra miles into your account. It doesn't hurt to ask.

Flight Delays

What do you do if your flight is delayed? This is something I have dealt with perhaps hundreds of times and now I want to share some of my secrets with you.

Flights are delayed for many reasons. It could be due to weather, airplane mechanical problems, or crew issues, among others.

Note that if the delay is due to weather, the airline is not required to offer you any compensation whatsoever. That means if you are stuck at an airport overnight, they do not have to pay for a hotel room for you. It is unfortunate but it does happen.

If you travel enough, anything can happen. Indeed, I have been stuck in airports overnight because there were no accommodations available within miles of the airport. Like everyone else, I just accepted it and did my best to sleep in one of the seats near the gate.

To minimize this problem, try to always have a backup plan. This consists of knowing alternative flights, first with the host airline and then with others. Also, it helps to never book the last flight of the evening. Here is where a travel agent, when engaged to book your tickets, can be invaluable for giving you options around the delay and to help with the re-arranging of your plans.

Sometimes it is only a matter of getting re-routed on another flight quickly if you know your options. But yes, sometimes it means waiting hours at the airport, or sometimes staying overnight.

What to do? Really, there isn't anything you can do about a delayed flight. Best to just accept it and make the best use of the time.

You may decide to visit the airport shops, which have gotten much better over the years. Another alternative: Buy a book or magazine and find a comfortable seat. Also, look for an available power outlet and either charge up items like a laptop or phone or just get some work done.

Some airports offer free Wi-Fi, others don't. For those that do, it certainly helps to pass the time by surfing the internet. Most airports at least offer Wi-Fi for a fee. This might or might not be worth it to you. In any case, it is a limited activity unless you have a power source.

One thing to consider, especially if you are a frequent business traveler, is membership in airport lounges. This allows access to comfortable seating, food, and drink, as well as to a power source. Most of the lounges offer one-day passes for travelers. If you are stuck at an airport for more than a few hours, it might be worth it to you. Note that the one-day charge is usually $30-50 per person (and can cost less if purchased online, either with the airline or sites like eBay).

Alas, not all terminals offer lounges. For those that do, their hours might be somewhat limited, definitely a drawback if you are stuck in an airport late at night.

If you do end up sleeping in an airport overnight, check out the airport's chapel. They may have pews for you to lie down on. At the very least, it will be quieter than the terminal.

Bumped from a Flight

Yes, it does happen. Sometimes flights are overbooked, causing the airlines to first look for volunteers to give up their seats so another connecting passenger won't be more inconvenienced. This "bumping" can be voluntary or even involuntary.

What are the odds of this happening? Pretty slim, about 1 in 872 according to the *Book of Odds*. As for being bumped involuntarily, the odds are pretty safe at 1 in 10,040. These odds vary depending on a number of things such as day of the week, time of day, and which airline. Some bump more than others.

We will look only at volunteering to give up your seat. Is it worth it to volunteer for this? Well, it depends. It is never worth it if you will be late for something else. Here are a couple of examples:

Let's say you have a connecting flight to Europe. If you miss the first flight, the next one available might force you to miss the connection getting you to Europe. That could be a disaster for your business meetings or vacation.

This is an obvious case where you would never volunteer to give up your seat, no matter what the airline offered as compensation. But what if your travel plans are more flexible?

What if the airline offered you a voucher for future travel plus promised to put you on another flight within a couple of hours, maybe even with an upgrade to first class? Then you certainly might consider it. I know I would, as long as I wasn't forced to miss something important.

The most common situation calling for volunteers is when the next flight is either many hours later or perhaps necessitates an overnight stay. These situations should be decided on a case-by-case basis.

Things you want to know before you agree to volunteer to miss your flight:

- How long before the next available flight?
- Will the airline check with other carriers to see if a flight with them is possible?
- What about meal vouchers while waiting for the next flight?
- Will the airline provide overnight accommodations if necessary?
- If an overnight stay is required, is it possible to get your checked bag off the plane or will your bag be forwarded to your destination without you?
- Do you have clothing and personal items in your carry-on bag?
- Is an upgrade to first class available?
- Can you get an amenity kit from the airline with a toothbrush and other necessities?

Here are some downsides...

The most obvious downside is you will arrive later than you planned. Sometimes that delay is not until the following day. Is it worth it to lose another day for traveling?

The airline may well offer you a meal voucher but I find these are nowhere near enough to actually pay for a meal. You pay the difference out of your own pocket.

Your checked bags will most likely remain on the first flight even though you won't. When your bag arrives "on schedule" and you don't, it will be taken to the airline's baggage claim department to await your arrival.

Yes, the airline may offer a hotel room if you stay overnight but sometimes your next flight is early the following morning, often before hotel shuttles begin service. That means you may need a taxi to get back to the airport, yet another cost out of your own pocket.

For all these considerations, there is indeed an upside. Besides the nominal meal vouchers, the airlines also are required to compensate you. I have been offered vouchers in the $200 to $400 range good for a future domestic flight (higher on international flights); though have also had airlines offering only $100 or $150. Others offer a free round-trip ticket, usually limited to the continental U.S. Voucher values have recently been increased, so you may hear about higher values being offered.

Of course, everyone would love a free round-trip ticket but each person has to decide if the cost is worth it. For what it's worth, I have said yes in several instances and no in most others.

Note, though, that there is also involuntary bumping of passengers. If there are no volunteers, the airlines might boot you anyway. Fortunately, this is very rare because there are normally enough volunteers but be aware that it can happen.

Wi-Fi on Planes

Is it worth it? My answer is always... yes and no. I'll start with the "yes" answer.

As I said on Twitter some time ago, it really is pretty neat to be tweeting at 36,000 feet. But seriously, Wi-Fi on a plane really is much more than that.

Here are some of the benefits:

- Opportunity to get additional work done. For example, just being able to respond to emails is a huge benefit for many business travelers. For some, it means additional time for billable work.
- Staying in touch with loved ones while you are traveling.
- Nice distraction to be on the internet rather than reading a book or magazine.
- Works quite well with a laptop computer, netbook, smartphone, tablet, or any device with built-in Wi-Fi.

There are some downsides as well. For example, it is very difficult to use a laptop in the economy class seats and nearly impossible if the person in front of you decides to recline their seat all the way.

TIP: If you want to use your computer, the smaller screen laptops or tablets are much better. Also, book an aisle seat if possible. This gives you a little more room because you can tilt the computer into the aisle a little.

If the Wi-Fi is free, enjoy it. If they charge for it, the cost for short flights is quite high for the time you actually get to use it. If you anticipate numerous uses of inflight Wi-Fi throughout a month, look into monthly fee plans vs. one-time use.

Remember, you can only use Wi-Fi above 10,000 feet. Discount the time leaving the gate until you get to 10,000 feet – and then take out the time when you are in approach mode for landing – this is at least 20 minutes, sometimes an hour and possibly more depending on weather and other issues.

That makes Wi-Fi near worthless for short flights of less than 2 hours or so. Between 2-3 hours, it is more of a personal decision. You get the most out of the fees you pay if the flight is over 4 hours long.

Then another potential problem may arise. Not all airlines have power outlets available. Most laptops are good for at least a couple of hours or so, but that's about it. With no source to build up the battery, you may be paying a lot of money for only partial usage. Also, the connection may not be very good. There are lots of possible reasons for this but the most common will be tower issues or the weather.

My experience so far has been quite pleasant but there is no guarantee it will work well on all flights. Just be aware, you may be paying a lot for a slow connection.

Note, too, that some airlines have blocked certain sites. This will not be a concern to most people but if you like surfing *certain* sites, your Wi-Fi experience may be a disappointment.

One more thing: You cannot use Wi-Fi for talking on the phone, for example, using Skype. This is actually an FCC rule but strongly supported by the airline industry and many frequent travelers. There is just no support to encourage passengers to engage in loud conversations while flying.

TIP: If it is required that you complete an application with the Wi-Fi carrier to use it on the plane, do it before you board. It can take anywhere from 10-30 minutes to complete the application process by the time you enter your name and credit card info over what can be a slow connection.

You don't want to be using precious Wi-Fi minutes just for the application. Indeed, in most cases it costs nothing to do the application. Better to have it done beforehand so you are good to go at 10,000 feet.

Best Overall Airline Tips

There are so many things I've learned over the years, and I want to share them all! Here are the tips most useful to frequent travelers and tips that I follow the majority of the time:

- Generally, fly early in the day if possible, though Monday mornings can be very hectic due to other business travelers and returning vacationers. If there is weather or other delays across the country, the first flight is the least affected. This gives you more options in the event of a flight delay or cancellation.

- The riskiest flight is the last one of the day.

- The least busy days to fly are Tuesday and Wednesday followed by Saturday. Also, they may be the least expensive.

- When are airports usually most crowded? While some business travelers fly out Sunday evening, I typically see much larger crowds on Monday morning. Other busy times are Thursday evening and most any time Friday. That's when business fliers usually return home.

- Travel around holidays is always hectic. This includes any long weekend with a holiday as well as the worst times, which are over the Thanksgiving and Christmas periods.

- Non-stop flights are less likely to be delayed because there is no interim flight to your destination. Sometimes these flights cost more but there is that peace of mind factor to consider, too.

- Noise-cancelling headphones can be your best friend on an airplane. Even some of the less expensive brands do a decent job of drowning out noisy engines, crying babies, and chatty seat neighbors.

- Spend a little time and research for a back-up plan in the event your flight is cancelled or delayed too much. The same airline might offer another flight that becomes more attractive to you, or you may have an option with a different airline altogether.

- To save some money, go through the TSA lines with an empty water bottle. Fill it up on the other side at a water fountain after you clear security. This saves money and helps reduce waste.

- This is a little strange but true: Sometimes it is less expensive to purchase 2 one-way tickets than 1 round-trip ticket. Try it both ways before you book your flight, even checking different airlines for each direction.

- Avoid using the seatback compartment. It is very common for passengers to leave all kind of things in the seatback pockets (wallets, mobile phones, game systems). Occasionally the items are returned, most often they are not.

- Purchasing a first class ticket usually means checked bag fees are waived. The extra cost on some flights may not be much greater than the bag charge, especially for shorter flights, and you get a much more comfortable ride.

- If you have checked bags and need to pick them up at the baggage claim, use the time waiting for your bags to confirm hotel reservations, car rentals, taxis, shuttles, someone picking you up, etc.

- If your luggage does not arrive when you do, file a claim immediately with the airline before leaving the airport. They will begin a search right away and may be able to offer some temporary assistance.

TIP: Have a photo of your luggage in your mobile phone for easily describing it to airport baggage personnel.

- The same applies if you ignore the suggestion to not use the seatback pocket on the plane. In most cases, items left behind are turned into the airline's baggage claim office. This might not be a problem if that is your home airport but it can be a major issue if it is somewhere else.

- If you are traveling with a small computer, best to keep it under the seat instead of in the overhead compartment. There are more than a few stories of passengers who realized too late that the laptop they had stored above was not still in their bag upon arrival.

Always check in for your flight as soon as possible, preferably online up to 24 hours in advance of your flight time. Then be one of the early birds when arriving for your flight. There are many reasons for this:

- This is your best opportunity to get a seat change in case you were assigned to a middle seat. There are often several passengers moved up to first class because of their status with the airline, which can open up some preferential seats in coach. The bulkhead seats are often held back until the last 24 hours as well.

  With so many flights full today, it is nearly impossible to change seats at the gate or after you have boarded the plane.

- Sometimes the airline changes the type of plane that will be used for a flight. This can happen for many reasons but the point here is a different type of aircraft may mean a different seating arrangement. In other words, even though you have a seat assignment, it might not work for the replacement plane.

- When you are an early bird at the airport, you are more likely to get a seat in the waiting area near the gate and much more likely to find a seat near a power outlet to charge up your electronic gadgets. These seats can fill quickly as the time for boarding approaches.

- If you were unable to get a desirable seat online when you checked in earlier, now is the time to talk with the gate agent before they get busy boarding the flight. The gate agent knows all the seat assignments and may be able to put you in another seat or help you get adjoining seats for family members.

When it comes to flying at holiday times, flights on the actual holiday can actually be much less expensive than days before or after. A couple of examples are flying on Thanksgiving or Christmas day.

I actually did this a few years ago on a late flight out of O'Hare on Christmas day. I enjoyed Christmas eve and most of Christmas day with my family, then headed to the airport for an evening flight home.

O'Hare Airport in Chicago is one of the busiest airports in the world. On Christmas day, not only was the flight much less expensive than the following day but the airport was nearly empty. It took less than 5 minutes to get through the TSA security line. On a normal day, it can take 30 minutes or more.

More benefits: The flight was on time and not full so I had the entire row to myself in coach. I could have slept across three seats if I had wanted to.

Another way to sometimes save money on a flight is to use a different airport. This is not possible for everyone but for those who may be within 100 miles or so of another airport, it just might pay to look for flights out of both. (For example, Chicago's O'Hare and Midway airports, even Rockford and Milwaukee, Wisconsin, are all within a reasonable driving distance for many in the Chicagoland area.)

This only works if someone is picking you up at the airport or you are renting a car. Otherwise you will need to pay for a taxi or, in some cities, a subway or bus. The savings by flying into an airport further away may disappear when you add in the extra cost of getting to your eventual destination.

Always look for a non-stop flight that meets your fare or airline requirements. Of course it isn't always possible to find one, but there are many instances where a single airline may offer direct flights between the two cities you need.

Connecting flights can be problematic. Whether it is due to weather delays, mechanical problems, or crew issues, the bottom line is that many connecting flights are delayed throughout the day.

It is always a good idea to have a book or magazine with you at the airport. Delays happen not only at the gate but sometimes sitting on the tarmac. I am sure you have heard some of the horror stories about delays.

This is a "tweener" time where you are sitting out on the airport tarmac but not allowed to use anything electronic. Your backup can be a new book or magazine to keep you entertained at least until the plane reaches 10,000 feet.

Speaking of magazines, here's a tip for those magazines that you subscribe to: Always remove the address labels before packing them in your bag for a trip. Why? For the same reasons mentioned elsewhere in the book. If someone can read your address label on a magazine, they will know you are out of town. Burglars like to have this information. Don't make it easy for them.

Instead of trashing your magazines when you are finished, give them to the flight attendants. Many of them enjoy reading something different so they will appreciate the gesture.

Keep your important items that you want in-flight readily under the seat in front of you, not in the overhead compartment. Some of these items may be a laptop computer, iPod, DVD player, earphones, magazines, books, etc. It's just easier to have ready access instead of climbing over someone to get into the overhead bin, then doing this again when your bag needs to go back up.

Note that only small, lightweight items can be placed in the seatback pocket. This is an FAA rule, and more airlines seem to be enforcing it. Their concern: additional items in the seatback may come out during turbulent moments, which can include takeoff and landing.

Reading the rule, it is clear that laptop computers cannot be placed in the seatback because of their weight. Instead, put it either under the seat in front of you or in the overhead bin until you are allowed to retrieve it in flight.

I always try to avoid checking a bag when I fly. Some of the pitfalls of checked bags include losing the bag, damage to your luggage, stolen items, and sending them to the wrong destination.

The last pitfall is avoided with this handy tip: When your bag is checked, always look at the tag. First you want to make sure it is heading to the correct destination. Second, check to see that the flight tag matches your exact flight. Anything different, it is a guarantee your luggage will arrive possibly before you but most likely after you, maybe even by a couple of days.

This does not happen often but in the rush to move passengers through quickly, it can and does happen. It takes only one time for it to happen to you to realize that this is a tip you will never forget.

4

LOCAL TRANSPORTATION
AT YOUR DESTINATION

*A*fter signing the car rental agreement at the counter in Minot, North Dakota, the agent tossed an extension cord over the counter at me. "What's this for?" I asked. He replied, "You're not from around here, are you?"

I was handed instructions on connecting the cord into the block heater in the car and using the plug-in located in the hotel parking lot. This would keep the engine warm overnight in the cold January weather.

As I drove off and headed into town, one hotel after another was advertising free plug-ins on their signs. Wow, who knew?

Many business travelers drive to their destination cities. Others might have someone meet them at an airport or train station. Still others may take a shuttle or subway.

However, there are many more business travelers who don't do any of the above. This chapter is for those who must arrange their own transportation when arriving at their destination city.

Taxi Services

Many business travelers prefer using taxi services. Some are simply uncomfortable traveling to unfamiliar cities and do not want to deal with things like traffic and relying on GPS to get them to certain destinations.

Indeed, some travelers don't own a driver's license, much less a car. I know people in New York, for example, who do not bother with either. Instead they rely on public transportation or taxis exclusively.

For these and other reasons, taxis are popular with business travelers and in some cities, provide the primary support of the taxi industry. Like any mode of transportation, there are things to think about before hailing the first cab that comes along.

Do you climb into a cab with trepidation? Do you expect the driver to be surly and seemingly not happy to see a new customer? Do you dread the moment when you slide into the seat and look around at the less than sanitary conditions? Do you have suspicions about the route being taken or the anticipated fare? If so, you're not alone.

When you board a plane, you would never question the route the pilot is going to take. The fare has already been paid and will not change based on traffic backups or extra miles flown. The environment looks generally clean and you're not too scared that you'll find something totally gross when you reach down for the seatbelt. And the flight attendants, while maybe not ecstatically greeting you at the door, are not usually surly.

When getting in a taxi, all of these things need to be considered.

Tips for Avoiding Tangles with Taxi Drivers

To help you become a confident back-seat taxi passenger, here are some tips for avoiding problems with your next taxi driver:

- Be very specific about where you want to go. Have a hotel business card with an address, a printed itinerary, or a clearly written address. This is better than saying "The Hilton downtown" as you may think there is only one but in fact there may be two or more.

- If paying by credit card, ask if credit cards are accepted and if there are any credit card fees before getting in the taxi. [See more about using credit cards below.]

- Ask if the fare is by meter or a flat fee before you get into the cab. If by meter, ask for an approximate fare. Keep reading the next tip for how to have confidence in the estimate you're given.

- When taking a taxi from the airport to a hotel, call the hotel ahead of time and ask for the approximate fare. If the driver gives you a very different fare, say something like, "Hmmm, the usual fare is around $xxx, isn't it?" If there are no traffic issues such as construction or rush hour backups, any higher estimate may seem reasonable to you. Too low of an estimate and the driver may not be clear on where you want to go.

- If you know that your destination is only a short distance away – and that the taxi driver may have been waiting in a queue for a very long time for a fare (this is common in many airports and at hotels):
  - Call your hotel to see if a free shuttle bus is available.

- ◆ Check with the taxi coordinator onsite (typically this is only at the airport) on what the rules are. They will usually not tolerate a taxi driver who refuses to take passengers on "short runs."

- ◆ Get in the cab; say that you know it's only a short distance but that you'll provide a generous tip. You shouldn't have to tip extra, but this may be the lesser of the evils and get you to your destination with less stress.

- Always take down your taxi driver's permit or registration number. This is typically attached to the vehicle's visor or other visible spot near the driver. If not easily seen, ask the driver for it. Why?

  - ◆ If they do not have a taxi permit or registration, it is possible they are operating without a taxi license. While this is unlikely in a taxi queue such as at an airport or train station, it is surprisingly common on the streets of many cities.

  - ◆ You might have forgotten an item in the taxi and need to call the company to search for it.

  - ◆ You may have a question on the actual credit card billing if it differs from what you thought you paid.

  - ◆ You may need to file a complaint if any serious issues or bad driving occurred.

  - ◆ You might feel unsafe so the information can be sent to a family member or colleague via text or email.

- Better yet, ask the driver for a business card. This is especially valuable for the above reasons, but also gives you their contact info if they are a truly great driver and you would like to use them in the future. Most drivers appreciate being asked for their card, especially when they are hoping it will lead to future business.

A quick, real-life story on why it is important to note a taxi driver's name and number:

My husband dropped me off at the departure area at LAX and helped me get my luggage out of the trunk of our rental car. A hug and a kiss and I headed to my flight. He got behind the wheel, waited for the adjacent taxi to drive away, then pulled away from the curb to exit the airport.

CRUNCH!

He stopped when he heard the noise and felt a bump under the tire. The girl who alighted from the cab came screaming after him. "You ran over my bag!"

Seems the taxi driver, who had by now driven away, placed her laptop bag on the street in front of our car and not on the walkway where it would have been safe.

Police were summoned, and my husband was questioned. This was deemed an accident, though the taxi driver might have been found at fault. But his passenger, who now owned the thinnest laptop ever, had paid cash for her ride and had not noted down the taxi driver's name or number.

Taxi drivers in more and more cities are accepting credit cards. That's good because it means traveling with less cash. Most of them have transaction machines in the cab. Just slide your card the same as in a store.

However, I have seen a couple things I don't like with cabs and credit cards. First, some of them charge an additional fee for using a credit card. This may or may not be disclosed, so ask!

Second, many have built-in *"proposed tip"* calculations. Most of them begin at 20% but I have seen them as high as 35%. Just touch the % button and the selected amount is added to your charge.

Of course, no one is required to tip a taxi driver – and the amount can be changed to 10% or whatever you want – but you need to do that manually. They are counting on your simply using the touch screen to be finished with the credit card transaction sooner.

If a taxi driver will not accept your credit card or says the machine is broken (I can't believe how many times I have heard this line!), get another cab if paying by credit card is important to you.

Similarly, another line often heard is, "It's going to take a long time to run your credit card through." If you hear this, say in reply, "Sorry to hear your machine is so slow. You could already have another customer if they gave you a faster machine." Funny how quickly the credit card approval is done.

There are many great taxi drivers, though there are lots of the other kind, too. When I think back over all my travel horror stories, many involve taxis. Had I known the above tips before many of these unfortunate events occurred, most of them never would have happened at all.

Car Rentals

Of the "big four" in travel – airlines, hotels, cruise lines, and car rentals – only the last one has been pretty profitable during the economic recession. How do they do it? They have an advantage over the others.

Hotels and cruise lines cannot sell off the parts that aren't making money. Both have fixed expenses with their number of rooms. While hotels may close off a wing or a floor of rooms, their real estate costs remain the same.

Can you imagine only three-quarters of a ship sailing out of port? No, they either fill their cabins or they don't. In economic downturns, they just have to get through as best they can.

Airlines can't fill their planes in difficult economic times either but let's face it, there is not much of a market for used Boeing 757s. All the airlines can do is take the planes out of service and park them in the desert, awaiting better days. The remaining planes can fly full, minimizing operating costs.

Comparatively speaking, car rental companies have it much easier. When their business falls off, they simply sell the unused cars at auction. That leaves them with just enough rental inventory approximately equal to what they need. With no excess cars on hand, there is no reason to reduce prices. Thus, the price of car rentals has remained steady.

The first question you want to ask when renting a car is where do you go to pick up the car? It may be onsite at your destination city and it may be located some distance away.

For example, many airports offer onsite service. You may need to walk a bit but they are usually somewhat near the baggage claim area. On the other hand, there are many airports that set up their rental car facilities off-site. To make this a little more confusing, there are some airports that have multiple off-site car rental facilities.

Most often, there is a shuttle service from the airport to the rental location. However, even this is not the same everywhere. For example, at some airports like Chicago O'Hare and Los Angeles International, there are shuttle buses for each rental car company. Then there are other airports like Las Vegas and Houston that use a central shuttle to take you to most of the rental car companies (not always all, so ask if you're not sure).

Also, remember to ask where to return the car at the end of your trip. Again, some returns are onsite at the airport while others may be a few miles away. Plan for additional time when returning a vehicle, even more so if you are unfamiliar with an off-site return location.

Features to Look For

Before you go searching for a rental car, know what features you're looking for. Your needs will determine car availability and costs. Here are some things to consider before selecting a vehicle:

- Determine the type and size of car you need. Larger cars, of course, cost more to rent and are usually more expensive to operate because they use more gas.

  If you will be sharing a car with one or more colleagues, it may make sense to have a larger car since you may be transporting a lot of luggage.

- While a smaller car or even a sports car may appeal to you, consider whether it is big enough to hold you and your luggage. Even some larger cars may have relatively small trunks. Ask about this if you have more than a few bags, perhaps only a large one, or you are traveling with children or others.

  Some rental car agencies offer upgraded cars at no extra cost but this might not be a bargain. Why? The vehicle costs more to operate, and parking it is often a challenge, especially when full size sedans exceed the boundaries of small downtown parking garages.

- The majority of cars for rent in the U.S. have automatic transmissions; outside of North America, a manual transmission is the norm. If you can't drive a stick shift, read the car's features before booking. If you are booking a car for an international trip and do need an automatic transmission, book early as many agencies have only a small number of these cars.

- If you have more than one driver, inquire about age restrictions for drivers. Many car rental companies used to limit this to drivers at least 25 years old. Today, many companies allow for drivers as young as 21, even as young as 18, though expect additional fees.

  I have been on consulting projects where a teammate is not yet 25 years old. They can vote, drink, have a family, an MBA, be working on a major global project . . . but cannot rent a car.

  Some corporate customers may be exempt from the underage limitations or fees, so check with your corporate travel coordinator if you are not yet 25 years old.

- Think about the weather. If you are renting a car in winter, an SUV with 4-wheel drive may be necessary to get around certain locations. Also, don't forget to ask if you need something like a ski rack or other car-top mount. A remote starter is also a very nice feature in cold winter weather.

A popular and very functional accessory you can request at the time of booking is a GPS navigation system. It can be very handy when you are traveling in an unfamiliar city to have a Global Positioning System. It also can be pricey, usually about $15 a day, but can save you from driving around lost, wasting valuable time or missing a key meeting. Some of the navigation systems also have features for weather, mapping out the best driving plan if you are making multiple stops, and setting up the itinerary online for easy downloading to the GPS.

Don't wait until you pick up the car to request a GPS; there may not be any cars with GPS or portable units available.

Here's an alternative: If you own a portable GPS unit, consider packing it for your travels. If you don't have one already, today they are readily available for less than $100. That is less than the cost to rent one for a week, and now you own it. Just remember to pack the car charger when you travel.

Another alternative: There are GPS apps for many mobile devices. However, my experiences have been that sometimes they work, sometimes they don't. GPS vocal instructions are very helpful but not if you are using the phone as well. Hearing both voices in your headset can be annoying. Also, this quickly drains the battery.

A feature that comes in handy in many major cities is a toll pass. It is usually a transponder that attaches to the windshield or the front bumper of the car. Some car rental agencies include them; some do not, so ask at your car rental agency.

These transponders incur a daily charge for each day you have the car once you use the toll pass at least one time. You can skip the toll pass lane and pay all tolls with cash or with your own transponder, so even when it's attached to the car its use is optional.

It may take only one long line at a toll booth when you're running late to a meeting or catching a plane to see the value of a transponder. It's a nice feature if there are several toll booths to go through but an unnecessary expense if there are only one or two and traffic is not heavy.

More Questions to Ask

Do you only need a one-way rental? They are often available but can be quite expensive due to the rental car company's "drop off charge."

Some rental companies have restrictions such as one-way rentals only within the same metropolitan area or between major airports. Generally, larger rental companies offer more choices because they have more facilities and more cars.

Picking up your car at one location and dropping it off at another may not cost anything or it may cost more than the rental itself. Picking up a car at a rental car location in a Chicago suburb incurs no additional cost if the vehicle is returned to the airport. However, if the vehicle is picked up at the airport and returned in Milwaukee, for example, there may be a drop-off charge.

Do you require different hand controls or handicap options? Book ahead to ensure the features that you need are available.

Does the vehicle come with unlimited mileage? Most car rentals allow for this but others allow only a certain number of miles included in their rate. Unlimited mileage may be important if you are driving any long distances, say a couple hundred miles or so.

Do you need a car seat or booster seat for your children? Car companies almost always provide these for a daily fee. Providing your own can save a lot of money.

Planning to use a debit card to pay for the rental? Some locations accept debit cards, some do not. Rental agencies have different requirements for customers who have only debit cards at the time of pickup. Some, but not all, debit cards may be accepted, your credit history may be checked, and a significant authorization hold may be put on your bank account.

ABC's of Booking a Car Rental

Before arranging for a car rental, know the dates and times for pickup and drop-off. The time matters!

Rental car companies usually work with a 24-hour period starting from the time you pick up the car. If you need a car from 12:00 pm on Monday to 4:00 pm on Wednesday, this is a 3-day rental. Usually once you are past the 24-hour mark, you will be charged for another whole day.

How can you reduce this down to a 2-day rental? Either pick up the car a bit later or return it earlier. Consider working in an airport lounge for a couple of hours before getting the car or return to the airport earlier when your business is completed.

If you are generally within 2 to 3 hours past the 24-hour period, most agencies will charge a per hour rate for the additional time. Over a few hours and it usually becomes equivalent to a full day charge anyway. This is why you want to know the dates and times for pickup and drop-off before you rent your car.

Now for booking:

You can arrange for a vehicle online or via telephone with all car rental companies. If you select online, fill out the screen information for each of the rental agencies to get their quotes and then compare them.

If your organization contracts directly with car rental companies, enter the firm's rate code. While this is speedy for business travel, you will want to know the other methods for occasions when a specific vehicle style is not available from this company or you are traveling for personal reasons.

Check out consolidators like Expedia, Travelocity, Orbitz or Kayak. These sites offer the convenience of comparing rates for different car rental companies in a side-by-side matrix. They also may have access to special deals offering better prices than the car rental company itself. However, these sites may charge a booking fee on top of the quoted price.

Some travelers prefer using these sites for their comparison feature, then book directly on the selected car rental's website. Changing or cancelling a reservation made via the consolidator sites may be more troublesome than booking directly through the car rental company. Typically you are charged for the car at the time of the rental, not at the time you actually need it. These rules may change so read them before booking.

Another option is to rent through a name-your-own-price online site such as Priceline or Hotwire. This is a viable option that may save money if you are not choosy about the type of car you will be driving. However, be prepared to be billed immediately upon reserving a vehicle. Also note that in most cases, your selection might be non-changeable, non-transferable and non-refundable. Express service and loyalty programs (frequent flyer points, frequent rental points, etc.) usually are not available for these types of rentals.

With car rental companies, it is very important to shop around. At any given time, one or another may offer special deals or promotions. See if these are available on the dates you need the car.

Another option: Use a travel agent. They can search all the car agencies quickly to find the best deals. Letting them do the work may save you valuable time. However, there may be a booking fee charged.

Demystifying Car Rental Insurance

A study in 2007 by the National Association of Insurance Commissioners (NAIC) found that 42% of the respondents were "either thoroughly confused or had only a rough idea about insurance." Moreover, 34% of consumers surveyed by telephone bought a rental car company's insurance just to make sure they were covered, even though they may already have had sufficient coverage through their own auto insurance policy or their credit card.[9]

This begs the question: Is the rental agency's insurance necessary? I don't know about your personal situation but in many cases, the coverage you already have will extend to rental cars.

If you currently have comprehensive and collision insurance for your own vehicle, it may not be necessary to request similar coverage from the rental car agency. In other words, agency coverage may be nothing more than duplicating what you already have. If you do not have this coverage, the rental agency coverage will be your primary risk protection.

What if you do not own a vehicle and have no coverage? The rental agency will offer primary coverage so this might be worth the money. Compare products offered by your credit card company, rental car agency and a non-owners auto insurance policy from regular auto insurers.

While insurance is one of the most profitable add-on features from rental companies, it's best if you look at this more from a risk protection point of view. First, check with your own insurance carrier. If you have coverage already, it is very possible the rental insurance will not pay off anyway, since your own policy is considered the primary coverage.

A TIP ABOUT INSURANCE: Many credit card companies include rental car coverage as a benefit. Obviously this applies only if this is the card used for the rental. Also, corporate renters may have coverage as part of their contract with the corporation. If applicable, check with your travel department.

If you are planning to rent a car outside the U.S. – even if only Canada or Mexico – ask your insurance company about coverage for a rental vehicle. Also ask if the deductible for your own car applies to a rental car.

ANOTHER TIP: When I began driving a lot for international travels, especially driving on the left side of the road in the UK, I called my credit card company. They have low-cost insurance applied to each rental that offers collision coverage in most countries. Interestingly enough, this coverage becomes primary over that of a standard auto insurance policy.

Here's a quick line-up, in layman's terms, of the most common coverages offered:

- Loss Damage Waiver (LDW): Covers loss or damage to the vehicle and releases you from responsibility for these costs. There is a daily fee for this, possibly with several levels of coverage.

- Party Auto Liability Claims: Protection involving accidents with other people.

- Accidental Death and Personal Passenger Protection: Covers your life and your stuff. Typically, your own health insurance may cover medical costs, regardless of what car you're driving. Your homeowners or renters policy most often covers personal property if it's stolen or damaged while in your car (likely with a deductible). Of course, your own life insurance will pay off as well in most cases.

If you elect any or all of the coverages available from the car rental agency, you must accept these types of insurance at the beginning of the rental. Once the vehicle is off the lot, it is too late.

And please, remember to pack your insurance card when renting a car in the event you are involved in an accident. Also, at the time of rental some car agencies ask to see proof of insurance, especially if you elect out of their coverage. Obviously you also need copies of driver's licenses for each person who will be listed as a driver of the vehicle.

One warning about all vehicle insurance: If you do have an accident and it is determined that you were speeding, driving under the influence, or it was due to some other reckless error on your part, any car rental coverage may become void.

Additional Costs

Yes, there are other costs that can go into car rentals. Here are a few more:

What is the cost to add an additional authorized driver? This depends on the rental agency and the relationship of the other driver to you. Some do not charge if your spouse or partner is the additional driver, some will. Some exempt a spouse but not a partner. There are differences for corporate employees using company rate plans, children over age 25 and companion drivers for disabled renters. Also, charges vary by state. Always check each agency's rules if there is the possibility of an additional driver.

This varies wildly between agencies as well as states but rental companies are generally consistent in their practice that the younger the driver, the higher the additional costs. Do the math to see if it is worth it.

 TIP: If you are tempted to skip the cost of an additional driver by just not telling the agency – don't! Any insurance you may have will most likely be void if it's found that an unauthorized driver was behind the wheel at the time of an accident.

A little known fact is that there may be upper age limitations when renting a car. This is not very common (yet) in the U.S. with major rental companies, but some domestic franchises and various international countries do impose maximum age limits. If you are 69 or older, check with your rental agency before booking a car.

Is there a charge for returning the car early? Yeah I know, this sounds like a strange question. You would think they would be happy to have a car back early so they could rent it again sooner.

Sometimes reality is weirder than... common sense? But seriously, some companies will charge an early return fee. This most often applies in conjunction with discounts like a weekly or special weekend rate.

The rental company will re-calculate what the cost would have been at the normal daily rate. Perhaps by no coincidence, the new calculation seems to be the highest possible rate they can charge. That daily rate is now multiplied by the number of days the vehicle was actually used. When the benefit discount disappears, the new day rate is more expensive.

But wait, there's more. Some companies may add an early return charge of $10-15 per day. Even simple math shows it is possible to actually pay more to keep the car for less time. Search online for each car rental company's "early return policy" to know the rules ahead of time.

What's the charge for returning vehicles late? There are a couple possible charges here. Expect to see a late charge fee as well as an hourly or daily rate for the extra rental time. Many rental car companies have short "grace periods" – 29 minutes is the norm – but the grace period does not apply to optional charges such as collision protection plans and GPS rentals. For these, expect to pay a full day's charge if you return the car late.

What about a refueling fee? Generally, you receive the vehicle with a full tank of gas and they expect it to be returned the same way. However, some rentals include a minimal amount of driving, perhaps 75 miles. Staying within that minimum may mean no refueling requirement though there may be a nominal charge.

Most agencies allow renters to pre-purchase a tank of gas at the time of rental (not once you've driven off the lot), sometimes at a cost per gallon a little less than at the pumps. This is usually a good deal if the expected driving approximates a tank of gas. Use less than three-quarters of a tank, and this becomes expensive. Note that some agencies, such as Hertz, now offer a pre-purchase of a half tank of gas at the time of rental.

If you are unsure about the amount of driving expected, the best option is usually to refill the tank just prior to returning the vehicle. Just to be safe, always get a receipt if you fill the tank.

A final option is to return the vehicle without refueling. Absent any other special deals, this is usually the most expensive choice. It is not uncommon for rental agencies to charge an extra dollar or more per gallon just because they need to fill the tank.

A frequent flyer fee, really? Some travelers take advantage of certain car rental company policies that include receiving frequent flyer miles with a favorite airline. [Note: Some hotels offer this as well.] Sadly, some agencies now charge a fee for this. While the cost isn't high, it might be more than you would pay an airline for additional points. Check this out before you sign the rental agreement.

If you arrive late, will the car still be there for you? The answer may depend on how prepared you are and how late you arrive. For example, if you are flying to your car rental destination, always tell the company your airline and flight number. Most – if not all – online car rental booking sites include a place to add your flight information. If your flight is late, the agency will know about it, which minimizes the chance that they will give your car to someone else – but doesn't necessarily guarantee it.

Of course, always call the rental agency directly if possible. Like all the other important phone numbers to have when you travel, be certain to have the rental agency confirmation and central reservations phone number handy.

What if the car isn't available because of a late arrival? Most rental companies try to work with customers when problems arise. First, of course, they will go through their own inventory but it is not unusual for a company to work with other vendors to help find what you need. As discussed in Chapter 12, loyalty program members are more likely to receive better service.

The bigger issue is when the rental car office is closed for the night. If they know your flight number, they may remain open, especially if there are several customers all on the same flight. Again, though, no guarantees.

What if you cancel the car? This varies substantially. Know the cancellation rules before making any reservation. Failure to meet their minimum cancellation notice could probably result in a fee.

More Considerations

There are a few more things to consider no matter what size and type of car you select. The first thing is to look over the contract. If you have any questions, ask before renting the car. I know, most of us are not lawyers but it is still worth a few minutes to review your rental agreement; always ask questions if there is something you don't understand.

Note that the rate you are quoted may be different the next day. Most companies have a system that monitors their inventory. As the number of vehicles available goes down, the rates can go up. In other words, the rate tomorrow might be higher or lower than the rate today. Yes, it can change that fast.

Here's another recent development with some car rental agencies: Their contracts now include opt-out boxes instead of opt-in. What that means for you is that they will automatically add in certain charges and fees unless you specifically say no.

It used to be that you had to agree to those charges. Now you have to agree not to have them. It doesn't seem to be a very ethical way to do business but apparently it is not illegal. This is another reason to check your contract very carefully.

Rental agencies are well aware that most people simply sign or initial where they are asked to do so. Indeed, many learn the hard way that they agreed to something they didn't want or need.

Of course, always look for whatever discounts may be available. These include AAA and AARP, as well as special coupon codes you may find through online searches. The Entertainment coupon books, available in many cities throughout the U.S., usually have discounts off daily and weekly car rentals.

TIP: If you are staying at a hotel that offers a free shuttle service from an airport, think about using that instead of renting a car at the airport.

Why? Well, there are two good reasons: First, you can rent the car the following morning. This alone could save you one day's rental costs.

Second, you may be able to rent the same car at a non-airport location for a lot less money. The reason is airports add huge fees to their rental cars. You will almost certainly pay additional airport taxes (I saved 22% in Chicago by renting off-airport). Also, some rental companies charge a "convenience fee" to use their shuttle services. Note that even downtown city rental locations are often less expensive than airports.

As mentioned elsewhere in this book, many hotels charge parking fees at their properties. This can be another very expensive, unexpected cost of renting a car. There may actually be instances where the parking fees are greater than the rental fees. In any case, add this cost to your budget if it applies.

Now That You've Booked, What's the Total Cost?

The daily cost for renting a car is just the start. Yes, there's more – much more!

Car rental companies actually have more add-on charges than airlines. For example, expect to see fees for sales and use taxes, local taxes, excise taxes, value added taxes, airport or facility taxes, surcharges or similar fees.

In some locations you also may find special types of tourism taxes, drop-off fees, seasonal surcharges, various administrative fees, and even "customer facility charges," whatever that means. All these extra charges can add 30-50% to the cost of a car rental. Take this into account before renting.

Each company is different, of course, but here are some additional charges to look for, especially from those who offer particularly low rental rates: reservation charge fees, administrative costs, servicing charges, even miscellaneous things like tire disposal fees.

Getting a quote for total cost is sometimes difficult. For example, some agencies offer special weekend rates but they are very specific, such as Friday to Sunday or Monday. Yes, it actually may cost more to pick up a weekend rental on Saturday instead of Friday. I know, I don't understand the logic either.

As you can see, it is very important to ask about the *total cost* of renting a vehicle. At a minimum, you can be certain the total cost will greatly exceed the amount of the simple rate quoted.

Before Driving Off, Check Out the Car

Car rental companies claim that there is substantial damage to vehicles by renters. Be aware that they are enforcing this more by seeking reimbursement from renters. It is very important to inspect the vehicle for damage prior to driving it off the lot. Report any damage immediately.

At an absolute minimum, a good tip is to photograph the car before it leaves the lot (your mobile phone's camera can be used for this). If the company later claims you damaged the vehicle, and you can prove the damage was already there, your chances of their dropping a claim against you are much improved.

Mostly due to flight time considerations, it is not uncommon that cars are returned either before or after regular business hours. For example, having a 7 am flight might mean returning a vehicle at 5:30 am, before the agency opens. Since this is before anyone arrives at work, vehicles are not officially checked in by anyone. All you can do is leave it there all locked up. But this is often where the problems begin.

Cars can be damaged after you drop them off but before the locations are officially open, especially if vehicles are left in an unsecured area. It is difficult to prove the damage occurred after the vehicle was returned but you can do a couple of things to protect yourself.

The best thing you can do it take photos of the car when it is returned. Cover everything, from the bumpers and sides to all the windows. Better yet, use video if you have it.

If the rental company files a charge against you, use your own photos or videos as proof that you returned the car in the same condition you received it. It is still no guarantee they won't pursue an additional charge but it will put you in a much stronger position to argue your case.

In addition to checking out the condition of the car, make sure you know how to operate everything. This includes door locks, headlights, wipers, emergency brake, gas tank release and the radio. It's not safe to be trying every button or switch when it starts raining and you are on an unfamiliar highway.

Many of the national chains offer only non-smoking fleets, with hefty cleaning fee assessments if they find evidence of smoking or the presence of tobacco odor. If you receive a vehicle with a smoky odor, let the agency know right away so that you are not charged an assessment for a previous renter's smoking.

TIP: Traveling in cold or snowy weather? Look inside the vehicle for a brush and scraper for the windows. You don't want to discover their absence when already on the road. This is when you will learn that a credit card can become an ice scraper alternative!

ANOTHER TIP: Make sure the fuel tank is full when you get the car. If it's not, insist that the agency rep note the fuel level on your rental contract so that you don't wind up paying for the last driver's gas as well as your own. Then return the car with the fuel level up to where it started.

Returning Your Car Rental

If you have to fill the gas tank, generally try to do it within 10 miles of the return location. In some cities, this is easy. In others, it may be difficult to find a gas station that close to the drop-off location.

TIP: If the vehicle is to be returned to the same location from where it was picked up, look for nearby gas stations as you leave the car rental facility that can be used when you return.

For peace of mind, check the vehicle for personal items when it is returned. It is amazing how much is left behind. Look in the console, glove compartment, under the seats, and definitely inside the trunk.

In fact, check everything twice, especially if you are traveling with someone else. The last thing you want to hear a companion say is, "I didn't check the car because I thought you did." Best if both of you check behind each other.

One soon-to-be bride left her wedding veil in the back seat of a rental car. Much to her dismay, she didn't realize it until after going through security at the airport.

Of course she went through obligatory bridal panic but was smart, having had the foresight to record the telephone number of the rental agency in her phone. The veil was found, and the agency sent it to her overnight. Disaster averted.

Alas, her story is the exception. Rental agencies report that dozens of items are left in cars every day. These include sunglasses, wallets, laptop computers, mobile phones, car charges, even luggage.

Remember to turn in the keys! Car rental agency employees don't appreciate not being able to move the car. Yes, sometimes there is no backup key available, most certainly if the return location is different than the pick-up site. Besides, you want to avoid the hassle and additional expense of sending it back.

Always review your final bill. It is helpful to get a print-out at the time the car is returned but there may be additional charges anyway. Fuel charges, fees for smoking in the car, exterior damage, parking fines, and other items may be added after the fact. Auto responder toll charges usually post to your credit card days or weeks after your rental and are not part of the rental car bill itself.

Compare the final bill with the amount on your credit card statement. If there is any discrepancy, make an inquiry to find out why.

Hopefully, differences can be worked out to everyone's satisfaction but if not, consider filing for an adjustment with your credit card company. In any case, email is preferable for correspondence because it is immediate and leaves a paper trail, as attorneys like to call it.

Phone calls also are quick but sometimes lead to disputes over what was actually said. If calls are necessary, always obtain the other person's name along with the date and time called. Finally, document any discrepancies.

One additional fee that might show up after the vehicle is returned is for traffic tickets. For example, the rental car company may receive notice that one of their vehicles was caught running a red light. Unfortunately, this notice may not arrive for a few months after the car was rented. Imagine a driver's surprise on seeing this belated charge on a credit card statement. However, this surprise ticket charge is often minor compared to the "administrative cost" added by the company. It is sometimes hundreds of dollars. Review all rental car charges very carefully.

Hiring a Car Service

Some business travelers do not want to rent a car nor do they want to deal with trying to find a taxi, especially in certain neighborhoods or perhaps late in the evening. I know from experience it is no fun trying to hail a taxi when it is pouring outside.

For a relatively few lucky travelers, there may be a private driver available for their needs. Usually this driver is provided by an employee's company or a client to specifically provide transportation as needed. Needless to say, this is the ultimate in local transportation. In truth, sometimes the vehicle is actually a van – and it is probably shared by other employees – but for a moment here, let's just enjoy the fantasy that this is your own private limousine.

This driver is there to cater to your needs with door-to-door service available as needed. Besides thick, comfortable leather seating, some include luxury amenities such as satellite television, Wi-Fi, video conference calling, and a bar with your favorite libations.

These drivers are willing to sit in horrible rush hour traffic with no road rage while you relax in the back reading a newspaper or magazine, enjoying a refreshing drink, or perhaps catching up on some email or social media.

Yes, it is nice to dream about such great service but time to get back to reality. Actually, there is an alternative and it many not cost as much as you think.

Many cities offer local car services for hire. While it is unlikely they are less expensive than most taxi services, their advantages may be worth the difference. Most local services allow you to rent by the day. In other words, you have a vehicle and driver available as needed for the entire day.

Perhaps you need to travel to several locations in a single day. Maybe some of these locations are not on high-traffic taxi routes. Also, it is possible you are unsure how long you will be at a specific location so having a driver waiting for you is necessary.

While this may be seen as too expensive for many who are traveling, consider being able to share the cost with others. With a group of four to six people, the cost may well be similar to taxi fees for each, possibly even less expensive. Check it out next time you travel to another city.

You may not need a car service for a day, but would like a nicer ride to and from the airport than in the back of a taxi. There are numerous car services available in all major cities where the car service acts in a similar capacity to that of a taxi (though with a much nicer car).

See the *Business Travel Success Ultimate Travel Resource* for car service sources or call your hotel and ask who they recommend. This latter tip is how I found drivers in two different cities who I used repeatedly over several years.

5

HOTELS

After seeing that many colleagues from the same company were traveling to the same city on a recurring basis, my previous company decided that renting a home for all of us to use would be much more economical than separate hotel rooms.

A 4-bedroom split-level home was secured in a decent neighborhood; 3 bedrooms upstairs and 1 down.

While this may have made economic sense, it sure didn't make sense in other areas:

- I was the only female colleague amongst about a dozen guys who might be rotating through this house.

- Maid service was only twice a week and some bedrooms might have a different occupant nightly.

- The downstairs bedroom was off-limits to the guys and deemed as mine since I was the only female sharing the house. However, this didn't always work as I learned when I'd smell men's cologne on my pillow.

- You never knew when you'd hear the garage door open (which was right next to my room) and it was usually at all hours of the night due to late night flight arrivals.

- Cell phones were not yet in existence. There was one wall phone in the kitchen for us all to share. When the phone rang, we were all scared to answer. Would it be my husband or his wife? Try explaining this household sharing situation to spouses!

The situation finally remedied itself when the neighbors ranted loud and clear. Seems they didn't like people arriving at all times of the day and night. Nor did they like seeing one *woman (yes, me!) with a vast assortment of guys (every race and age) coming and going. They said it wasn't a good impression for their kids.*

Needless to say, the company finally conceded that individual hotel rooms were the better route to go and that was the last time I "slept with" the CEO of our firm.

Think about this: You will typically spend more hours each day in your hotel room than anywhere else during your business travels.

It is in your hotel room where you have some quiet time at the end of each day and get revved up for the next day. Your hotel room is also the place where feelings of loneliness can sneak in and where you may feel cutoff from family and friends.

Your hotel room is a functional part of business travel that becomes a personal part of your life. The goal is to make the most out of the functionality while also creating a good experience.

For most travelers, a hotel room is more than just a bed and a shower. It's a place where you relax, enjoy some alone time, work out, expand your network and take advantage of offerings not available at home. Many hotels offer more amenities than we realize or take the opportunity to enjoy.

For example, hotels may offer:

- In-room fitness equipment or workout television shows
- Wine tastings
- Business networking happy hours
- Live music in the bar or lounge
- Books, videos or games to borrow
- In-room massage or full-service spa
- Wellness, nutrition or sleep advice
- Exercise classes
- Holiday events

Your hotel also may offer partnerships with local restaurants, fitness centers, museums and a variety of other venues that help increase your enjoyment of not only the hotel but the city you are visiting.

Start by reading the in-room or on-screen listings of the hotel offerings. Also check with the hotel's concierge or front desk. Simply ask them, "How do I make the most out of my stay with you?"

You may not need to bother selecting a hotel or other overnight accommodation. If you are traveling for a conference or other meeting, the organizing group usually selects a hotel for you – sometimes a few hotels depending on attendance – and you simply book a room where everyone else is staying.

Some companies and government agencies make it easy for business travelers by contracting for certain long-term accommodations at destination apartments or condos. Basically this is company-paid housing and offers features such as separate bedrooms and perhaps a full kitchen. Most are far larger than typical hotel rooms and more home-like, though they may lack some of the amenities of a full service hotel.

Others companies may restrict accommodations to a limited geographical area. It is not so unusual for employees to be required to stay within only a short distance of a destination city. Other firms may require a stay within a shuttle ride of an airport.

Limits on maximum hotel rates also may be in place. Some limits include taxes, internet, and tips, while others are for the room rate only. Limits by city are also in some travel policies, with higher room rates allowed in New York City or San Francisco, for example.

In the most common corporate scenario, a list of "approved" hotels is provided. This approved list is the result of annual negotiations between internal travel managers and selected hotel properties. Rates have been agreed upon based on anticipated usage and other factors.

The number of hotels on the "approved" list may be small or may be extensive. It usually depends on the size of the company doing the negotiations and how many travelers they expect each year in any one geographic area. No matter how long the list, it may limit your choices on where to stay or limit the reimbursement amount should you decide to stay elsewhere.

When it comes to selecting a hotel for your business travel and conferences, work with your travel department or agent to find a hotel that's within budget but has the amenities you want. You'll enjoy the time at the hotel much more if it meets your minimum requirements.

As with other travel providers such as car rentals and airlines, always check with your company before making any reservations. Know the guidelines because mistakes can be costly.

Which Amenities Are Important to You?

Assuming you have a choice in hotels, wouldn't it be nice if you had an unlimited budget to choose whatever you wanted for overnight accommodations? Yes, very nice but not very realistic. Fact is, each traveler wants something different than the next one. The good news is there are lots of choices, and many of them add no extra cost to your stay.

Take, for example, hotel bedding. One traveler may want a bed with soft pillows while another likes only firm pillows. Some prefer a soft mattress while another wants something harder.

If you're a big screen movie watcher, sports fanatic or channel-flipper, the size of the in-room television, along with the choice in channels, may be what you base your hotel choice on. For those who rarely watch television or just turn it on to have noise in the room, this gets bumped down on your list of must-have hotel amenities.

Possibly the most popular amenity for business travelers is internet access. And free Wi-Fi always trumps paid Wi-Fi.

Listening to some of these road warriors, you would think that the internet was more important than a bed or a shower. Okay, knowing some of them, Wi-Fi probably *is* most important to them, but at least the travelers who I know always remember the shower, too. And yes, there are some hotels that do not offer internet at all (free or paid), or maybe have it only in the lobby, so check before making a reservation.

Many hotels today offer in-room coffee machines with regular and decaf coffee, along with tea bags. There are as many brands of in-room coffee as there are hotel chains. Some guests actually base their hotel choice on which one offers their favorite coffee.

When it comes to kitchen amenities, preferences may be:

- In-room refrigerator and microwave for keeping a small amount of food and storing/reheating leftovers;
- A full kitchen including a stove and dishware for cooking meals (great for longer term stays when you get tired of eating out each day); or
- Nothing that resembles any kind of kitchen stuff.

Speaking of food, a number of hotels include breakfast in the price of the room. Some make it available to all guests, while others may limit it to those who enjoy the hotel's executive lounge access. Either way, it is a popular amenity.

There are many other considerations to think about as far as where you stay in your travels. This list is certainly not exhaustive but does address many of the choices that may be available. Hopefully it will help you to think about what's important to you:

- Is there a shuttle service available from the airport? If so, what is the cost? What are the hours? Does the shuttle stop at several hotels?
- Does the room have two double beds or perhaps one king size bed? Maybe only twin beds in the case of some international hotels?
- Do you prefer a ground level room or something higher up?
- Does the room have a balcony?
- Is parking available? If so, is it valet or self-parking and what's the cost of each?
- Is smoking permissible in the room?
- Is there an elevator?
- Do you want to be near or far from an elevator or stairwell?

- Is there a door to the adjoining room? If so, it is double-bolted?

  Note: Beyond security reasons, many travelers prefer rooms with no adjoining doors as this keeps the noise level down and odors (smoking, smelly foods) away.

- Are there kitchen facilities, or at least a refrigerator, in the room?

- Is there a restaurant on site? If not, how far away?

- For on-site restaurant, can they prepare foods with dietary limitations?

- Is there a particular direction you prefer to face (away from the morning sun, for example)?

- Noise: Is the location near a highway or train? Is there construction in progress?

- How much does it cost to use the in-room telephone?

- Is room service available? If so, what are the hours of operation?

- Are internet services available? If so, what's the cost?

- If they have internet, is it in the rooms or only in the lobby? Wireless or wired? Is there an extra fee for better (i.e., faster) wireless service?

- Is there a hotel lounge for guests and if so, how much extra does it cost?

- Is there a fitness center? If so, what are its hours and what equipment is available? Is there a daily cost?

- Are upgraded rooms available and if so, how much extra do they cost?

- Are there in-room coffee makers?

- Is there a hair dryer?

- Are there padded hangers or a trouser press?

- How many power outlets are available in the room?

- Are in-room movies or games offered? If so, what's the cost?

- Is the heating and air conditioning room controlled or hotel controlled?

- What amenities are available for children? Are there parks or playgrounds nearby?

- Does the facility offer daycare services? If not, do they have recommendations for babysitters?

- Is there a pool or hot tub? If so, indoor or outdoor? Is there a lifeguard on duty?

- Is there a spa or sauna? If so, is there an additional cost?

- Are there on-site laundry facilities? Dry-cleaning or self-service washer and dryer? If not, how far away?

- Do they offer 24-hour security? If not, what hours do they work?

- Do they allow pets? If so, are these rooms on dedicated floors?

- Are business services available (printer, copier, fax, and shipping)?

Making Your Own Hotel Arrangements

For those who arrange their own hotel reservations, there are many options. Take time to do an internet search for useful information about the community you plan to visit, as well as places to stay. Search for the city's convention and visitor's bureau or local Chamber of Commerce websites for copious information.

Needless to say, there are many hotels and chains to choose from. Unless you desire a specific hotelier like Marriott or Holiday Inn or Four Seasons, selection can take quite a while.

There are a variety of hotel selection and booking methods:

- Online at a travel booking website (Hotels.com, Travelocity, Expedia, booking.com and the like);
- Online through a review site (TripAdvisor, Oyster and others);
- Online through a bidding site (Priceline, Hotwire, etc.);
- Online at a particular hotel chain's website;
- Call the hotel chain's toll-free central reservations number;
- Call the specific hotel property directly; or
- Call a travel agent.

If a corporate booking code is available, usually it is best to make a reservation through the hotel's main website. However, you may also want to check out other methods because the corporate rate may not always be the lowest.

While most conferences have group codes offering discounts, occasionally other discount rates are better, especially if you are traveling for governmental purposes. Take a couple of minutes to try it both ways before making a reservation.

Travel booking sites may offer good deals because they acquire a block of rooms and then resell them. Make sure you know the full cost of the room including any booking fees and taxes. *Always* read the rules for changes or cancellations as these may be extra or may not be allowed at all.

Online bidding sites are for the gamblers among us. These sites often will not tell you which hotel you're staying at until you have booked and paid for it. However, you can request the general location and quality (three-star, four-star, etc.).

Sometimes it is possible to save a significant amount of money over other booking methods. Nevertheless, these sites are used more often by vacation travelers when a specific property or exact location is not as important.

TIP: Many hotels/motels offer some form of discount off the printed rate. These discounts may be for AAA or AARP members, active military, or government. Check out each one that applies to you to see which gives the best rate. (Be prepared to show proof of your eligibility upon check-in.)

Also, do an online search. Some hotels offer discount or promotion codes online. And watch your email box. If you have an awards program with a property, you may receive special offers by email.

ANOTHER TIP: When you call a specific hotel directly, ask for a better rate. Sounds simple, and it often works! A hotel property may offer last-minute specials that they don't submit through their centralized reservation services.

Plus, agents at a hotel chain's central reservations number are typically not authorized to negotiate. If a booking service or central reservations service says that a property is sold out, call the hotel directly as there may be rooms available.

Another reason you may get a better deal directly from the hotel property rather than the main reservation number is because the hotel is independently owned.

This is surprising to many but most of the hotels are not really owned by the hotel chains. Instead, they are owned by others but managed by, say, Marriott, Hilton, or Omni, for example.

A travel agent may be able to get you the best rate and include extras that you may not have seen online – perhaps breakfast and a room upgrade.

Many hotels now offer a lower, non-refundable rate. Usually this is better than other discounts but it can be risky.

Non-refundable means just that. You may be responsible for payment for your stay even if you fail to arrive. While the rates may be lower, take advantage of them only if you are certain your itinerary will not change. (Note: For weather systems that affect travel in either your origination city or destination city, it _may_ be possible to change the dates of your hotel stay. Ask for the rules.)

Like all travel, booking with third parties comes with certain risks. If you book your reservation directly with a hotel, any issues you have are directly between the two of you. If you choose to use a third party to make the reservation, e.g., another online site, the hotels say any differences or issues need to be taken up with that site, not the hotel, since they were not involved in the reservation. Sometimes this becomes a nightmare to resolve.

Once you think a great deal has been found, ask about any additional charges such as taxes, resort fees, parking costs, energy surcharges, and other odds and ends that will be applied to your final bill. Even if one hotel has a lower daily rate, it may end up being a more expensive option once all the extras are added in.

Since no one method for hotel reservations always works the best, a good general rule is to shop around for the best rate using a combination of the above methods. Try to shop at only a few places. Time is valuable. You could spend hours looking for a rate that is $10 less a night, then add more time trying to find the rules on the lower rate. Know when good is good enough.

What else do you need to know about booking a hotel room?

Regardless of how you book your overnight accommodations, always become a member of their loyalty program before you make the reservation. This can be very helpful to you in many ways, from better rooms to upgraded suites.

The more you stay at a particular hotel group, the better the benefits. Some of these include nicer rooms, better views, quicker check-in and checkout, executive lounges, computer usage, and maybe a free breakfast. It is also much easier to work out issues when they know you are a frequent guest.

For more about loyalty and award programs, see Chapter 13.

Many hotels let you add additional information to your reservation. For example, if you desire additional towels, foam pillows, a refrigerator in your room or more, the hotel can have these items ready for you when you arrive.

Also let a hotel know if you are celebrating a special event. They may tell you about event packages or give you a room upgrade.

TIP: If you are staying at the same location for more than a couple days, get to know the staff. The more you relate to them on a friendly basis, the more they are likely to help you in time of need.

A simple 'Hello' followed by their name is all it needs to be.

Ah, Those Unexpected Costs

I briefly mentioned resort fees, parking fees, energy surcharges and more above. What's with all these charges?

Like many other travel vendors, hotels look for ways to increase their revenue. Be aware of possible add-on charges that can really increase your total bill.

Hotel mini-bars can trigger a charge to your room with their new motion and weight sensor technology. Merely opening the mini-bar's door to check out what's inside may trigger a cost just by your pulling out the item to look at it – even if you put it back. A time lag of 30 or 60 seconds is usually in place, so look fast and put the item back exactly where it was if you don't want it.

Some travelers are used to removing items in the mini-bar to make room for their own food and drink. While that may have worked in the past, this would be an expensive alternative now with this technology in place.

Non-refrigerated items such as snack crackers, nuts, and cookies may be sitting on top of a cabinet or minibar. Assume that the motion and weight sensor technology is in place there, too. Don't shove the items to the side to make more cabinet-top or refrigerator space for your stuff. You may find yourself at the front desk disputing the mini-bar charges. This I learned from experience.

And dispute you can. Just know that it takes time at the front desk to get your bill worked out. You can always bring the unused items down to the front desk to prove you didn't eat or drink them.

Children love checking out the mini-bar. Keep a watch on this or you could easily see a $100 charge on your room. Better choice: Ask the hotel to lock the mini-bar if you have children in the room. Best choice: Ask them to remove it.

Think twice before touching that seemingly "complimentary" bottle of water that the hotel has left on your desk. There is usually a tag around the neck of the bottle with its price.

If you're an elite member of the hotel's loyalty program, bottled water and a small snack may be included gratis. Ask if you are not sure.

This reminds me of a co-worker who had recently come to the U.S. from another country. He thought the hotel for our company conference was fabulous because of all the "free" snacks on the counter. He enjoyed many of the items over the course of the conference. I was behind him at the front desk when we were checking out and I saw his eyes become the size of saucers when he saw how much he had been charged! No disputing this bill. It was an expensive lesson learned.

To help resist the lure of the minibar edibles, make a quick stop in the hotel gift shop or a local store. Pick out your favorite snacks and enjoy them at a comparative bargain. Enough about food and drink, on to other hotel charges.

Before using the room's telephone, make sure you understand what the fees are. A toll free number may still have a charge associated with using an outside line. It is usually better to simply use your own cellphone if you have one and hope the reception is good enough.

Many hotels today offer guests the use of internet-connected computers, usually in their lobbies or nearby. In many instances, there is no charge, limited only by availability.

In the business center, expect to see charges for printing, copying, or backing up data to a disk or flash drive, or for sending faxes.

Certain hotels add daily charges for service support, energy surcharge and administrative fees. Each hotel calls it something different but the result is the same: You will have another daily charge to your room that might not have been quoted in the original price. Always ask about fees before using any hotel service.

There was a time when hotels would gladly hold your luggage if you checked out but were staying in town for a few more hours. Now some hotels charge for this service. What used to be a relatively small tip now may be quite a charge. If you need this service, ask about the fees.

Another more frequent charge is hotel parking. Valet parking typically has a fee, but now more hotels are charging for self-parking as well, especially in downtown areas.

The parking fees can be really high. How high? The most expensive I have seen so far is $58 a day in San Francisco, plus tip on top of that. In some cases, the parking charges are more than the cost of the rental car!

It is very common to see hotels charge for late cancellation of a reservation. However, the definition of *late* is changing. It used to be 6:00 pm on the day you expected to arrive. Now some charge a fee as much as three days before the arrival date. If you have a non-refundable rate, cancellation at any time may cost what you already paid. Add a reminder in your calendar for the cancellation date just in case your plans may change.

Yet another way hotels are adding revenue is with early check-in. If you arrive early, especially coming in from an international flight and wanting to get into your room before the more typical 3:00 or 4:00 pm check-in time, some hotels charge an additional amount.

On a side note, some airport hotels offer a half-day rate. These can be terrific whenever you may find yourself stuck at the airport for hours and would like a shower or a nap in a real bed. Usually this is found at hotels attached to airports but may apply to others only a short shuttle ride away.

And yes, I've stayed in hotels that appeared to be the type that charge by the hour but those can be the subject of someone else's book!

Good Night's Sleep

After spending a day traveling, sitting at a desk, walking a convention floor, and eating a drawn out dinner with business colleagues, it can feel great to finally get to your room for a night of peace and quiet. Unfortunately there are times when that is not to be. Been there, done that far too many times to not list a few.

Let's begin with noisy neighbors. To be a little fair, sometimes the walls are way too thin. The most common complaints are neighboring televisions and loud phone conversations. As a guest, you should expect to have reasonable quiet when you want to rest, much less sleep.

Most of the time, the irritating noise is periodic. This could be anything from neighbors to people walking in the halls to being too close to an elevator, stairwell, or ice machine. Other examples include loud children (especially if your room overlooks the pool), barking pets, maybe even being too close to a lounge that offers live music.

Usually these noises stop within a reasonable time, so turn up your television or music. Hopefully within a short time you'll find the noise has subsided. If not, a call to the front desk should take care of the problem. If the noise is really excessive, the hotel will usually get their security people involved. Try to work with the hotel if this is an issue, and they will try to work with you.

What are your best defenses? Of course, the first thing would be to have a room away from whatever is creating the noise. Unfortunately, sometimes that is impossible or at least impractical as it may mean relocating to another room in the middle of the night.

Fortunately there are still options. Many who fly prefer to use noise-canceling headphones. Not only do they drown out noise in an airplane, they do a pretty good job in a hotel room, too. Alas, they have a drawback to many travelers. The best of these headphones tend to be bulky, and some people just can't seem to sleep while wearing them.

Sometimes ear plugs can be your best friend. They are small, inexpensive, and can turn a horrible night into a tolerable one. They are usually foam inserts, just enough to keep out most of the loud noise while still being able to hear things like a telephone, alarm clock, doorbell, etc.

For some travelers, a little background noise is a welcome pleasure. Some leave the television on all night, perhaps as much for safety reasons as for noise. For bedtime listening, think about using a pillow speaker, which allows you to listen to music without headphones. This is what I travel with.

Others just want a little background noise. Consider turning on a fan if one is available. Many units have individually controlled heat/air and most of the time, the fan is set to Auto. That means it comes on only when you need additional heat or air. Change the setting to On and you can have a little fan noise all night long.

Still others prefer drugs, either prescription or the over-the-counter variety. Be careful here, the sleep can be too deep and too long. There is also the risk of sleeping through safety concerns such as a hotel fire alarm, someone trying to enter your room uninvited, or even missing your morning wakeup call.

Can I Steal This Stuff?

A question that comes up often is whether it is okay to take the hotel amenities. Put more bluntly, can we take this stuff because we already paid for it in the room rate or do the hotels consider this to be stealing? I have posed this question to many hoteliers over the years and here is how most of them see this issue.

Most hotels want you to feel comfortable and at home in your room, so nice amenities are provided. They're so nice that you might be tempted to take many of them home with you. Before you start loading up your luggage with goodies, know what's okay to take from your hotel room and what's not.

The toiletry items that hotels provide are generally included in the room rate. This includes soap, shampoo, conditioner, shower caps, body lotion, mouthwash, etc. Some hotels may include additional items like toothbrushes, razors, and sewing kits.

Some hotels offer two bars of soap, one for bath and another for facial. I know some travelers who use one for double duty and just take home the other.

Some travelers take these amenities because of personal benevolence. Yes, they remove some of the amenities before checking out but then they donate the unused items to local non-profit groups such as homeless shelters or others in need. I have been to conferences where the hotel shampoos, etc., were collected at the end of the conference for a local shelter.

Hotels also do not generally have a problem when guests remove things like snacks that may be provided for free or perhaps a bag that was intended for laundry. Most say you might as well take the slippers, too, since they can't be reused by another guest, though it is a bit greedy to take two pairs if there is only one person staying in the room.

In fact, some hotels want you to take small items like these. Because they went to a lot of expense to have their name placed on many of these items, some are quite happy that when you use them at home, you think of their hotel.

Sometimes the toiletry items are in a basket, often on a sink counter. Can you take the basket as well? No!

Okay, so if legitimate guest "thievery" is limited to the toiletries, how about if you see the maid's cart in the hall while you are going out. Is it okay to take a few items off the cart? The hotels not only frown on this kind of behavior, it actually bothers them quite a bit.

The carts are loaded with planned supplies, such as tissue, towels, soap, and shampoo, based on the needs of a floor or a wing. It is one thing when a guest asks for an additional towel or perhaps just ran out of tissue. It is something else to raid the cart with handfuls of anything you can grab just after the housekeeper goes back into another guest's room. If you need something, ask. Either call the front desk or ask a housekeeper.

For those who just can't resist the temptation to leave the cart alone and to take as much as possible —beware, you may be on camera.

Those hall security cameras are there to protect you as a guest, which means they may be recording all hall movement. That includes your lust for shampoo or toilet paper. At a minimum, you may not be invited back as a hotel guest. At worst, they will give you an additional room charge, hopefully along with that souvenir photo.

Coffee mugs and water glasses in the room belong to the hotel, not the guest, as do all the hangers in the closet along with the iron, hair dryer, and clock radio. It should go without saying that all furnishings and anything attached to the room belong to the hotel, too.

This includes televisions and stereos. And yes, the Bible in the drawer also belongs to the hotel. If you love the hotel's logo on the glassware or ashtray, look to purchase them at the hotel gift store.

What about towels and bed linens? Hotels tell me they are generally forgiving if a room is missing a towel (as in *one*); not forgiving at all when more towels are missing or the sheets are gone from the bed.

While waiting at the airport for my ride, I watched a man take his bag off the luggage carousel. White hotel towels were bulging out of the zippers. The main zipper wouldn't even close due to his big stash of towels. He kept trying to stuff them back in so he could leave the carousel area. It looked like four hotel towel sets were on their way to a new home.

Though this is tame compared to what one hotelier shared: They had a mattress stolen and an old mattress put in its place. It's unreal what some people will do!

Bathrobes, padded hangers and shoe trees always belong to the hotel unless you have made prior arrangements. Some hotel chains offer their bathrobes, bedding, and other products for sale. Look for their in-room catalog or ask at the front desk.

One tony Beverly Hills hotel bucks the trend, not only giving bathrobes to certain guests but even having them monogrammed, proving that prior arrangements and enough money can get you just about anything from the room. And no, I do not have one of these monogrammed robes.

Other Considerations

When traveling to a new location, first check out the hotel's website. You want to know what the place looks like, both inside and outside. Many of the sites today have virtual tours showing off most of the property's features.

Of course, they won't be saying anything negative about their hotel. That's where a website like TripAdvisor may be helpful. Check out the former guest comments, both positive and negative.

A note of caution: There has been a great deal of discussion about whether these comments are accurate. For example, their rating system allows a hotel manager and other employees to write anonymous glowing reviews while competitors are free to write scathing reports. Use this information carefully.

Tips on room locations:

- If you book your reservation directly with a hotel (as opposed to a central reservation line), ask about the room you will have. If your reservation is booked enough in advance, they may offer you choices of views or floors or at least note your preference on your reservation record.

- You may have more room location choices if you are traveling on less busy days or non-peak travel periods. This is also true if you are reserving for a special event like a honeymoon. However, be prepared to back it up with documents, though some hotels don't even ask for them.

- Some properties have multiple buildings. This might be either multiple towers or many small buildings. Ask about how far away you would be from activities like the pool, fitness center, restaurants, meeting rooms, and parking.

- *Safety tip*: You may not want to book a room above the seventh floor or so. In the event of a serious fire, fire truck ladders can only extend perhaps 100' from where the truck is parked. They may not be able to reach you on higher floors. Even if you do not need to be rescued, any evacuation will have you walking down the steps so lower is better.

- Some people prefer convenience so a room located near an elevator, exit door, ice machine, restaurant, bar, or laundry may be preferable. On the other hand, others want to get away from noisy and high traffic areas. Ask about your choices and also ask about the view from the room and the direction it faces.

- *Weird tip*: If the view is important to you, go to Google maps and get an idea of what the hotel looks like and the direction everything faces. Once you know that and see the view you like, tell the hotel you want a room facing in the direction you prefer. It never hurts to ask.

- If you have any doubts about your room, ask to see it before you check in. If it turns out to be less than you expected, ask about another room. You might get lucky.

Then there is the matter of actually finding the place you are staying. At the very least, make sure you have the address and phone number of the hotel along with your confirmation number. Better yet, if you have a GPS unit, put in the hotel address before you begin traveling. Or have the hotel's address in your mobile phone to take advantage of mobile apps such as Google Maps.

Want to sleep in for a bit in the morning? No problem, just remember to put the Do Not Disturb sign on the door. You may still hear some activity in the halls in the morning – after all, housekeeping still has work to do for the other guests – but at least you will be assured that they won't bother you any more than necessary.

Some people prefer no maid service so the Do Not Disturb sign is always hanging on the outside of the door. If you prefer this, tell Housekeeping so that they're not constantly checking your door during the day.

Is That You Crawling Under the Desk?

Think about all the things today that need electrical power. They include cellphones, music players, hair dryers, cameras, computers, razors, and game systems. I am sure you can add more to this list.

One of the most frequent complaints from business travelers is the lack of power outlets. Indeed, some hotels have done extensive renovations, which hopefully included adding more outlets. These renovations can't come soon enough because sometimes the only available outlet is tucked away under a desk.

Some hotels really do get it, adding outlets in various locations around a room, some perhaps more convenient than others but at least they are there. If this is important to you, don't forget to ask about it.

It is always a good idea to ask about room power outlets before you travel but you also might want to consider traveling with an extension cord. It might not be enough to charge up everything but it sure helps. If you have a laptop, think about using the USB ports to charge up some of your smaller electronics.

Very popular today are small, travel size extension cords. Usually they have three outlets, easily enough for most travelers. Since they are compact and light, it is easy to slip one in your travel bag.

Even More Hotel Tips

After a good night's sleep, you are ready to visit your new city. Here are a few more tips.

When leaving your hotel room, always check to see that the door closes behind you. Make it a habit to always pull it shut once outside the room. Do not learn the hard way that some doors do not close all the way and lock on their own.

Never put the "Make Up Room" sign on the door. Yes, it might be helpful to the cleaning crew but honestly, they will find out about your vacant room anyway. Instead, simply let someone at the front desk know your room is ready for housekeeping service.

Why not use the sign? Because all it does is tell everyone – including local burglars – that your room is empty. No reason to give them an invite.

If you need assistance on any aspect of your stay, the best hotel people to ask are at the concierge desk, if one is available. They are an amazing source of information about the town you are visiting and the hotel itself.

Here are a couple examples. Some travelers want more of a local feel to their journey so they want to hang out with the locals. Also, some tourists want to know the best local restaurants or get tickets to shows that are in town. A good concierge can be your best friend in any city or town across America.

Most hotel rooms have alarm clocks. If you need to get up early in the morning, either figure out how to set it or use the wake up service of the front desk.

LESSONS LEARNED ABOUT HOTEL ALARM CLOCKS:

- The time displayed may not be correct. Check it against your phone or watch.

- The person who stayed in the room before you may have left the alarm set – for 4:00 am! Check the settings so that it's right for you or turned off.

- The most accessible electric outlet may be where the clock is plugged in. Unplug the clock and you will have to figure out how to reset it or it might be blinking 12:00 at you all night.

By the way, many hotels today use an automated system for wake up calls. That means you can be rude and complain about the call all you want because there is no one on the other end of the line. However, some hotels still use a personal service for calling. They would appreciate it if you aren't rude when they wake you up as you requested. Ask what kind of system your hotel uses.

Especially nice is the wake up service that asks if you would like another wake-up call in 10 or 15 minutes. This is a great service if you are the type of sleeper who loves hitting the snooze button a few times in the morning.

Learn about the value of a shut-down call in Chapter 12, Time Management.

As I mentioned earlier, many hotels offer computer usage to their guests. If you are flying out of town, using their computer for airline check-in can be a great time saver.

If the hotel also has a printer, consider printing your boarding pass even if it costs you a couple of dollars (or get an electronic boarding pass sent to your phone for free, if available). That peace of mind will be worth it when you are running to the airport.

Check Points for Checking Out

Always check your room charges before you check out. Indeed, check your bill the day before you check out. Use this service throughout your stay if your visit is more than a couple of days.

The best time to review your room charges is when the day or evening staff is available to help resolve any issues. Later in the night there may be no manager around who has authority for room charge modifications. During the day, you will almost always be working with the regular staff.

TIP: Some travelers end all of their room charges with a specific number – let's say "07". After adding a tip to each bill, the total ends in this number. When scanning your hotel charges on your bill later in the week, it makes it much easier to verify that the charges are correct.

Some hotels offer on-screen viewing of your bill on the television. This makes it easy to check your charges frequently. If there are questions about your bill, bring them to management's attention immediately. You are more likely to get them resolved if you can do it in person rather than waiting until after you return home.

Unfortunately, most travelers review the bill when they are checking out. This is the worst time. Why? Because if there is a problem, you may have to wait to speak with a manager or they may need to review their records. In some cases, they may ask for something additional to support your claim. I know of one case where a hotel guest showed time-stamped pictures proving he was at a theme park when the hotel claimed he was sitting in their restaurant running up charges. I've had charges for in-room movies that I never ordered and minibar food I never ate.

My point here: The last thing you need is a hotel delay at the time you are planning to either move on to your next destination or are perhaps rushing to the airport to catch a plane.

As for the key to your room, most are now electronic key cards. Do you leave these behind or take them with you upon checkout?

One option is to leave your room keys at the front desk when you're checking out. If you have no need to go to the front desk, drop the keys into a key drop-off box, often seen in the lobby or near the elevator or even at the exit point of the parking garage.

There has been much discussion online and in the media over the past several years about the information stored on the key card's magnetic strip. Every front desk staff that I have ever asked says that only the room number and activation start and end dates are on the card. However, there are so many reports to the contrary that good safety sense says it is better not to leave the keys in a hotel room.

Another option is to take the key card home with you, either destroying it or adding it to your hotel key card collection. Few (if any) hotels demand that key cards be returned or charge guests who fail to do so. If you are more comfortable keeping or destroying the card, do so.

MY FINAL TIP: When checking into a hotel, ask for two envelopes. One can be used for business receipts, the other for personal receipts. This makes it easy to reconcile business expenses and verify personal credit card charges.

6

TRAVELING ALONE

When I lived in Chicago and traveled to Detroit for business, my mother would always say, "Be careful, you're going to Detroit!"

"But Mom, I'm working in one of the most upscale suburbs of Detroit. Besides, we live in Chicago. There are unsafe areas here, too."

I am still a very frequent solo traveler and my mother still worries about me. Once a mother, always a mother.

Some trips require traveling with others for business. Perhaps you fly or ride together with a co-worker, maybe even share a hotel room. Other times, family members are part of the journey. Most of the time business travelers are on their own, maybe out of necessity, perhaps out of preference.

Indeed, 68% of women travelers reported traveling solo at least once in the past three years. Significantly, nearly 4 out of 5 wish they were traveling with someone else.[10] This chapter is about those who spend significant time alone and examines both the downsides as well as the upsides.

Disadvantages

Admittedly, traveling solo requires additional considerations. Very simply, you are on your own.

For example, there is no one to remind you about checklist items. There won't be someone else to look at maps or GPS or travel plans. No one else can contact your various travel providers. There won't be anyone to get the rental car while you pick up the checked baggage.

For many, the most painful part of traveling without someone else is the inability to share the experience. Many things happen along the journey that are often more pleasant when shared with family or friends.

Thanks to the internet and gadgets like digital cameras and video recorders, it is possible to make others feel like they are part of the trip. See some of the later chapters for more about this. Nevertheless, it is not the same because most of the sensory portions are missing.

If driving is a component of your trip, you are doing all of it. This might not be a big deal for shuttling between a hotel and some nearby destination, but for those who travel from city to city for hours at a time, it can be a chore if the driving is not split. For those on tighter budgets, overnight accommodations can be expensive because the costs are not shared. This is even more painful financially when you consider that hotels rarely charge for a second person anyway.

Some single travelers develop bad habits like not working out or not eating correctly out of either boredom or depression from being alone. It is not difficult to turn into a hotel couch potato (or bed potato) when others are not around to share activities.

One quite common experience is dining alone in a restaurant or lounge. It begins on a negative tone when someone at a restaurant asks, "Table for just one?" Something about that makes some travelers defensive, feeling like others believe they have no friends. For those who find a restaurant where this is not an issue, they still might get into a rut by frequenting the same place every time because it's comfortable. Being with other travelers tends to open up group curiosity.

Others become room-service hermits, eating dinner while sitting on the bed watching television. Room service is handy now and then for conference calls during dinner time, but it's easy to become isolated when the greatest thrill of the evening is lifting off the silver plate cover to see how your meal was prepared.

As for bars and lounges, men are generally more comfortable heading out solo and engaging in conversation with others sitting near them. This is much more challenging for women for many social reasons.

While women traveling alone may choose not to initiate a conversation, it sometimes seems that just appearing alone is a magnet for others. I could wear my wedding band pierced through my nose and there would still be guys coming up to me.

Not trying to be unfriendly, but really, male or female, traveling alone doesn't automatically mean seeking company. While some single travelers might be looking for someone to share an evening with, it certainly doesn't apply to everyone.

This leads to some safety issues that need to be considered if you are traveling alone. Many are included in Chapter 7 but a few that are specific to solo traveling are mentioned here.

- In many cultures, women traveling alone are seen as targets by certain men, some with honorable intentions but also by predators with much less than honorable intentions. At an absolute minimum, it is essential for all travelers to be aware of, and sensitive to, their surroundings.

- When traveling by yourself, look like you know where you're going. By this, I mean don't get overly distracted traveling in a new city, captivated by the sights and sounds. When walking, do it with purpose so as not to give the impression that you are lost. Stopping to read maps is a dead giveaway that you are a tourist.

- Getting out and socializing is a great way to grab a break from business travel. If you are unsure about where to go, some of the best resources to ask are local hotels and visitor's centers. They are far better choices than someone you just met in a bar.

- Some single women who prefer not to get involved with what they consider obnoxious behavior by locals or other business travelers resort to wearing an inexpensive wedding band when they travel. I can't say that this will ward off all attempts but it might help.

- It is always a good idea to avoid showing a wad of cash when traveling. If you must reach for cash, take out only the amount necessary and keep the rest from view. Credit cards are generally safer so use them when possible.

- Consider very carefully your choices for jewelry. The flashier it is, the more likely others will notice. While this is flattering, it also could be dangerous for a lone traveler.

- When traveling alone, it is especially smart to have a cellphone. If you feel someone may be following you, take out the phone and pretend to speak with a caller. As long as you are having a conversation, others are more likely to leave you alone.

- Another good tip is to see if the price of the hotel room is the same for two guests as well as one. If it is the same, make the reservation in two names and get two keys when you check in. This gives the appearance that you are not in your room alone.

- What do you say if the other person isn't there to check in with you? Just tell the front desk that they are on a different flight and will be in later. If you are already checking in late at night, say they missed their flight and will be in the next morning.

- If driving, park only in well-lit locations. If you need to park in a hotel parking lot, especially late at night, ask one of the hotel security people to accompany you into the building.

- Let someone else know where you are going. If you don't know anyone in your destination city, call someone in your hometown, email them, or leave a message at the hotel desk. At the very least, this will tell someone where you are supposed to be in the event of a problem.

- Be watchful of your purse or laptop shoulder bag. If you are in a restaurant, place the leg of the chair through the strap. Alternatively or combined, you also can use your own leg. Either way, it makes it impossible for the bag to be removed without your knowing about it.

None of these negative things should scare you away from traveling alone. Yes, you need to be more careful but it takes almost no time before this advice becomes second nature.

Advantages

Most of my business travel is solo but I really don't think of myself as being alone. There are many other passengers when on an airplane or train, sometimes even an engaging seat neighbor. And the hotels have hundreds of other guests.

The real difference is that traveling alone means not always having someone else tied to your hip. As you will see, traveling alone is not the same thing as being lonely.

I have a great husband but the fact is, we are different. We have different likes and dislikes. Our choices for food, movies, and music are not the same. We enjoy travel but may to go to different places and do different things.

We get along very well, but we have to work at compromising to meet each other's needs. When traveling alone, all that flies out the window. Each of us is free to eat what and where we want or go somewhere that the other might not enjoy.

My husband and I rarely fly together, usually out of necessity because we are traveling from different directions. That's okay because flying alone has some wonderful benefits, including:

- Not being forced to have a conversation.
- Enjoying the choice of a good book or taking a nap.
- Not feeling responsible for providing the entertainment when traveling with others.

Driving to work also has an upside to being alone. It means traveling at your own pace. You stop when you like, take a side trip, or wail along with a tune on the radio if the mood hits you.

Traveling alone means working and sleeping when you desire without worrying about pleasing a partner. You go where you want, when you want, and stay as long as you like, subject to work conditions, of course.

When I am working, that is exactly what I am doing. I am paid to perform certain assignments. This is not the time that best lends itself to having family or friends around. Workdays are long with maybe some evening time to meet with others when possible.

For many, it is true independence to not rely on someone else. This means selecting your own restaurants for meals and eating when you want. You also define your own entertainment. It can be anything from enjoying an evening drink in a lounge to sightseeing or shopping. It can also mean choosing to do nothing.

The primary advantage of traveling alone is control. Since work typically defines the day, really all we are talking about is the time when work ceases and individual control begins.

That time is most often in the evening when on a business trip. This might mean dining with co-workers or choosing to eat alone. Occasionally it may be necessary to do work in the evening, in which case staying in your room and ordering room service is another option.

Traveling alone certainly doesn't mean you need to be a hermit. Telephones are readily available to communicate with anyone, and internet voice or video calls are an option for those with laptops, tablets, or smartphones. This alone time can also be used to update your social media, surf the net, go to a fitness center, or anything else of your choosing. For that matter, you could decide to get together with someone else. This might be a co-worker or someone you met at a conference. And some solo travelers really enjoy meeting local folks.

Contrary to some people's fears, eating dinner alone in a restaurant is not a curse and actually can be quite relaxing. You order what you want and enjoy the meal at your own pace. Maybe you seize the moment to order a special wine or dessert.

Other travelers like to use this solo-dining time for people watching, particularly in a new city. In nice weather, look for a restaurant with outdoor dining, especially with beautiful scenery. You may choose to read a book or magazine or use the time to plan your next day. I do some of my best journal writing over an after-dinner coffee.

This is not to say you can't be sociable when you dine alone. If you prefer, it is an excellent opportunity to engage others in conversation. While many solo travelers seem to lean toward the introverted side after a long workday, others are quite pleased to have some company. This is a great way to meet other business travelers. It can be exciting to learn where others are from and what they do. And who knows, what begins in a social setting may turn into a business opportunity.

A hotel's executive lounge, accessible by frequent users with elite status or by paying a special rate, is another great place to have breakfast and evening snacks. It is typically a very comfortable environment with people just like you – other business travelers.

If you happen to work on long projects that bring you back to the same hotel often, it is very common to see familiar faces in the executive lounge. This is a great way to make new friends or find a companion for dinner if you desire.

It is also easy to begin conversations just by seeing someone else's company badge. I do it all the time with my alma maters, Oracle and Deloitte. Overhearing someone talk about where they live or may be traveling to is another opportunity to chime in and join the conversation.

Hotels that don't have a lounge level may offer something like a manager's reception event. Usually it is a dedicated room similar to a lounge, though usually without the comfortable seating. Nevertheless, it is a bonding area for business travelers where they can munch on appetizers, enjoy a free drink, and meet other road warriors who share similar lives.

Those who are more adventurous may choose to wander the streets of a new city in the evening. For many, it is the only time to get out and meet local people or see new sights. Ask the hotel concierge or front desk for safe places to enjoy evening outings.

A day off from work could mean visiting local attractions or museums. Solo travel means you get to see the sights that interest you, spending as much time (and money) as you feel comfortable with.

Solo time also brings some welcome treats. Sure, you probably miss your family but an hour or two soaking in the tub or a spa treatment can be a gift to yourself that you would never have time for at home. If the spa is not your thing, maybe a local ball game would be a welcome treat.

Many choose to go to the movies alone. Find an appealing movie, then sit where you prefer while enjoying your own goodies. And really, since you have to be quiet in a movie theater anyway, what's the difference if someone is sitting next to you if you can't even talk to them?

Compare these experiences with times when you travel with a companion. It is inevitable that they will want to spend more/less time somewhere than what you have in mind. Or they may want to do something you had not even considered. As a solo traveler, these concerns become non-issues.

Perhaps the best part about traveling alone is choosing what you do with your spare time. This is about meeting your own needs rather than accepting compromise because your mate or travel partner wants to do something else.

One last advantage of solo travel – well, for women anyway – is a benefit I once received. After arriving at a hotel in my rental car, the front desk told me self-parking was $13/day and valet parking was $20/day. Typical so far, but then they offered me a service I had never heard of before.

Since I was traveling as a solo woman, they offered valet parking for the self-parking rate. In other words, since the cost was the same, there was no reason to use the self-parking at all. They have eliminated the potential risk to women being alone in the parking garage by allowing them to leave their cars at the entrance instead of parking by themselves, especially late at night.

This is a very smart move by this hotel, and very much appreciated by all women traveling solo. The next day I was already recommending the hotel to other women because of the parking benefit. It would be nice to see more hotels offering this to their female guests traveling alone.

Make the Best of Solo Travel

Traveling alone offers so many opportunities, including perhaps a unique chance to do something you've always wanted to do. Create your bucket list and cross things off as the opportunities present themselves. Try things that you finally have time for. Not only will your business travels be more pleasurable, you also will have fond memories of the cities and towns you visited.

Give yourself the gift of self-care. Here are a few self-indulgent things that can be done just hanging around many hotels:

- Enjoy an extra hour of sleep
- Swim a few laps in the hotel pool
- Make an appointment for a facial or massage
- Get a front row seat to enjoy a sporting event in the lounge
- Better yet, get a front row seat to enjoy a live event

Take advantage of the hotel amenities. Ask at check-in for ways to increase the experience of your stay. You will learn much more from a concierge or front desk agent than you normally would by reading a hotel's guide in the room.

Think about extending your trip. There are fun and interesting things to do in virtually every city. Try to tack on an extra day for personal time, even if this is at your own expense. For the cost of an extra night in the hotel, you can plan out and enjoy a day of seeing the sights.

If meeting people while traveling is what you desire, opportunities abound. People are everywhere so your contact list is limited only by finding others who enjoy your interests and a desire to know more about someone. Here are some great sources:

- Restaurants
- Book stores and coffee shops
- Shopping malls
- Museums
- College lectures or events
- Film festivals
- Concerts
- Professional speaking events
- Sporting events
- Alumni and professional associations
- Hobby groups that share your interests
- Hotel lounges

- Local tours – maybe sightseeing, historical society, or zoo
- Bowling alleys
- Singles groups
- Social/religious groups
- Volunteer with a local organization

Some hotels offer group runs, exercise classes and evening socials to get travelers out of their rooms and meeting others. Holiday Inn, for example, rolled out a "social hub" concept in 2011 offering flexible work/play lobby areas that offer opportunities for networking. You can even meet people while walking the streets. People are everywhere. Feel free to extend yourself and make new friends wherever you go.

If in a restaurant, eat at the bar and talk with the bartender. Having a conversation with someone while eating may break up the monotony of an evening alone. Another benefit, bartenders can be a great resource for information about local restaurants and happenings in the area.

Use the internet to find out about local events. There are often tweetups on Twitter being talked about. Check out the ones that are in your area of interest.

Search LinkedIn for professional get-togethers or Facebook for more sociable events. Meetup.com has an amazing number of get-togethers that are worth checking out. However, best to err on the side of safety and go where there is likely to be a group instead of a one-on-one meeting.

Is it more difficult or uncomfortable for women to meet people than it is for men? While I do know several women who are less at ease talking with someone they don't know, I also know many women who are Chatty Cathys and seem to make friends in no time.

My best advice for those traveling solo is to first decide if you want activities with others. If not, there are many examples of things you can do alone.

If you prefer being around others, find an activity you enjoy, then go out and do it. Whether you meet up with other people or not, at least you will be spending time on something enjoyable.

The point to take away here is that traveling alone gives you more choices. Most importantly, I hope the message is clear that traveling alone is not synonymous with being lonely.

7

TRAVEL SAFETY

*E*arly on a Monday morning, the hotel shuttle bus approached Terminal 1 at Los Angeles *International Airport and the door opened. Within seconds, a traveler exited off the bus with his luggage and hustled into the airport for his flight. The shuttle bus door closed and we headed to the next terminal.*

"He took my bag!" screamed a woman from the back of the bus. The bus driver kept driving.

Another passenger jumped up towards the driver, yelling at him to stop the bus. Frantically, the woman looked for her bag and yes, it was gone. The bus driver finally stopped the bus, halfway to the next terminal.

Luckily for the woman on the bus, the gentleman who took her bag quickly realized he had the wrong one. We saw him running back towards our bus.

The correct bags exchanged hands and all was well. I realized then that this could happen to me, to you or to anyone in a matter of seconds. And the results could have been much worse.

Not only is our property at risk for being lost or stolen, but more importantly, we are at risk ourselves. While this can happen whether we are a block away from home or thousands of miles away, the truth is that travelers feel less secure when they're on the road.

Let's get one safety myth out of the way. It may be tempting to believe that concerns about thieves, pickpockets, and robbers apply only to destinations outside the United States. Yes, much has been written about certain cities in Europe, as well as some Caribbean destinations, but the fact is, this happens everywhere.

Popular destinations like New York, Las Vegas, Orlando, and other major U.S. cities certainly have their share of criminals, too. While you may blend in a bit more traveling across the U.S., do not think that safety issues are a concern only if you travel outside our borders.

Safety Before You Leave Home

Stories abound about laptops being stolen, jewelry theft, purses and wallets gone missing, luggage that goes astray and more. Nothing can ruin a trip faster than having possessions lost or stolen. Here are easy ideas to implement to keep your possessions safe.

Travel only with items you are willing to lose. I know this sounds harsh. Indeed, I can't imagine ever going anywhere without wearing my wedding ring even though I would be absolutely heartbroken if it was lost or stolen.

Of course, things like this happen only to other people. Yes, we unconsciously believe that only other people will become victims. That assumption, of course, is dangerous in itself.

Items you may want to think about leaving behind include jewelry, family heirlooms, and expensive electronics, including cameras. Those that are truly the most valuable are those that cannot be replaced at any cost.

Most business travelers have a cellphone and some also use a laptop computer as well as a tablet. When traveling for business, it is not unusual that there might be sensitive company data stored on these devices. Sadly, it happens that they might be lost or stolen. If you travel with any of these items, at the very least you can password protect them. It won't stop everyone from accessing your data but it may help. Some devices offer a remote lock feature. See if this is available for any that you may be traveling with.

Ask yourself how you would feel if an item were lost or stolen. If it is a concern, perhaps it's better to enjoy your trip without fear rather than risking something that could absolutely ruin your journey. Here are some more safety tips before you begin traveling:

- Always document all your travel valuables. At the very least, make a written list. Even better, photograph them. They can be saved as digital images that can travel with you if you have a computer, flash drive, phone, or any electronic device that stores images.

- Some insurance policies may provide coverage when you travel, others might not. For particularly valuable items like jewelry or cameras, separate insurance riders are common. Each policy is different so check with your carrier.

- Attach a business card to the bottom of your laptop and include your cellphone number. If you travel through an international airport, add your international dialing code along with a phone number and any known foreign translations of your name.

- Make a copy of all credit cards, front and back. Store them in your laptop tote in a hide-away pocket. Better yet, scan them into a password-protected document on your laptop.

- Photograph all jewelry and valuables that you are taking with you, as well as your luggage. The luggage photo comes in very handy when reporting a lost or delayed bag to an airline. Keep a photo of your luggage in a mobile phone for easy retrieval in case your checked bag gets delayed.

- Have all your reservation numbers and phone numbers with you at all times.

Keeping Your Home Safe While Away

Safety begins before you ever leave home. Here are some valuable tips if your home will be empty while you are away:

- Turn off or unplug electronics.

- Cancel your newspaper and any other scheduled deliveries.

- The post office has a handy online method to hold your mail for the length of your trip.

- Contact your local police department (non-emergency number) to let them you know you will be away. Ensure your house alarm company has your mobile phone number in case of any emergencies.

- Use a timer for your commonly used lamps or lights. Set the timer to turn the lights on and off at typical times based on your typical at-home schedule.

- Close all drapes and blinds part-way. This gives the appearance during the day that the house isn't vacant, and yet also gives the impression in the evening that the windows are primarily closed.

- Check that all windows and doors are locked. Set your house alarm.

- Sometimes a garage door fails to go down all the way, getting stuck on something and going back up when you leave. Ensure that your garage door closes completely after you pull away from your home.

Luggage and Airport Safety

Most baggage today is soft sided luggage, making it easier for someone to simply cut open your bags and remove the contents. Nevertheless, if you use locks to secure all openings it might act as a deterrent for some vandals.

Unfortunately, the use of locks is limited when flying. Locks on carry-on bags are prohibited when the bags pass through TSA screening. Before or after the screening is fine but not for those moments when TSA demands access to them.

An alternative to keeping your luggage zippers locked is using twist-ties or round key rings to secure the zippers on your luggage and to make it difficult for a passer-by to open your luggage. These solutions work well, keeping the zippers closed and costing a lot less than replacing TSA-approved locks.

 TIP: Keep a few extra twist-ties in the outside pocket of your luggage since they wear out after a few trips and need replacing.

TSA tells us that tens of thousands of items each year are left behind on the screening conveyor belts. Most common are small ones like loose change, wallets, and keys. Nevertheless, cellphones and even laptops also make that list.

TSA claims that a surprising 78,000 laptops are left behind by passengers each year. Having traveled through TSA lines perhaps a thousand times myself, I certainly understand how passengers can be distracted.

On a recent trip through Houston's Intercontinental Airport, there was a page over the intercom system requesting that the person who left their laptop at security return to pick it up. Follow the procedures outlined in Chapter 3 and this will not happen to you.

You don't want your luggage to be out of sight any more than necessary. It is sad but just too many things can happen--anything from someone simply taking your bags to cutting them open and removing the contents.

Here are a few more airport security line tips:

- Keep your laptop and purse within your sight. Avoid sending your laptop and purse in advance of going through the TSA scanner.

- If you are delayed in getting through the security machine, keep an eye on your bins as they come out on the belt and watch for anyone who might be lingering around the exiting bins.

- If you are selected for additional screening, ensure that the security agent collects all of your belongings for you before they lead you to the additional screening area.

Checked bags in the U.S. can only have TSA-approved locks. I have used these locks before but each time they have been removed by security personnel and never put back on. Many of the newer bags today have built-in locks, the best of both worlds.

Caution: If the bag lock is not one that TSA can access, they may break it open and check the bag contents. I have seen the results of this from an international tourist unaware of our rules. It is very destructive to the lock and the bag.

Unfortunately, there is little protection for checked bags with airlines. There are numerous complaints filed each year against TSA and the airlines for missing items. Some are no doubt true, perhaps others are not, but the bottom line is you don't want to be in a position of needing to file a claim.

I know this is mentioned elsewhere in the book but it is well worth repeating: Never, ever put valuables in checked bags. At best you are looking at a disputed claim if something is missing. At worst, you will learn that the airline's contract of carriage specifically omits coverage for certain valuables such as jewelry and electronics.

Far too many claims each year are outright dismissed when the airlines refer passengers back to their travel contract. It is heartbreaking for travelers to learn there is no coverage. Please don't become one of these depressed travelers.

Another source of lost bags is transportation services. For example, if you use a taxi service at the airport, don't get into the cab until after you see that your bags are placed in the trunk and it is closed.

The same concerns apply to tour buses. Most people leave their luggage next to the bus, waiting for the driver to load it. Unfortunately, there are other people hanging around the bus posing as tourists, looking like everyone else in the group.

These are the people who will snatch your bag and walk away with it. Since they look like other tourists, no one even thinks about their stealing someone else's luggage. It is best to stay with your bags until they are securely on the bus.

Finally, a few more airport tips:

- When using a public restroom, keep all of your items with you inside the stall. Wrap a purse around the hook twice or place your coat over your purse. This eliminates the chance that someone on the outside can reach over the doorway and grab your purse.

- Keep your driver's license and/or passport in the same location all the time. In the haste to get through airport security, it's easy to place these items in a pocket or other quick spot. Instead, place them in the same compartment all the time so there is no doubt where they are.

- If you realize you forgot your laptop or any other item while you're still at the airport, head back to TSA as fast as you can, assuming you have time before your flight leaves. If not, call the TSA Lost and Found office for the airport where you forgot your item.

Driving Safety

If you are using a rental car, locate all the following and know how to turn them on and off:

- Door locks
- Headlights
- Wipers
- Emergency lights
- Emergency brake

It is very unsafe to be fumbling around trying to figure out how to turn on the headlights when you are driving as it becomes dark. It is distracting to you as a driver to be turning on the wipers accidentally and not knowing how to turn them off.

Always have your car keys in your hands before heading out to your car. Have the key ring around your finger and the keys pointing forward in a firm grasp.

- This eliminates fumbling for keys while outside at your car;
- It allows for quick access to the Panic button on the car key; and
- It's good for jabbing an attacker.

Have you ever noticed that many rental cars seem to look alike? Knowing that the car you rented is a white, 4-door compact sedan won't help much in a parking lot with a sea of other white cars. Here are some travel and safety tips that will help:

- Write down the toll-free number from the rental car key or put it in your cellphone in case the car key needs replacing.
- Take a photo of your rental car and parking space with your mobile phone.
- As you walk to the car, act as if you are talking with someone on your cellphone, even if you are not. Let a would-be attacker think that you are not alone and that you have someone to hear you scream.
- Place your laptop bag in the trunk of your car as you depart your hotel, home or office. Do not wait until you reach your destination (such as a restaurant) to put your laptop bag in the trunk. Would-be thieves may see this and know that there is something valuable in your car and you've just walked away.

  Three consultants I've worked with each had their laptops stolen out of their rental cars (two were in the back seat, the other in the trunk of the car) while they were having dinner in restaurants. One laptop contained sensitive employee data. The consequences of this event were very costly to the company and its thousands of employees.

- Place maps, car rental agreements, GPS systems and anything else that marks you as a tourist into the car's glove compartment or your bag so it is not visible.
- Buy a local newspaper and leave that on your car seat. This gives the appearance to some that you are a local.

- If you have an auto club membership, add the telephone number and account number to your cell phone in case your car is stranded. Also, phones are doing a lot these days with applications. Auto clubs such as AAA have applications for mobile phones, for example, that allow stranded drivers to easily contact AAA and have them determine your location.

- Add your hotel phone number into your mobile phone in case you need directions to your hotel. When nearing your hotel late at night, phone ahead and ask for a security escort to meet you at the main door. Hotels would rather have you do this than risk your safety in their parking lots.

- Whether you travel with your own GPS or use a rental car's navigation system, store your hotel information into the GPS when you first arrive at your destination. In addition to having the GPS direct you to your hotel upon arrival, each day or evening's return trip to your hotel will be easier by quickly searching the recent history and selecting your hotel.

When traveling for business, it is not uncommon to need local transportation. Here are some safety tips if you use buses or taxis:

- When traveling via bus, know the fare and have it ready upon boarding. This is better than searching through your purse and looking like a tourist. Also, try to sit up front near the bus driver to avoid other passengers bothering you.

- Carry two hotel business cards, one in your bag and one in your pocket. When hiring a taxi to return you to your hotel, show them the business card. This is especially useful in a foreign country where you cannot distinctly pronounce the hotel name or street.

- Never get into someone's car who claims to be a taxi driver. It is common at airports, bus stations and busy tourist areas for someone to say that they will drive you, but they may not be a licensed taxi driver. Only go with a taxi from a taxi stand or one that you flag down. Remember the important tips from Chapter 4.

- Have an idea of the direction your taxi should be going and the approximate time it will take. Ask the driver for information such as, "Are you taking Highway xxx?" This gives the impression that you know where you're going, and the taxi driver is less apt to take you the long way around.

- Be alert when using taxi services. Make a note of the cab or driver number. I once had a cab driver take a turn down an alley in downtown Chicago in the evening when there were no traffic issues that would warrant this. That's a good time to make a quick exit, which I did.

Hotel Safety

Hotel room safety is the number one concern of women travelers. The good news is that hotels are safer today than ever before. Part of this is in response to consumer demands while some, sadly, is in response to lawsuits. Whatever the reasons, they are far more secure now.

The first big change came when hotels began using cards instead of keys. Before the days of room cards, some hotel guests made copies of the old style keys, then gained entry into a hotel room long after they had checked out. The card system is much safer. These cards are coded when you check in and most are automatically canceled at check-out time on the day you are scheduled to depart.

Are these cards safe? Well, if you compare them to keys the answer is definitely yes. Keys often had fobs on the key ring which indicated not only the hotel but the room number. If you lost that key – or someone took it from you – there was no protection against someone getting into your room.

Cards might have the name of the hotel on them but never a room number. If you lose the card, simply contact the hotel and they will re-code another one very quickly. If your room number is written inside the key jacket given to you with the key, either toss this or leave it inside the room. Instead, note your room number in your mobile phone.

There have been reports that some hotel key cards may contain data such as credit card information. One incident that comes to mind was a criminal organization that had a reader able to pick up this data. Once they had the credit card information, the thieves went on a spending spree while the hotel guest was oblivious.

No hotel admits that there is any credit card data on the room key card. We have to take them at their word here since we can't read the cards ourselves. Nevertheless, I always turn in the card at the front desk when I check out rather than leave the card in the room. Better to be safe.

Most hotels lock many of the secondary outside doors, especially after dark. This means the only way to enter the property is with a coded card. Although this is a great security feature, note that hotels are inconsistent in how this is applied.

Some hotels require use of a card to enter the building from every door except the front door to the lobby. Others do not require use of a card for any outside door. Some change their policy to require card entrance at night, others don't.

Here are some more basic hotel safety tips:

- Keep a close eye on your luggage, laptop bag, and purse when checking in. Do not get so distracted looking for your credit card and identification that you do not notice someone lurking nearby intent on taking your valuables.

- If the front desk staff announces your room number out loud, ask for a different room. Instead, ask them to write down the room number or point to it inside a key jacket. Ask for two keys to give the impression to anyone nearby that you are traveling with someone else.

- Do not leave your credit card lying on the check-in desk while completing any paperwork. Make sure that you get it back from the hotel desk clerk.

- Ask for a couple of business cards that have the hotel name, address and telephone number on them. Keep these with you so that you have the necessary details to give a cab driver when returning to the hotel or in case you get lost. Keep an extra hotel business card in your purse or laptop bag in case these get misplaced or stolen.

- Another safety feature at many hotels are in-room safes. Definitely ask about fees before using this service but if it costs nothing, this is a good way to protect your valuables. Even a small daily fee may be tolerable when you consider the cost of your valuables.

- Ask for a room away from the stairways but near an elevator. However, you do not want to be so close that you hear elevator noises all night long. Request a room that is close enough that a long hallway walk is not involved.

- If staying in a motel with an outside entrance to your room, ask for a room near the hotel's office, where there is more activity going on, rather than a more remote room.

- Select a room no higher than the 7th or 8th floor. In case of a fire, most fire department ladders cannot reach beyond this height.

- Ask for a room that has no adjoining door to the next room (unless you are with family and want access between rooms).

Here are some safety tips for inside your hotel room:

- Upon entering the room, use only the double bolt when you have checked that there are no unwanted visitors inside (behind the drapes, in the shower, in the closet). Then latch the door with the bolt.

- Female airline crews suggest looking under the bed for any unwanted visitors. Frankly, I have yet to get on my knees to do this but I pass along their words of wisdom.

- Check that the door lock is functioning properly. Also check that windows and sliding doors are securely locked. For sliding doors, look for a metal bar across the inside of the door that prevents the door from sliding open from the outside.

- If you have a room with an adjoining door to a neighboring room, check that the lock is secure. Then place the luggage rack in front of this door. If someone tries to enter, a falling luggage rack will make noise and hopefully scare away a would-be intruder.

- Make sure that the telephone has a dial tone and is working correctly. Know how to call the front desk and also how to make an outside call.

- Know where the nearest stairway and fire exit are in the event of an emergency.

- Never leave the door to your hotel room propped open. It may seem easier to leave the door open while you run down the hall for ice or await a porter, but anyone can enter your room during this time.

Sometimes business travelers learn these things the hard way. Consider the experience of this veteran business traveler...

"After arriving at my destination airport the day before I was to speak to a large group, I discovered my luggage had not made the flight. My silk blouse and panty hose that I had with me could be washed and re-worn the next day if necessary.

"Panicking at the thought that my bags might not arrive for days, I asked the front desk to deliver my bags no matter what time they arrived. Sure enough, the bellman delivered the bags late that evening, and after pressing a fresh suit for the next day, I went back to sleep.

"While getting dressed that morning, I decided to wear the washed panty hose rather than rummage around in my re-packed case, since they were now clean. Fully dressed at 7 am, I called down for the bellman to come for my bags and propped the door open a few inches.

"While putting on my mascara, I realized that the cotton part of the panty hose had not dried completely. Since I am a speaker on time management and organization, I felt the easiest thing to do was to grab the hairdryer and blow my panty hose dry.

"I forgot the door was partially open. Of course, in walks the bellman to retrieve the bags. He took one look at me with the hair dryer between my knees and said, 'Lady, I promise I won't ask if you promise not to tell me what on earth you're doing!'"

Linda from Virginia Beach, Virginia

- Place your room key in the same place every time. I leave it on the hotel desk next to my purse when I am in the room and place it in the outside pocket of my purse when I depart. This way the key is handy when leaving the hotel in an emergency and easy to find upon returning.

- When inside a hotel room – no matter if for just five minutes or overnight – always use the deadbolt or security chain.

- Look through the eyepiece before opening the door. If the person says they work for the hotel, ask them their name. Call the front desk to verify that this person does work there before allowing entry.

- When ordering room service, ask the restaurant to phone your room when the room service attendant is near your door.

- For overnight walks to the bathroom where lack of light can cause bumps into doors or stubbed toes, pack a small nightlight that gives off just enough light for safe bathroom trips.

- In addition to a nightlight, bring a small flashlight. Keep this on the nightstand next to your bed. You can use it to find your way to the bathroom at night or in the event of an emergency, to help you find your way in a dark hallway or stairway.

- Never use the "Clean Room" cards that many hotels provide. That tells everyone that your room is vacant and only serves to increase the risk that someone will get into your room.

- When you are entering or leaving your hotel room, always check to make sure the door has closed all the way and is locked. Nearly all hotel room doors use a vacuum tube, and over time these tubes wear down.

Hotel parking lots are also a concern, especially for women traveling alone. Here are a couple of tips:

- Using the hotel phone number already entered in your cell phone, call the hotel when you are within minutes of arrival. Ask for someone to escort you in from the parking lot.

- Use the hotel's valet service. It may cost more to use valet service but your safety is of utmost importance.

With many negotiated hotel rates, the cost of valet parking may not be included in the room rate but perhaps regular parking is. In this case, drive up to the valet stand and ask one of the valet staff to escort you to the regular parking area.

This provides additional comfort knowing that a hotel employee is with you when navigating the parking lot and also saves on the valet charge (though do offer a tip to the staff). If you're not sure if your hotel offers this service, just ask a manager ahead of time. Hotel management places high priority on your safety as well.

Out and About

As one who travels all the time, I know it is easy to be distracted when faced with unfamiliar surroundings. There is so much to see that sometimes we forget about the world around us.

Remember that while you are focused on your journey, there are others that are focused on you. It is easy to spot travelers, as opposed to locals. Many experts suggest that travelers be on the lookout for potential pickpockets and thieves.

When people travel to a new destination, they are intent on absorbing so much that is new. Virtually all the senses are in high gear, taking in new sights, sounds, and smells. Because most people want hands-on experience, it is not too likely they will use their internal warning system to question whether each person they encounter is friendly or is after their valuables.

Nevertheless, at least be sensitive to the area around you. For example, travelers may not be dressed like local people. Also, travelers often look at maps and guidebooks while they are walking, not to mention stopping at tourist shops. Do the opposite and more people will ignore you.

Always be identifiable. What if you forget to carry identification and something terrible happens...

- Out jogging one morning with your identification left at the hotel, you slip and fall, hitting your head on the pavement;
- You suddenly become sick and feverish, having trouble speaking coherently;
- You are driving a rental car and are involved in an accident; or
- Worse yet, you are mugged.

Here are some tips to help with identification...

- Give a copy of your itinerary information to a trusted relative or friend so that someone knows your travel schedule.
- Wear a wristband, ankle band or shoe pouch that contains your name, mobile phone and contact's information.
- Carry hotel business cards. Keep a card in your pocket, another in your purse. If anything happens, someone coming to your aid will find the hotel name and have a contact to call. If you are mugged and your purse is stolen, the hotel name inside the purse may aid in the recovery.
- Keep key information in your mobile phone. Add a contact called "ICE" (In Case of Emergency) into your contact list. Add the phone number of your spouse or key contact. Repeat this for additional key contacts (ICE2, ICE3, etc.).

Many police, fire and paramedic personnel look for the ICE number as an emergency contact in the event of an accident. Without ICE, how would they know that your spouse, entered only by a first name in your phone, is your emergency contact? Less than 25% of people are believed to have emergency contact information in their cellphone, so this is a quick and easy key safety strategy.

Criminal activity is rare but it can happen anywhere. Perhaps the most common is pickpocketing. These thieves are often found in areas frequented by tourists though they have been known to work popular local areas as well. Whether you are in the airport, on a train, in a busy convention area or city center, you are vulnerable.

A colleague had his wallet stolen from his suit pocket. While on a train, he hung up his jacket on a hook just slightly behind his seat. Busy on his Blackberry checking emails before a meeting, he never realized his day had just gone downhill.

Some pickpockets work alone but most work in small groups. It is not uncommon for one of them to distract or bump into a tourist while another uses the opportunity to take items out of the unsuspecting tourist's pocket. Sadly, it is somewhat common to see children pickpockets in some European cities.

Travel expert Peter Greenberg talks about a situation in which a woman was carrying a baby in a blanket. Seeing a lone female traveler, the woman tossed the baby into the traveler's arms. Distracted and holding the baby, the traveler watched helplessly as the thieves ran off with her belongings. The baby, of course, was merely a doll.

These types of thieves like to work crowded tourist areas such as theme parks, museums, and certain areas known for high street traffic. However, some prefer to work local transportation like buses, streetcars, and subways.

Another common type of criminal is the snatch-and-grab purse snatcher. Sometimes they walk along a sidewalk toward you, only to reach over at the last moment, grab a purse or other easy to reach possession, and run off.

When I worked in the Sears Tower in Chicago (now the Willis Tower), there was a run of purse snatchers who would operate in the area of the revolving doors. A woman with a long-strapped purse would enter the revolving door, her purse swaying behind her. Just as she started pushing the door forward, a purse snatcher would cut her purse strap and run. What could she do but keep going through the door? By the time she got fully around to where she had entered, the thief was long gone.

In another variation, a local resident rides by on a bicycle or motorbike and slices the straps off a bystander's purse, then rides away. If there are other travelers around, they might drop their bags and chase the perpetrator. That's when the bike rider's accomplice grabs the bags left on the ground and takes off.

Other purse snatchers might come up behind you. Knowing you can't see them coming, they may actually cut a strap to grab your bag and off they go. Still others watch for tourists riding in cars with the windows down.

When the car is stopped at a light or in traffic, the thieves reach into the car, grab whatever they can, and run away. Where is your purse or mobile phone typically? Yep, on the passenger seat beside you.

Some of these criminals are bolder, breaking car windows to gain access. Yes, while you are still in the car, usually stopped at a traffic light behind other cars. Of course it will scare the daylights out of you but for what it's worth, all they want is your property, not your life.

Your best protection here is to be aware of strangers who approach you. Most importantly, remember that thieves often work in groups so if you are in a crowd, be particularly careful when you stop. And of course, make sure your valuables are protected. Hold your bags tightly at your side and place valuables on the floor of the car when driving.

In some cities, you may run into phony taxi cab drivers. These are unlicensed drivers who pick up mostly tourists. Some will take their passengers to a destination and charge a greatly inflated rate while others plan to rob the passengers.

Other taxi drivers have a different scam. You give them a $50 bill. They fumble with the money and show you only a $5 bill. They threaten to call the police if you don't give them the rest of the fare.

In most cities, police are not part of the scam so despite what the driver says, most really don't want the police involved. Nevertheless, most tourists simply pay the difference because of fear and language differences.

The best protection against scam artist taxi drivers is to ask a hotel to contact a cab for you, though this probably won't be necessary if there are cabs already lined up outside the hotel. At an airport, use the designated taxi line. Better yet, hire a car service by either having your hotel arrange this or having the hotel provide you with their contact information. I have found that a car service is usually not much more of a fare than a taxi and it's almost always a much nicer and cleaner ride.

You may run into street vendors in many areas. Some offer to sell you expensive items like luxury watches for a fraction of the general selling price. This is definitely one of those things that if it sounds too good to be true, you can bet it is a fake.

I have actually met vendors who are at least honest enough to admit their products are fakes. Even so, they often want a steep price for an otherwise inexpensive item simply because it may have a name like Rolex, Louis Vuitton, or Gucci on it.

There have been reports of travelers getting arrested for handling merchandise in duty-free shops in Thailand. After paying a fee, the travelers are then let go. That fee is split between the merchant and the police. The only way to avoid this is not to handle any merchandise in these shops.

Yet another scam is when someone "accidentally" spills coffee or something else on you. While helping you clean up, their partner walks off with your bags.

Another type of criminal gaining more attention is the one who breaks into rental cars. This is common even in the U.S. These thieves look for tourists parking at the beach for the day or perhaps just in a parking lot.

After the tourists leave the car, the thieves go to work. If the car is locked, they often just break the windows to get access. If the trunk is locked, they pry it open. Unfortunately, these thieves have lots of practice and know how to break into a car and be gone in merely seconds.

In certain locations, rental car companies will tell customers not to lock the vehicle and to never leave anything valuable in it. If you hear this warning from a company, you can be sure it is one of those areas with a severe problem.

In various parts of the world, someone may seem to offer assistance to you in a retail setting. Only later do you find out that if you refuse to buy something, they will tell the police you stole something.

In a similar scam, someone tells you your car is not running properly. Of course they know someone who can fix it. Your car is "repaired" at an inflated cost and the person and the shop split the fee.

Travel guru Rick Steves reports on a woman, usually elderly, who "accidentally" falls down in the London subway. People, of course, want to help but alas, it is a setup designed to separate you from your valuables while you are distracted.

Women, carry your purses over your head, across the shoulder, and closed tightly. You might also buy a purse that has wire in the strap so it is not as easy to cut. Men: Keep your wallets in a front pocket, zippered if possible.

Carrying a camera? Always keep the strap tightly around your wrist for small cameras. For larger cameras, keep the strap around your neck. Both of these will make thieves think twice about going after your camera.

Carrying a nice DSLR with extra lenses? Bags that say Nikon or Canon on them are magnets for thieves. Least safe: A bag on your shoulder. Safer: A sling-style bag or a backpack.

When you stop at a restaurant, always wrap the straps of your bags around the legs of your chair. That way no one can simply reach down and run off with your bag. When using the restroom, wrap your purse strap twice around the door hook. Thieves have been known to reach over a door, grab a purse and run.

Carrying Money and Cards

Women tend to carry wallets and other valuable papers in their purses. Men typically use their rear pockets for the same things. If I know this about you, thieves do, too.

There are a few options here. Consider using your front pockets instead of those in the back. This is a great place to store money, credit cards, and your passport. These pockets are more secure and much more difficult for thieves to access.

Some people like to use old fashioned money belts. This is an excellent option as long as it remains hidden and your shirt or blouse is tucked in. The biggest downside here is when you need to reach your money or credit card, it can be awkward.

If you like the money belt idea, look for one that is lined. This is especially important if you are traveling in a humid climate because sweat can seep through the belt. Not many people want soggy, sweaty money.

Other travelers prefer something worn around their neck. Yes, they are easy to reach, but again, most thieves will think that's exactly where you would put your valuables. The downside here is that it is very easy to cut the cord and rip it away from your body.

Sometimes a combination of methods works best. Keep a little money and possibly a credit card in your front pocket if you have one. That is simply for ease. The remainder, along with your passport and other important items, is secured elsewhere.

As for what to carry, minimize cash and credit cards based on need. While people have an average of six credit cards, it is usually not necessary to have that many when you travel. With cash, small denominations are always better. It is very common, for example, to get short changed using large bills when the host currency is different.

I prefer having two credit cards. The first is my primary card and the second is a backup just in case I run into any problems while on the road or the establishment does not take the primary card. I have never found it necessary to have more than two.

Like everything else, credit cards have a downside. On a trip, it can be very easy to get carried away with spending. After all, it's only plastic, right?

Also, be aware that if your travels are lengthy, you don't want to get caught up missing your payment date. While many people today use the internet for online banking and credit cards, remember that the internet may not be available to you while traveling. You can also ask your credit card company for an extension of your due date when you are away for an extended time, though finance charges will most likely continue to accrue.

For those who prefer debit cards, just be aware that if someone gets your card and PIN, it is as good as cash to them. Be very protective of the card and PIN number.

Never include a PIN number for credit or debit cards in your data. If someone gains access to this information, the results can be disastrous. The bank offers less protection on a debit card. If you do not have a cellphone, carry this information just as you would any other valuable papers, but again, memorizing your PIN numbers instead of having them written down is very, very important.

Some travelers prefer to store this information in an email. This might seem safe at first glance but it really is less secure than you think. Since email is easily hacked, if someone gets access to this information, even without the card, they may be running up charges without your knowledge.

If you use the internet for online banking and credit cards, check your statements as frequently as possible when you travel. Any suspicious transactions should be reported immediately.

Using ATM's is a good way to minimize the amount of cash in your pocket. While they provide some protection, thieves have become more creative about accessing your private information without having the ATM card.

For example, some use tiny cameras set up on ATM machines that can read your PIN number as you type it in. Yes, technology can be wonderful when used for good purposes but crooks always find a way to use it for doing evil. For this reason and others, always use your other hand to cover the keypad while typing in the number. Other reported incidents with outside ATM machines include devices that make your card get stuck. While you search for someone inside to help you, the bad guys access your card and drain your account.

Another thing is something called a false reader. No one will be able to recognize this but basically it is a device on top of the real readers. This is only possible with machines on the outside so when possible, do all your transactions inside instead.

Some travelers prefer traveler's checks. Unlike cash, they can be replaced if lost or stolen, making them safer. However, I have noticed increasing difficulty over the years trying to use them, especially internationally.

I assume traveler's checks have become much easier to counterfeit, which is why merchants are less likely to accept them over cash or credit cards. Just be aware that this may be an issue for you when traveling.

This is also a good time to remind you to keep phone numbers for all your credit and debit cards. If you use traveler's checks, I would record those numbers, too.

When traveling, it is best if you can leave this sensitive information with someone you trust back home. In the event you need it, a simple phone call will retrieve the data. Some people keep this information in their cellphones. It is easy to do with a fake name – just bury important information like the card number inside the contact's data.

Others keep the data on a traveling computer or flash drive. Some prefer to scan the information while others use a camera to photograph digital images of everything.

Whatever makes you most comfortable is what you should use. However, never include PIN numbers anywhere. Anyone who has your card and PIN can clean out your account before you ever know it has happened.

Identity Theft

A recent story in the news describes an airline ticket agent who was caught after stealing $480,000 over a 3-year period by skimming credit cards. She got away with it for so long because passengers failed to check their credit card statements.

Are you protecting yourself? Here are some of the ways you may be vulnerable:

- Using free Wi-Fi?
- Paying bills online?
- Having your social security card in your wallet?
- Checking your online bank statement?
- Using online credit card statements to do expense reports?
- Shopping – online or in stores?
- Using Wi-Fi in-flight?
- Storing sensitive data on your laptop?

- Riding elevators or subways?

- Failing to stop your mail when out of town?

- Downloading movies to your iPad?

If you answered yes to any of them, you are a candidate for identify theft.

Oh, you answered yes to ALL of them? Your risk just skyrocketed.

Maybe you have wondered about your exposure to identity theft. You have taken what you think is a precaution or two:

> You look around to ensure no one is watching when standing at the ATM.

> You make sure there is a little "s" behind http when doing online shopping.

> You run a virus check on your laptop on a scheduled basis.

> You password-protect sensitive documents, including the one that holds your account numbers.

Phew ... you should be safe. Not so fast!

Sorry to be the bearer of bad news but all of us are vulnerable every day – and it doesn't matter if we're on the road or sitting on our back porch. Whether you travel a little or a lot, all you have to do is be in the wrong place at the wrong time.

Our risks increase as we move more and more into an online world and have an ever-growing wallet of mileage-accruing credit and debit cards. Will we ever be completely safe against identify theft? Unfortunately no, but we can be smart about it.

There are people who make it their business to thwart thieves who steal your personal identification. To get specific answers for identify protection, I spoke with the experts at Lifelock® -- the people who provide proactive identity theft protection.

Smart tips for warding off identity thieves from attacking you:

- Realize that identify theft is not just about credit cards – that's only 15-16% of identity theft crime. Now it's about someone stealing your social security number to get a job or file for benefits.

- Never carry your social security card in your wallet or purse. Leave it in your home safe or safety deposit box.

- Don't use debit cards. They provide thieves with a direct pipeline to your bank accounts. It is also more difficult and time consuming to resolve fraudulent purchases made with debit cards. Instead, use a credit card for reduced liability.

- If asked for your social security number on paper or online applications, leave it blank. If they want this information, ask these questions:

  - Why do they need it?

- ◆ How are they storing this data, e.g., laptop, desktop, paper file?
- ◆ If something happens and you get a letter saying your data is lost, how will they protect you?

- Get an annual credit report and review it carefully. You are entitled to one free report annually from each of the top agencies in the U.S.: TransUnion, Experian and Equifax. Ensure all of the account numbers are valid and that the credit cards are in your possession.

- Remove yourself from direct marketing lists. Contact the Mail Preference Service of the Direct Marketing Association for how to do this.

- When using Wi-Fi, ensure you are selecting the right connection from your computer's list of available Wi-Fi connections. You don't want to be connecting to someone who is "sniffing out" your information.

- Avoid banking or shopping online when using free Wi-Fi.

- Get an air card (also known as a laptop card, wireless internet card, USB modem) from a mobile service provider. While there is a monthly service fee, you have more secure internet-on-the-go access even when no Wi-Fi is available.

- Chips in credit cards and passports were designed to be safer but criminals have developed RFID readers. They can walk by you and read the credit card or passport information right out of your wallet or purse. This is why everyone who answered Yes to the "Ride elevators or subways?" question is vulnerable. They even build antennas and drive by your home or office picking up the RFID signal.

You can place fraud alerts on your credit card accounts and freeze your credit file to prevent thieves from establishing credit in your name. Also, keep an inventory of credit cards and other important numbers in a safe place at home or safety deposit box. Enlist the help of experts such as Lifelock or similar companies to help protect against identity theft.

Get smart. Be vigilant. Be safe.

8

INTERNATIONAL TRAVEL

A hotel building engineer stopped me one morning in a busy hotel lobby in northern Scotland to ask me a question. With people milling all around, he asks, "Do you want to have sex or sex?"

I reacted with a very loud "Did you just ask me if I wanted to have sex or sex?"

This certainly got the attention of everyone standing around us.

"No, lass," he said laughing. "I asked you if you were in room six-oh-six."

And so goes the challenges of international travel. Even something you expect to be the same is different, as seen in the above exchange I *thought* we were both having in English.

International travel presents exciting opportunities to learn about different cultures, most of them much older than ours in the U.S. While foreign travel offers great opportunities to see faraway lands, it is also loaded with challenges and potential pitfalls.

Navigating the Passport Maze

Travel outside the U.S. always begins with a passport, even for children and babies. How do you get one? It is as simple as filling out an application (and paying a fee). The best place to learn about your foreign travel requirements is the website, www.state.gov/travel.

Most important thing here: Allow sufficient time for the application to be processed. The State Department tends to be busier during certain times of the year such as right before summer and/or holiday travel. Their website provides up-to-date information on their processing times.

Note: Many nations require passports to be valid for at least an additional 3 to 6 months before their expiration date.

 TIP: Apply for a passport renewal when you are down to the last year before it expires.

In addition to a passport, many countries also require individuals to have visas, which is a document that allows you to travel within a foreign country. However, there are different visas for different types of visits.

First, there are visas for personal travel. In other words, designed for vacationers. Sometimes there are limits as to where you can travel, and there are always limits on lengths of stay.

Then there are visas for business travel. These are often for longer or more frequent visits to a foreign country yet with requirements that may be more demanding.

For example, some nations require you to not only state your business purpose but also where you are staying, who you are visiting, and to provide dates. It is not unusual that a foreign business or organization will need to provide supporting documentation for your visa application.

In addition, some nations require U.S. citizens to provide health certificates as well as proof of certain immunizations. Your source for the latest travel requirements for each nation is the U.S. State Department's website. If you are in the last year of your passport, get it renewed before applying for a visa and you won't be charged twice for it.

What If You Lose Your Passport?

This happens to numerous travelers each year and the results can be anywhere from mildly irritating to severely annoying. Here are a few tips that can save you days of being stuck in a foreign country:

- Before ever leaving home, entrust a photocopy of your passport and other travel-related documents with a family member or friend.

- Take photos of your travel documents, including your passport and driver's license, with your mobile phone. That way you always have a backup in case of emergency.

- When you realize the passport is missing, contact the police. There might be someone at the station who speaks English, very helpful if you do not speak the language. Also, hotel personnel often can bridge the language gap.

- If you are not sure whether the passport was lost or stolen, tell them the last time you know you had it. They will write up your statement and give you a copy. This is a legal document officially stating that your passport is missing. (*Note*: The same applies in the U.S. if your driver's license is stolen.)

- This police statement is usually needed at the Embassy when you request a new passport. Also, use the police statement when checking into a hotel. Many countries require guests to show their passports.

- After having your police statement written up, get two ID photos taken, similar to what you did when you initially applied for your passport. Ask for where to get these photos taken. For example, in Switzerland you must find a special booth or photo store to have passport photos taken. Note that in some countries the passport pictures are smaller and the American Embassy might not take them.

- Go to your Embassy or Consulate. Since they typically work normal business hours, you may be waiting a few days to get home. Once there, you will fill out a replacement form to provide your personal data. This is where it really helps to have a copy of your passport, either in paper form or digitally.

- Rebook your flight. Call the airline and explain what happened. Ask them what it will cost to rebook you on a different flight.

- Hang on to your replacement passport! Losing a passport a second time raises a red flag with Homeland Security. You do not want them to think that you are helping outsiders get into the United States.

U.S. Government Assistance

One of the best programs ever created to assist travelers returning from foreign countries was created by the U.S. Customs and Border Protection (CBP). There are a few Trusted Traveler programs that may apply to you but the most comprehensive is called Global Entry (GE). GE is a fast track for re-entry back into the United States because it bypasses the regular immigration lines, which are frequently clogged with other travelers.

The application for GE is quite simple. There is a questionnaire that must be completed online. Go to **www.cbp.gov** and they will direct you to the registration site. Once the application is reviewed, CBP will ask you to come in for a personal interview and explain how the system works.

If you qualify for GE, CBP will put their sticker on your passport. It is this sticker that allows you to go to a special kiosk and record your re-entry into the United States. The time savings can easily be 30-60 minutes or more each time, particularly critical if you have a tight connecting flight. The cost is very nominal and covers a 5-year period.

Another great feature is offered by the U.S. State Department. You can record your foreign itinerary in a password-protected online account. This way there is a record of where you are when traveling. Well, rather, where you *should* be.

No, they don't follow you around. Rather, you tell them about your flights and hotel plans, and they allow you to register that information with them. It is called the Smart Traveler Enrollment Program (STEP).

The online registration is simple and free. Go to **https://travelregistration.state.gov** and record your itinerary. In the event there are problems or emergencies, someone from the foreign Consulate or Embassy can assist you or your loved ones who may be trying to find you.

It takes only a few minutes to complete an international itinerary with the State Department. In my opinion, this might not be as beneficial for those traveling to fully developed countries in groups, but is essential for those traveling alone, especially to areas known for not being friendly to Americans.

In addition, there may be situations where registering allows the State Dept. to help find you if there is an emergency back home or in the country you are visiting.

 TIP: Any time you travel outside the U.S., it is always a good idea to make sure you have the telephone numbers and addresses for the U.S. Consulates and Embassies wherever you will be traveling. The State Dept. offers emergency services to U.S. citizens through its Embassies and Consulates. This can be anything from contacting loved ones back home to assisting with obtaining emergency funds if necessary.

They also issue travel advisories for those visiting certain countries. It is always a good idea to check out their advisories before planning a trip abroad.

Some business travelers take extra precaution by registering their personal items with Customs and Border Protection before they leave. These items generally include jewelry and electronics such as laptop computers, watches, digital phones, and camera equipment.

Why go to all this trouble? Because when you return to the U.S. and go through customs, CBP may allege these items were purchased outside the States, and they may want to impose a duty on them.

Personally, I have never had an issue with this, but if you want to be proactive and avoid a potential fight with CBP, register each item on their Form 4457 before you leave the country. When you return, this will not be a problem.

TSA PreCheck

In late 2011, TSA introduced PreCheck, an experimental program allowing passengers to speed through TSA lines by removing the very requirements that slow down the security process. American Airlines and Delta Air Lines each were permitted to designate two of their hubs as entry points, and then select the qualifying passengers from their frequent flier ranks.

While Global Entry membership is not a stated requirement, it appears most passengers who qualify for PreCheck also have a Global Entry card. Indeed, some airports even direct those with GE to the expedited TSA line.

So how does PreCheck help? The PreCheck lane does not require passengers to remove liquids or computers from their bags. These passengers also are not required to take off their shoes, belts, or even coats. The only requirement is to remove items like a cellphone from clothing pockets before going through the security scanner.

Obviously these TSA PreCheck security lines move very quickly, seldom requiring more than sixty seconds total for a passenger. This reduces the wait time for everyone else as well because the other lines are now shorter. At the beginning of 2012, TSA announced an expansion in the number of participating airports where PreCheck lanes will be installed. If proven successful, presumably the program will be made available to other airlines and airports.

Power Adapters and Converters

One travel accessory you will need in most foreign countries is a power adapter and maybe also a power converter. The power adapter is a *"must"* item when traveling to Europe, Asia, and other continents. It is a gizmo that converts the U.S. 2- or 3-prong wall connection to whatever the foreign country uses. Simply plug your electrical cord into the adapter, and then plug the adapter into the wall. It's that simple.

Well, nothing is really that simple. It wouldn't be a challenge if they didn't make it at least a bit more difficult.

They did. There are quite a few different power outlet types around the world, depending on location. Canada, for example, is identical to the U.S. In the United Kingdom, however, they use 220v with very different outlets.

Like the U.K., the rest of the European community uses 220v but their power connections to the wall are different. France, for example, is different than England. In parts of Asia, it is yet another type of connection. See, it really isn't that simple.

Power adapters are readily available in many stores. Some adaptors are sold as individual items, meaning a connection good for one nation or region. Others are sold as packs with perhaps 5 or more of the most common types of connections.

Because there are so many types of electrical wall connections out there, some manufacturers have created all-in-one adapters. They are designed to be universal, meaning they have numerous types of prongs that can be used nearly anywhere in the world.

Note: Many of these adapters are 2-prong. This is not an issue for most items but there are still some small appliances, such as certain laptop computers, that use a 3-prong. If you have one of these, it also may be necessary to buy another adapter that will convert your 3-prong to a 2-prong.

There may be another limitation: The power adapter works only with electrical items that work on both a 110v and a 220v system. I'm no electrical genius so I asked my husband what this means. Basically, he told me that most appliances, like cellphones, laptop computers, and hairdryers, made today can connect to both the 110v and 220v power systems. Unfortunately, there are always exceptions. It is those exceptions that also require a voltage converter.

How do you know if your travel electronics and other small appliances also work with 220v systems? Some products will say so right on their power cord. For others, refer back to their manuals.

See, it's never really that easy. If it doesn't say anything on the power cord and you cannot find a manual for it, then you need to contact the manufacturer. If available, go to the manufacturer's website to see if the information might be there. If not, look for a way to contact them.

As I said in the beginning of the book, some things are learned the hard way.

I was in Europe once and plugged a portable blender into one of these adapter gizmos, then plugged it into the wall. Everything was fine until I turned on the appliance.

To this day I don't know exactly what happened but when I turned it on, sparks went flying everywhere. It looked like the Fourth of July in my hotel room!

At that moment, I wished I were wearing Depends, seeing myself about to implode along with the entire hotel. Fortunately, it only shorted out the electricity in my room. A kind gentleman from maintenance helped me out by resetting all the circuits but of course, the blender was DOA and my in-room breakfast smoothies were a bust.

If you need a power adapter/voltage converter, it is probably better for your peace of mind to pick one up in the U.S. before you travel. However, they are usually available in most host countries. In fact, there are some hotels that will let you use one of theirs while you are a guest.

Also, if you are visiting an international airport lounge, adapters are often available for borrowing in exchange for their holding your boarding pass. Note, though, it is not likely anyone outside the U.S. will provide a 3-prong to 2-prong adapter.

Learning the Language

Rule #1: Don't expect people outside the U.S. to speak English. Well okay, they will in places like Canada and the United Kingdom but in non-English speaking countries, they may not know any English. They may, but just don't expect it.

Usually you will find that in many places around the world, English is spoken quite satisfactorily in hotels and in retail and restaurant venues in tourist sections of town. However, once you venture outside the door, you are on your own.

If you find people who do speak English, remember their language version might be different than ours. It is important to be careful not to use our slang expressions or idioms. Phrases that mean one thing to us may mean something totally different to them.

Likewise, it is very common that they won't understand our jokes. Telling a religious joke in the Middle East may be more blasphemous than funny to them. However, it is also possible their understanding of our language may be little, if any, better than our understanding of theirs.

This is not only important when meeting locals but suppose your purpose is to deliver a speech to a foreign audience. While you may have a translator assisting you, some of your thoughts may not translate well. Worst case scenario: They are translated in a way that is seen as offensive.

Before traveling to another country, learn something about the language, culture, history, and customs. If you intend to do any business in a foreign country, also take the time to learn about their business practices and regulations.

For example, in China, a person's last name is customarily spoken first. In other words, they announce themselves using their last names first, then their first names. That is exactly the opposite of how we indicate our names, which explains why they call me Mrs. Carol over there instead of Mrs. Margolis.

In most cases, it is not necessary to be proficient in the foreign language unless you expect to transact business in that language. If you are there to conduct business where speaking the language is a must, either learn the language fluently or hire a translator.

Nevertheless, it is still very helpful to have at least a rudimentary understanding of a language. Translations for simple terms such as *please, thank you, good morning*, etc., go a long way toward showing your hosts that you care. Generally they will be very pleased that you at least took the time to try to communicate with them even if your pronunciation is not perfect.

There are many sources available to help with foreign language translations. They include:

- Books.
- CD/DVD courses.
- Podcasts. Some are free, others may cost a little.
- Applications for today's PDA's and smartphones. Some of the basic versions are free; others often cost no more than a few dollars.

For those who have no way to speak a foreign language, there is always sign language. What I mean is using universal gestures as a way to communicate. For example, pointing to your belly or mouth might tell someone you are hungry. Pointing to another body part may tell them you need a restroom (or it may get you arrested, so be careful!). Be safe here and learn the word for toilet!

Even the most seemingly harmless gestures might be interpreted as something very different in their country. The results can have an adverse effect. For example, the way you simply hold up your hand or fingers may mean nothing to you but in another country, it can have great significance. Indeed, in certain parts of the world, which hand you use to eat or pick up something with may convey an unintended meaning.

In Thailand, simply pointing your feet at a person, religious icon, or worse, Buddha, is considered an insult. In the Middle East, South America and more, giving a thumbs-up is hideously offensive. If you try the gesture method, hopefully it will be no more damaging than getting a good laugh. On the other hand, your harmless gesture may be seen as a major insult. Do yourself a favor and do some research before your visit.

There also may be issues with colors. Yellow flowers have a very specific meaning in France – jealousy. Not exactly how you intend to show your love. In China, you would never wrap a gift in white because it signifies death.

For this and many other reasons, it is common to hire translators when you travel. They can help not only with language but also with how to deal with some of the local customs and practices. This is particularly important for business, where misunderstandings can destroy relationships, as well as prove to be very expensive.

If you choose to hire a translator, get a recommendation from someone you know, if possible. Using someone recommended by your international business connection host may turn out to be less favorable and indeed, even may be one of their employees. Needless to say, looking out for their best interests means they will be much more loyal to the host than to you.

Another consideration is to hire a bi-lingual personal guide. This can be anything from assistance with travel hotspots to help with shopping. Prices vary depending on location and need.

Then there are people who just love to travel to foreign destinations on their own. At the very least, a good guide book or some internet research would be very helpful.

While language in a foreign country is very important, so is the way you dress. In some cultures, our beachwear is simply unacceptable. In Europe, for example, expect to have your body properly covered when entering a church (no bare arms). In the Middle East, you may be required to wear even more covering just to walk down the street. Do your research before you go.

It also helps to be mindful of holidays in other countries. Making any business arrangements without knowing the other country's holidays and traditions can have unfortunate consequences.

Don't count on your contacts in the other country to let you know about national holidays. Sure, they may remind you a few days before a meeting but that is long after you have already booked your nonrefundable travel to meet with them.

This is what I call, "Oh by the way...." Those four magic words have killed many an otherwise good business relationship. Don't let it happen to you. As I said before, be proactive and learn about the country you are visiting. Just remember to include holidays as well.

 FINAL TIP: Always pick up a few business cards from the hotel. This is particularly important if you are in a non-English-speaking nation. They are invaluable when using local transportation to return to your hotel. Most taxi or bus drivers know instantly how to get you back after reading the card.

Oh Those Nasty Time Zones

There are many blessings when traveling internationally but there is one major curse: Time zone changes, many which are nasty.

For some travelers, just the 3-hour time difference between the east and west coasts in the U.S. is a major adjustment. If I just described you, you may really hate the extreme adjustments when flying outside of North or South America.

For many, the greatest time zone problem is jet lag. Basically, this refers to those times when your body clock is still on your host time but the clock in the time zone where you are is different.

Jet lag can cause mild disorientation to severe headaches, stomach cramps, nausea, and of course, insomnia. The conflict between body clock and physical location can even lead to depression.

When your body is telling you it desperately needs rest, that is often the moment when you find yourself in another time zone in the morning with the day about to begin. For example, you are flying from Los Angeles to New York. You leave at 7 am and arrive maybe five hours later.

Your body might be saying it is lunch time. However, the clock says it is already 3 pm, closer to dinner time. When your LA body tells you it is 10 pm at night and time to prepare for bed, the time is really 1 am the following day.

The next morning is no better for most travelers. If you normally rise at 7 am, it would already be 10 am in New York. By 10 am, chances are you are already late for work. More likely you need to get up between 6-7 am in New York. Put another way, this would be only 3-4 am for your Los Angeles body. Many business travelers sum up jet lag in one word: Ugh!

According to a British Airways poll in July 2005, 23% of business travelers said they had fallen asleep in a meeting and 14% had missed a meeting or a flight because of jet lag.[11] There was nothing in this poll to suggest the reason for the fatigue was jet lag but it does highlight how difficult it is for some to get back on track when there's a time conflict between mind and body.

As I mentioned, travel only within the U.S. is problematic for some. Let's look at the impact if you travel to Europe.

Traveling to Europe adds 5-10 hours to U.S. time, depending on your cities of origin and destination. If jet lag in the U.S. is an issue for you, travel across the Atlantic can be downright painful.

Note: Many countries that change to Daylight Savings Time do it a week or so apart from the United States. This actually can be fun if you happen to time your travel just right.

Let's say you happen to be in London on the Fall weekend when they set their clocks back an hour. Good part in this case is you've picked up an extra hour of sleep.

If you just happen to fly to the U.S. the following week, you pick up another hour because we change our clocks a week later. Okay, I admit this is rare but it is great when you can make it work for you.

In the examples above, the travel is west to east. Many travelers find that it is much easier to adjust to jet lag when they travel east to west. Going back to our first example, it is not as difficult to adjust to flying in the other direction, say from New York City to Los Angeles (JFK-LAX).

I admit to a preference for flying east to west. For an extended period of time I was flying from the east coast to Houston. A 6:30 am flight from home got me to Houston around 8 am local time, early enough that I could begin work that morning.

In contrast, what if the flight were going from Houston to the east coast? I would need to get up earlier because now it would be a 5:30 am flight to the east coast if I wanted to arrive by 9 am.

To help with time zone adjustment, some travelers prefer to get a one-day head start. Why?

- To be ready for meetings or other events scheduled for the following morning. A few examples include pre-meetings, setting up a booth for a trade show, or maybe the only available transportation to a specific destination is on that day.

- They are just not morning people and do not like early morning flights.

- They want to wake up in their destination city early for a good morning workout or jog.

- To allow a little time to travel around the destination city.

One more important reason: Flight delays and cancellations happen all too frequently. They are not predictable so if you plan to attend an important meeting or event, it's best to leave a day early. Gambling that your flight will be on time may yield pretty disappointing results.

Let's get back on track and discuss some serious jet lag. Europe is always a great example because there can be three time zones to deal with, depending on your destination. As always, the further east you travel, the greater the likelihood that you will pass through another time zone.

London is typically 5-8 hours ahead of the states. Paris is 6-9 hours ahead, while Athens is 7-10 hours ahead. Obviously, the smaller difference is based on U.S. east coast time while the larger is the time difference from the west coast.

From here it can really go downhill. Some examples include Dubai (9-12 hours), New Delhi (10.5-13.5 hours), Jakarta (12-15 hours), Hong Kong (12-16 hours), Tokyo (13-17 hours), Sydney (15-19 hours), and Auckland (17-21 hours).

I know, the last one makes no sense. How can Auckland be two hours later than Sydney when New Zealand is right next door to Australia? Looking at a map, it almost seems possible to swim between the two.

Speaking of New Zealand, that brings up another time zone matter. It was there that Daylight Savings Time began. However, some countries – and even a couple U.S. states – do not participate in Daylight Savings Time. While most adjust their clocks an hour either way, note that some don't.

To make this more confusing, countries that adjust their clocks for DST may not do it on the same date or even at the same time of day as in the U.S. Also, remember that countries on the other side of the world, like New Zealand, turn their clocks back an hour around the same time we change our clocks forward, because our Spring is their Fall.

What this means for you: Perhaps adjusting for time changes that may be an hour or two more or less than what you are used to relative to a foreign country. This may be important if you are doing business in these places, especially if you use the phone for doing business in the other country. It is also important to remember this for meetings that will occur around the time that the clocks change.

Like most people, traveling west is easier because you gain hours in your day. If you are like nearly every other business traveler, adding more time to even a single day is much more of a blessing than a curse.

I actually enjoy traveling from the east coast to the west coast, especially on a direct flight. An early morning flight means arriving on the west coast in time for a second breakfast. I know, I don't need a second breakfast, but my point is that having three more hours in the day is very helpful for both business and pleasure.

Three additional hours can add nearly 40% to the workday. For some, that means additional billings and more income. For others, it might make it easier to fit in an extra business meeting.

We flew west to Honolulu on our son's birthday. He loved having an extra 7 hours of celebration time on his special day.

Arguably the greatest benefit of traveling east to west is the luxury of more leisure time or a nap during a long flight. However, some would no doubt say the best advantage is not having to travel a day earlier. In fact, some who need only one day for work on the west coast will return on a redeye flight that evening. I'm not saying it is fun, since it is a very long day, only that it is doable. Plan for recovery time the next day.

Of course, traveling west to east has a different effect on the body. A transcontinental flight east to west takes only a couple of hours, adjusting for time zones. The same flight west to east is nearly 8 hours, the equivalent of a full business day lost in the air.

Suffering the Jet Lag Blues

I am asked frequently about a cure for jet lag. First, a bit on what jet lag is and how you know if you're suffering from it.

Jet lag is medically referred to as desynchronosis. For many travelers, this is when they feel that their body isn't synchronized with reality.

Jetlag is actually caused by disruption to your "body clock," a small cluster of brain cells that controls the timing of biological functions (circadian rhythms), including when you eat and sleep. The body clock is designed for a regular rhythm of daylight and darkness, so it's thrown out of sync when it experiences daylight and darkness at the "wrong" times in a new time zone.

Jet lag results from rapid long-distance (east-west or west-east) travel, most common when flying rather than driving through time zones. Jet lag is worse when you move from west to east because the body finds it harder to adapt to a shorter day than a longer one. It is not unusual for the condition to last several days.

Symptoms of Jet Lag
- Disorientation, lack of concentration or fuzziness.

- Becoming irrational or unreasonable – "Losing it" is another symptom reported by frequent travelers.

- Fatigue – Tiredness will make it difficult for you to concentrate and enjoy your business trip or vacation.

- Digestive problems.

- Dehydration – This can cause headaches, dry skin and nasal irritation, as well as make you more susceptible to colds, coughs, sore throats and flu germs that are swirling around you.

- Discomfort in legs and feet – Limbs can swell while flying and can become very uncomfortable.

- Broken sleep after arrival – Crossing time zones can cause you to wake during the night and then want to fall asleep during the day. Your built-in circadian rhythms have been disturbed, and it can take many days for the body to readjust to the new time zone

Jet Lag Time Warps

Since I live on the east coast, I will talk about jet lag traveling to Europe. Depending on destination, this means I lose 5-8 hours just because of time zones, in addition to the flying time.

I usually fly a redeye to Europe. It is approximately a 7- or 8-hour flight so I will typically lose 12-16 hours. If my flight leaves at 6 pm, I will arrive around 1-2 am the following day, according to my body. Actual local time will be 6-9 am, depending on destination.

So how do I adjust from an internal time of, say, 1 am, to a local time of 7 am? My body says it is time to sleep but the clock says the day is fresh and just beginning.

The jet lag adjustment begins by sleeping on the long flight. I usually sleep after dinner, which is a couple of hours into the flight. That means about 2 to 4 hours of sleep if I'm lucky before waking for breakfast on the plane.

I know, two to four hours is hardly a good night's sleep by most any standard, especially restless sleeping during a flight. Because of the toll on body and mind, I go to bed that first night in Europe a few hours earlier than usual and I avoid taking a nap upon arrival. By the second day, I am somewhat adjusted.

What if you are like my husband and just can't seem to sleep on a plane? Having traveled with him, I see how difficult it is for some travelers to adjust to extreme time zone changes.

Some experts suggest allowing one day for each time zone crossed. While this might indeed be appropriate for medical reasons, it is most likely impossible for practical reasons. When you consider that an international trip will mean 5-20 hours of time zone change, it is hardly realistic to set aside an equal number of days to allow your body to adjust to one time zone each day.

Reduce the Effects of Jet Lag

Here are several tips to help reduce the effects of jet lag:

- Start even before you fly with at least two good nights' sleep. Some travelers prefer to begin their time zone adjustment at least a few days ahead of time.

- Once on your flight, drink a lot of water. Because many travelers find it a pain to get up and walk to the bathroom, they don't drink when flying. That can be unhealthy because dehydration reduces your immune system.

- Bring along an eye mask, neck pillow, slippers, earplugs, and anything else that helps you sleep on the plane.

- Take supplements. Some people claim that melatonin will "cure" jet lag by promoting sleep. Others swear by a homeopathic product called No Jet Lag.

- Set your watch to the destination time as soon as you leave for a trip. This way you might trick your mind and body into believing you are already on the new time.

- Be as relaxed as possible when you fly. Wear loose, comfortable clothing. Noise canceling headphones are also very helpful for long flights where you want to get some sleep.

- If you are looking for rest, avoid the in-flight movies and settle for soft music. Others prefer no music at all. Instead, they practice meditation or quiet yoga. It can work wonders.

- Sleeping aids. Definitely speak with your physician if you feel this will help with the time adjustment and of course, never drink alcohol when taking any medication to help you sleep.

- Avoid alcohol altogether. While there are some travelers who believe it relaxes them, alcohol is known to dehydrate the body, not to mention act as a depressant. This can lead to the exact opposite result of what you intended.

- Avoid caffeine because it acts as a stimulant, not the best choice sitting in a pressurized airplane cabin where the air is very dry. The best choice is to drink lots of water or fruit juice. This keeps your body refreshed and hydrated.

- On long flights, periodically leave your seat and walk the aisles. This can do wonders for circulation and improve your overall well-being.

- Get on an eating schedule in your destination city as soon as possible.

- If you arrive early at your destination, a shower and change of clothing can help refresh you for the day. If you are at an interim stop, such as a connecting airport before your final destination, consider using either an airport lounge or perhaps a local service that provides showers and a place to relax for a little while.

The longer the journey, the more appreciative you will be to have some non-work days at the beginning of the trip. If your work week begins on Monday, perhaps you could complete your flight a few days earlier to allow some time for adjustment. Many employers are happy to cooperate because the relatively small additional cost up-front is returned many times over with more productive employees.

I want to emphasize something that is mentioned again in the next chapter: If you take any medications and are traveling across time zones, check with your physician to see if you should make adjustments to the time of day you take these medications.

Note that this may apply not only to prescription drugs but also vitamins, supplements, herbs, etc. As seen above, time zone changes can be quite extreme at 15 hours or more. Check with your doctors to see if a different time schedule would be appropriate for you.

On arrival, plan a good walk. Use the stairs and avoid the elevators, escalators and moving sidewalks. Jet lag hates fresh air, daylight, and exercise. Stay awake at least until the early evening. You will probably wake up very early on your first morning.

At your destination, walk barefoot on the ground, if possible, and/or swim in the ocean or soak in an Epsom salt bath. This will help ground your electromagnetic system. As soon as possible, stand in direct sunlight for 10-20 minutes without sunglasses.

Keep your mind off of the time difference. Don't think about what time it is at home (set your watch to local time!).

Keep drinking plenty of water.

Telephone Tips That Won't Break the Bank

Another important thing to consider when traveling outside the U.S. is using your mobile phone. While many of them will work, you may be shocked at the fees charged.

Some phone carriers use GSM cellphone card technology, the international standard for most countries around the world. Others use CDMA, which may limit your international coverage. Nevertheless, it may be possible to obtain a global phone for international use from all carriers. Before traveling, check with your phone carrier to see about available options.

Note that even if an international calling plan is available, it can be very expensive. If you are self-employed or part of a small business, this could be a major concern. If you are part of a larger organization, it might be something you can arrange through your own travel department.

If you have one of the smartphones, the cost may be even greater because these phones continually search for internet data, incurring what is called data roaming charges. They are a gold mine for the phone companies but may bankrupt you. Even if your phone just rings while you are outside the U.S., you may incur a charge.

Alternatively, if your phone has an Airplane Mode, consider using it. That eliminates phone calls coming in and avoids inevitable roaming charges from Push notifications (this is a setting in many current smartphones where data is automatically sent to your phone and updated). The safest alternative is to keep the phone turned off unless you are in a Wi-Fi spot.

Many travelers pick up a phone in the destination country. Usually you purchase a predetermined number of minutes. It is up to you to make sure you don't go over the minutes allotted.

One of the downsides to having a prepaid phone is if you don't use all the minutes, you will have paid for them anyway. In other words, you may purchase 60 minutes but only use 20. The cost of those 20 minutes is now 3 times as much.

Another downside is that the phone number will be different than the one you usually use. This might be an issue if people are expected to be able to contact you. The only way they will know the phone number is if you contact them first.

Some choose to purchase a SIM card for their phone. Your phone may need to be unlocked to use this option so check with your phone provider first.

The most frequent method for staying in touch internationally today is VoIP (Voice over Internet Protocol) and the most popular is Skype. If you and the person on the other end have Skype on your computer or cellphone, it is free and very easy to use as long as both ends have internet connections.

If both of you are using computers and have Wi-Fi available, there is an added benefit of video with Skype. You can see the other person as well as hear them.

For a nominal cost, Skype also allows you to call a land line back home. This is an excellent alternative when the person back in the U.S. does not have internet service available at the moment.

There is no one-size-fits-all here. After considering all the options, choose what works best for you.

Keeping in Touch Back Home

Mentioning the telephone is a great segue to the next topic, staying in touch with business, family, and friends back home. At best this is a challenge; at worst it can be impossible.

If you are like many, you believe that the greater the time zone difference between home and destination cities, the more difficult it must be to communicate. As you will soon see, this is not the case.

Let's say you are traveling and want to speak with your family in San Francisco, where it is 8 pm. That would be 11 pm in Boston, perhaps a bit late but often workable. If you were across the water in Ireland, it would be 4 am. Unless you are a *very* early riser, this might not work.

Let's change the scenario just a little: Your home is Philadelphia instead of San Francisco and this time you are in London. Now 8 pm at home is 3 am on the road. Unless you are a hardcore night owl, this won't work at all.

But it gets better...

Instead of Europe or even the Middle East, let's look at Asia. If U.S. west coast time is 6 am, it would be 9-10 pm in much of Asia. In other words, 6 pm in the U.S. would be roughly 6-10 am the following day in the Asian destination city. Now a phone call, email or Skype is looking very possible.

Even if we stretch this scenario to Oz and beyond, 10 pm on our west coast would be 5 pm a day later in Australia and 7 pm in New Zealand. Sounds like a pretty nice break from a crazy workday when you can get it.

So what's my point here? Communication between the U.S. and Europe is far more difficult generally than it is compared to most of the world further away. When my husband travels to Asia and we are 12 hours apart, that is quite easy for us. His 8 am is my 8 pm and vice versa, easy for us to have a nice morning or evening conversation on Skype.

Well, that is, it's nice until I throw a wrinkle in the works by flying to Europe at the same time he is on a trip to Asia. Now 8 pm for me is 5-6 am for him. Not the best of hours but still better than when he is in the U.S. while I am in Europe.

Currency

Currency exchange is important when traveling outside the U.S. Some countries, like Canada, gladly accept U.S. dollars in stores but typically at rates favorable to the merchants. Don't count on these merchants doing you any favors.

Many merchants around the world simply will not accept U.S. dollars. There may be many reasons why but in the end, they are unimportant. If you want to transact any type of business in these countries, you must convert your dollars to their currency.

Some travelers prefer using local U.S. banks to exchange dollars before leaving. Ask your bank for the lead time in ordering foreign currency as most do not have other currencies instantly available. If this is not an option, a bank in the foreign city might give you the best conversion rate. Not as good a choice: Using a currency converter kiosk often located in airports, sometimes within cities. They generally give lower exchange rates.

Another option is an ATM. The exchange rates may be better than the airport kiosks but weigh this against the additional ATM fees you may incur.

It is always helpful to know the approximate currency exchange rates. This is readily available from many sources online. For those with smartphones, there are many applications and most of them are free.

Alas, currency can be tricky. For example, most people have heard of *Euros*, the principal currency of Europe. However, generally they use *Pounds* in the United Kingdom. I know, if the U.K. is part of Europe, why don't they use Euros? Uh, because they don't. Just consider this another part of travel madness. In fact, 17 countries of the European Union use the Euro, 11 countries do not.

Making it more difficult, Pounds are not necessarily all the same. England has their own as does Scotland. Are they interchangeable? Not necessarily, even though both England and Scotland are located in the U.K. It seems that English Pounds are generally accepted in Scotland but the opposite is not always true. Oh, and Gibraltar has its own version of the Pound also.

Adding to the confusion (you were probably expecting more of this) is Ireland. For reasons way beyond the scope of this book, our Irish friends use the Euro as their currency. Well, they do in southern Ireland anyway. In the north, they use the Pound.

I know, I said the U.K. uses Pounds and Ireland is a part of the U.K. So why would they use a different currency? Because they do.

China is also confusing. We generally think of China as three primary regions: Mainland China (People's Republic of China), Taiwan (Republic of China), and Hong Kong, known as one of the Special Administrative Regions but part of the PRC. Unfortunately, each has its own currency.

Mainland China uses the Renminbi, abbreviated RMB or CNY, while Taiwan uses the New Taiwan Dollar (typically seen as TWD) and Hong Kong's dollar is usually seen as HKD. If you are ever in China and take a side trip to Macau (another Special Administrative Region), note that they have their own currency as well.

Yeah I know, four currencies in China? Honestly, I don't make the rules. Like everything else in business, just learn them and the rest falls into place.

Credit Cards

Any time you travel outside the U.S., contact your credit card companies before you leave. Not all of them require prior notification but best to be safe here. Some of your cards may not allow any transactions if you have not contacted them previously. Also note that calls to credit card companies from outside the U.S. may be quite expensive. (You may be able to call collect but then you need to figure out the international dialing.)

However, certain credit card vendors are notorious for charging very high foreign transaction fees. Initially you pay a fee to have the charge converted from the foreign currency back to the U.S. dollar amount. On top of that, many card companies add a fee merely because it is a transaction in a different currency. Combined, these fees can be quite steep. Check with your credit card company before traveling outside the U.S. to see just which charges may apply to you.

Certain credit cards companies are known to be a bit more traveler-friendly than others. For example, some do not charge foreign transaction fees. If you use credit cards frequently, this can be a significant savings.

Credit card company rules change often so I am not mentioning any by name. Instead, you might want to spend a little time on the internet researching this topic if you have interest in saving some money using credit cards when traveling internationally.

Nevertheless, note that not all countries accept credit cards for all transactions. Generally, they can be used for large purchases but it is not uncommon to find smaller businesses that do not accept credit or debit cards at all. If you must pay cash, it is almost always better to pay in the foreign currency.

Speaking of unfavorable, watch for credit card transactions where you expect the bill to be in the local currency but the credit card is calculated in U.S. dollars. You may be asked if you would like your credit card to be charged in dollars. This can happen in very upscale shopping establishments as well as in local bars and restaurants.

Always elect to be charged in the local currency and to have your credit card company do the conversion. Having a local business charge you in dollars will almost certainly cost you more.

Driving

Needless to say, driving in a new location is at best a challenge. A GPS navigation device is very helpful, though obviously not available everywhere. If you plan to rent a car for a long period of time, it may be less expensive to purchase a GPS unit instead of renting one with the vehicle.

Before renting a car outside the U.S., check with your auto insurance carrier and make sure you have coverage. Some policies may cover you only in certain locations.

It may surprise some readers, but it is not uncommon to find only manual transmission vehicles available. This is especially true for compact cars. If you need an automatic transmission, make this clear before renting a car and book it early.

Also, some countries may require you to obtain an International Driving Permit. Generally this is not required in much of Europe but to be safe, check with your local American Automobile Association office to find out the rules before you travel.

It is helpful to us that most other nations drive on the same side of the road as we do. While that makes driving easier, there are still many challenges.

You may have to convert miles to kilometers and gallons to liters, simple calculations but a bit unnerving when you already have so many other things on your mind.

You also need to know local traffic rules and regulations. Are you allowed to turn right on a red light (assume no)? Who has the right of way, vehicles or pedestrians? When are vehicles allowed to change lanes?

Adding to driving complexity, our friends in England prefer to drive on the left side of the road. This is prevalent throughout the United Kingdom (and most former British colonies), though not the rest of Europe.

It is quite the test if you haven't done it before. Just like the Brits who travel to the U.S. from the U.K., it takes a little time to remember to drive on the correct side of the road.

Alas, the U.K. and many other countries add another challenge to driving: They are very fond of roundabouts, circles located in the center of intersections that replace traffic lights. It is not unusual in some areas to see them every couple of blocks.

Naturally, locals are very used to this kind of driving but for visitors, it is quite a shock to see them everywhere. You must first remember to drive on the left side of the road, and then remember which lane to drive in so you can navigate through them.

TIP: This tip from a tour bus driver is great for successfully navigating through a round-about: Picture the round-about as a clock. If the exit you need is at 12:00 o'clock or after, be in the right lane of a two-lane road. If the exit you need is prior to 12:00 o'clock, be in the left lane of a two-lane road.

My suggestion for driving abroad: Be careful. If you have any doubts about your ability to drive safely, particularly in the U.K., better to leave the driving to someone else.

Driving in China is also interesting. Mainland China and Taiwan drive on the right side of the road, Hong Kong drives on the left side of the road. The first two jurisdictions may seem easy, but once you get out of a busy city district, it is unlikely you will find many – if any – people who speak English.

In mainland China, many of the roads are modern but you are on your own if you need assistance. Remember Rule #1: You may not find anyone who speaks English.

Actually, there are relatively few cars in Hong Kong because there is little if any need to drive there. An exception might be a day trip around the islands from the populous northern part down to the southern areas and back.

For business purposes, however, local transportation is generally excellent. They have a very modern high-speed rail system, and local buses and taxis are inexpensive.

Travel Insurance

There are many types of travel insurance. While most of them are targeted at leisure travelers, there are some designed to assist business travelers, too.

Most business travelers do not purchase additional insurance for each trip. However, there are a few exceptions, for instance, additional coverage for car rentals, life insurance, especially if flying to a destination, and health insurance.

The reason for not purchasing additional property insurance coverage might depend on your business. By that I mean if you are using equipment owned by a company, it is probably insured through the company. You may possibly have coverage through your auto or homeowners insurance, or even through a credit card.

If you are self-employed or work with a smaller firm, is your property covered for things like damage or theft? The answer is, I don't know. Call your insurance company to discuss this prior to your travels.

Because every insurance policy out there is different, review your coverage with your insurance advisor. In certain cases, it may be wise to purchase an international rider but this, as with all insurance coverage outside the U.S., needs to be determined on a case-by-case basis.

Ah, but what if you get sick outside the U.S.? Nearly all health insurance policies limit coverage to the states. If you work for a larger firm or even the government, there might be coverage available but check with your HR department to be sure. For smaller firms and for those self-employed, do not expect to have any health insurance coverage, though policies for such coverage are available.

In any case, medical treatment is generally available but unless it is an emergency situation, it might be best to contact the local U.S. Consulate first. They may be able to offer assistance, including help in finding English-speaking physicians.

What about auto insurance coverage? I don't mean to sound evasive, but again, it depends on so many factors. Certain locations outside the U.S. may be included in your current auto insurance coverage. Of course, they also may not be, but it is possible there is coverage through the credit card used for the vehicle rental. As you can see, it depends.

For these and many other reasons, it is always a good idea to review all your insurance coverage before traveling outside the U.S. You may or may not need additional insurance. Perhaps your employer or overseas business contact may have coverage that applies to you.

On the other hand, you may be self-employed and can't count on anyone to provide additional insurance coverage. Review this with your insurance carrier to see if it might be necessary to obtain additional coverage for things like personal property, driving, and health.

Miscellaneous

- There are many more considerations when traveling internationally. Some are important to know but not worthy of a long section. I am listing some of them here.

- Some countries require U.S. citizens to pay an arrival or departure tax. Also note that some countries require a certain number of blank pages in your passport, sometimes a couple of them together. Check with the State Dept. before you travel to see if these may apply to you.

- You may qualify for a refund for taxes paid on such things as clothing and gifts that you buy. For example, the VAT tax in Europe may be available for refund. You can collect it when you exit the country. Most merchants can explain the rules to you or you can read about them online. Allow for extra time at the airport to turn in your VAT refund claim.

- Each airline has its own luggage allowance rules. While the rules for U.S. carriers are generally better, you need to know the rules for every airline you are flying with.

  For example, most U.S. airlines allow passengers to bring two carry-on bags with a 50-70 lb. limit for checked bags. If you are flying on a foreign carrier – even if your reservation was made through a domestic airline – you may be subject to the foreign airline's carry-on and checked bag rules. Often this is one carry-on bag and lower weight limits for checked bags. Always check with the airline before flying because rules can change quickly.

- Tipping customs vary around the world. Some places simply add service charges in lieu of any tipping. Of course, they don't mind if you add a little extra though it may not be expected.

  In some countries, it is considered poor taste to simply leave a tip on a table in a restaurant. Besides, you don't know who will pick it up. It is always best to check with the hotel desk or other local source to learn about tipping customs at your destination. Know that in many places, a credit card machine is brought directly to your table for processing your card (a great idea for the U.S. to do!). Ask if you can add a gratuity at this time.

- Do you wear eyeglasses? If so, always pack an extra pair. It is not uncommon that one pair is either damaged or lost. In most non-English-speaking countries, repair or replacement may be close to impossible unless you know someone who speaks the local language and can accompany you to an optometrist. That is, if there is even one available.

- What we call restrooms in the U.S. are usually called toilets in the U.K. and WCs (water closets) in other parts of Europe. Traveling throughout Europe, look for the WC signs but if you need to ask for the location of a restroom or toilet, most anyone who speaks English will know what you mean.

Well, they may know what you mean but don't necessarily expect a restroom like we are used to. There are still many places in Europe – and even more throughout Asia – where it is quite common that the toilets are... uh... let's just call them holes in the floor.

Oh, and have some coins handy. Many parts of the world only offer public restrooms for a fee. This includes toilets in train stations, shopping centers, even some McDonald's restaurants.

Bring your own supply of toilet paper with you at all times. Wet wipes are actually best.

Also have a small bottle of anti-bacterial gel with you. This is very handy because there may not be soap or even a sink to wash your hands in after you use the toilet.

What can I say, what you may be used to is not considered the international standard.

- Traveling to a foreign country for the first time and need a taxi to get to a hotel? Contact the hotel and ask them to email you the address of the hotel in their language. Like the example above, you are more likely to arrive at your destination quickly.

- Some travelers use a dual time zone watch when traveling internationally. That way you can quickly see at a glance your new time as well as another time zone. Some use that second time zone for family while others might have it set for something like their company's home office.

To assist with this time zone issue, I created a one-page spreadsheet. Down the left side are the 24 hours in a day. Across the top are also 24 hours. Well, due to space limitations and an effort to get everything on one page, there are only 12 hours across the top but it is quite easy to convert those hours to am and pm.

Here's an example of how to use the spreadsheet. Let's say you live in Chicago and are traveling to Paris. That's usually a 7-hour time difference. If it is 5 pm in Paris – seen on the schedule at 17:00 – that means it is 10 am back home. Simply place an X or check mark in that box.

Indeed you can place marks in all the boxes for each hour of the day. That way you will always know at a glance what time it is in the other city without having to worry about the math. Some may find it helpful to place an am or pm in the box to serve as a helpful reminder of the time back home.

Have a copy of this time zone guide at home for your family. When your kids get home from school and want to call or Skype you, they will easily know what time it is where you are and can adjust their call time rather than wake you up in the middle of the night.

See the *Business Travel Success Ultimate Travel Resource* for this form.

9

HEALTH & FITNESS

My workout clothes have more air miles on them than most people have flown. They travel with me on every trip, but often arrive back home just as clean as when they left.

If my workout clothes could talk, they would say:

"Why do you take us out of our nice, cedar-scented drawer and throw us into a dark suitcase? We never know if you'll show us the sights of the city or toss us into a dank dresser drawer while you go out and have fun. We don't like the guilty glare we get when you throw us back into the suitcase clean before you return home.

If you would just put us on for a few minutes each day, you'd go back home feeling much fitter than when you left and actually enjoy your travels more!"

The majority of business travelers say it is more difficult to eat healthy and stay fit when traveling than it is when at home. You are in good company if this sounds familiar.

The same challenges you have at home, such as finding the time to work out, making healthy meals, and getting enough sleep, are multiplied when on the road. What with the germs aboard your flight, the late night dinners with clients and the reduced sleeping hours, it's no wonder that travelers complain the most (right after complaints about delayed flights) about health and fitness challenges.

For those with special dietary needs (gluten free, vegetarian, low carb, etc.), the challenges of eating away from home are even greater. Is it possible to eat better, stay healthier, and keep fit while we travel? Of course! That's why there is an entire chapter devoted to this.

It begins with a bit of planning before heading off on your next trip and a dose of discipline while you're away. This discipline is the most difficult challenge, especially with busy pre-planned days and nights. The tips offered in this chapter are lessons learned over years of many illnesses during my travels and the up-and-down yo-yo weight effect.

I once did a personal exercise where I listed all the things important to me. Narrowing it down to the top five, this is what I ended up with:

1. My health
2. My family and friends
3. My career
4. My home
5. My hobbies

I figured that without good health, the other four wouldn't matter much, at least not in the long run. Like most people, however, I find myself drifting into the unhealthier order of 3, 2, 4, and 1, with rare sightings of 5.

I share this with you because while I am pretty good at eating healthy when traveling, the fitness part is still a challenge. I am sure there are many of you who would most likely say your priorities are not what you would like them to be either.

Together let's focus on how to keep our bodies healthy and fit. It begins with an overview of the advantages:

- The ability to focus on our other priorities,
- Enjoying the sights and the foods of the places we visit, and
- Lots of years ahead to reap the benefits of all the mileage and flight awards accumulated.

Planning Ahead: Travel Health Kit

The U.S. Department of Health and Human Services Centers for Disease Control (CDC) recommends that travelers pack a health kit to treat conditions that may arise, especially for pre-existing conditions. Basic items relevant to business travelers include the following:

- Personal prescription medications in their original containers
- Over-the-counter anti-diarrhea medication
- Antihistamine and decongestant
- Anti-motion/anti-nausea sickness medication
- Acetaminophen, aspirin, ibuprofen or other pain/fever medications
- Mild laxative

- Antacids
- Bandages
- Lubricating eye drops
- Altitude sickness medication
- A first aid topical antibiotic ointment, such as Neosporin, available in individually sealed packets. This helps prevent infection in minor cuts, scrapes and burns.

A small amount of each item, kept in a small plastic bag or container, should fit into a carry-on bag and be available if you need it. It is always smart to keep prescription medications with you at all times. As mentioned elsewhere in the book, never put drugs – *especially* prescriptions – in any checked bag.

It is not easy to replace medications when traveling to a different city, traveling on the weekend, or traveling internationally. With heightened airline security, sharp objects and some liquids and gels may have to remain in checked luggage.

Every traveler (especially those with other special medical needs) should carry their doctor's phone and fax numbers as well as copies of prescriptions for medications that might be needed along the way. An email address, if available, is also helpful.

Stay Healthy Kit

Most business travelers manage to remain fairly healthy, despite exposure to germs, long hours and less sleep. Nevertheless, here are some simple precautions to minimize your risks:

- Instant hand sanitizer as a soap/water substitute. The FDA's standard of effectiveness is a minimum alcohol concentration of 60%.
- Disinfecting wipes for cleaning airplane trays, hotel television remotes and anything else before touching. The hotel room's TV remote is a prime incubator of germs.
- Vitamins. These may include Vitamins C and D (since it's difficult for business travelers to find a few minutes each day in the sun), as well as an overall daily vitamin.
- Supplements. Many travelers swear by Airborne or Emergen-C, a concentrated dose of vitamin C and minerals. Either one of these is good to take before going into crowded areas or at the first sign of a cold.
- Small container of petroleum jelly (Vaseline) for wiping a dab inside your nostrils with a cotton swab. This helps keeps your nose moist and may be a barrier to germs.

Many regular travelers, especially flight attendants, bring food from home to eat during their travels. For the plane, the following is a list of items that are portable and non-liquid. You may want to add more for a longer flight:

- Hard boiled eggs, peeled (eat these early into the flight so they don't become stinky)
- Berries, any kind, inside a plastic bag along with a plastic fork for eating
- Cut up vegetables
- Dried apricots
- Almonds or other nuts
- Protein or granola bars
- Apples
- Squares of dark chocolate (70% cocoa or higher are healthier)
- Instant steel-cut oatmeal (with a plastic spoon). Ask for two cups, each half full with hot water (6 to 8 ounce cups are typically available, neither of which is large enough for mixing in a full package of oatmeal). Split one instant package of oatmeal between the two cups and stir.
- Your preferred tea bags. Mix with a cup of hot water and lemon if desired. This may be helpful for digestion.

When leaving home mid-day or in the evening, a lettuce-wrapped "sandwich" is a great food source. Wrap up foodstuffs inside one or two large leaves of lettuce that will not spoil within a few hours, such as a variety of veggies (tomatoes, cukes, onions, peppers, mushrooms), and add some avocado. Wrap tightly with plastic wrap and bring extra napkins because they can be a bit drippy.

A good old fashioned peanut butter and jelly sandwich is also very travel friendly, especially when traveling with children.

Eating While Away from Home

It is certainly possible to eat healthy when traveling. However, it becomes most difficult when:

- Working long and late hours and the local restaurants are already closed;
- Rushing to the airport or train without enough time to pick up a healthy meal;
- Stranded by a delayed flight and, without any healthy food, running to the first food stand you can find;
- Meals are pre-arranged by a meeting planner and your dietary requirements are not fully met;
- There is a working lunch or dinner and sandwiches, pizza or other less-than-healthy meals are brought in;
- An evening of cocktails is planned for your group, lowering resistance to eating healthy.

With so many obstacles, it is easy to detour from healthier food choices. To help make those detours brief, I offer you some tips that help most of the time.

Before boarding a plane, look for a healthy meal or salad in an airport restaurant or take-away stand. Yes, healthy airport meals do exist, with more choices offered all the time.

TIP: Airport sit-down restaurants will prepare a meal for you to take on the plane, so ask for what you like and for what can be prepared in the time you have available before boarding your flight. Do not feel limited to the exact items on the menu as it never hurts to ask for what you want.

Remember to get utensils and napkins for your on-board eating.

At your hotel, find a nearby market and stock up on healthy essentials like fruit, raw nuts (avoid salted or roasted nuts) and low-sugar energy bars. This can serve as breakfast on the go or a healthy snack between lunch and dinner so you don't arrive at restaurant meals famished.

A local grocery store usually has what you will need. However, a store that specializes in organic and wholesome foods (such as Whole Foods or Trader Joe's in the U.S.) is great for healthful eating choices.

If there is a refrigerator available, include yogurt or milk with whole-grain cereal for an easy, in-room breakfast option if the hotel choices are not healthy. Request an in-room refrigerator if the room doesn't come with one and ask the cost. There may be no cost if it is used for keeping medicines cold.

Be sure to pack a few plastic sandwich bags in your luggage to portion out nuts and whole-grain cereal for an easy, on-the-go snack. If possible to shop ahead of time, bring a few packets of low-sugar instant oatmeal. Use coffee mugs to mix the oatmeal with hot water and stir with a spoon from a hotel restaurant.

If you will be attending breakfast or lunch meetings, try to find out what will be served and whether there is a healthier option. If not, eat breakfast and do the best you can with less-healthy lunch choices. You can also bring a couple of healthy snacks to eat before and after lunch so you can have a smaller lunch without feeling ravenous.

Healthy meals are very doable today in most hotel or city restaurants. Choose lean protein, vegetables and whole grains at meals. Limit high-fat preparation methods, including frying, sautéing and breading, and watch for hidden calories in sauces and dressings.

Ask your server to have the chef prepare your meal as you would like it, even though it differs from the menu. Most restaurant chefs, including those in hotels, are more than happy to accommodate.

You also may want to consider getting two healthier appetizers for dinner since restaurant portions are often large. Finally, try not to indulge too much in bread, dessert or alcohol, which is often much more readily available and appealing when dining out.

I know, I've just taken all the fun out of dining out, but you did want ideas on eating healthy, right? To not feel deprived, eat just half a roll or piece of bread, drink club soda with a lime as a cocktail replacement, and eat only three small bites of a dessert.

For healthier restaurant meals, order grilled chicken or fish with extra vegetables, no rice unless it is brown rice, and no bread. For breakfast, order a vegetable omelet (egg whites only, if possible), with no or little oil used when cooking, and sliced tomatoes instead of toast or potatoes.

More healthy eating tips to make any meal healthier with just a few "no big deal" changes are offered by Joanne "Dr. Jo" Lichten, PhD (**www.drjo.com**):

1. Get It Your Way:

- Ask the restaurant to not brush your fajitas, steak, chicken, or fish with butter (ask for some melted butter "on the side" if you're worried that the meat will be too dry).

- Ask for your pizza to be prepared "light on the cheese."

- Request *half* the meat and *double* the vegetables in your stir fry.

- Ask for the dressing, sauces, and butters "on the side" so you can "dip and stab."

- Order black beans or whole pinto beans rather than refried beans at Mexican restaurants.

2. Make Miss Manners Mad.

- Trim the visible fat off the meat;

- Pull the skin off roasted chicken and save 100 calories;

- Scrape off the breading and drain the excess sauce into your butter dish;

- Pat the pizza with a paper napkin – every little bit counts.

3. Control Your Portions.

- Order a la carte to get just what you want;

- Ask for luncheon or appetizer portions – even if it's not on the menu;

- Take just one roll or slice of bread and give the basket back to the server;

- Get the doggie bag *with* dinner and immediately put away half your meal (even if you won't be taking it back to your hotel – out of sight, out of mind);

- Use chopsticks – you'll eat less;

- To eliminate the temptation to keep nibbling after you've finished, salt your food heavily or pour on the hot sauce.

4. Check the "Price" Tag on your waist.

Did you know that:

- A large cinnamon roll has over 800 calories and contains more than a half a stick of butter?

- Your morning mocha or large fountain drink contains over 300 calories?

- Each of these has 100 calories – mayonnaise on your burger, cheese slice, two bacon strips, sautéed mushrooms, sliced avocado, one large onion ring, seven potato puffs, 10 regular fries, or 20 skinny french fries. Take your pick – not all of them!

- If you eat just 10 calories more than your body needs, you will put on a pound of fat each year.

5. Make Leaner Substitutions.

- Order fresh fruit instead of juice – lower in calories and more filling;

- Ask for egg substitutes instead of eggs – even in your omelet;

- Order Canadian bacon or ham instead of bacon or sausage;

- Instead of prime rib, order the sirloin or tenderloin;

- Request pasta with tomato sauce instead of cream – or ask for half the cream sauce;

- Instead of a full meal, order salad and a shrimp cocktail.

Driving and Healthy Eating

Start your day off right.

Begin your day with a carbohydrate feast and you'll be craving carbs again in a few hours. Put down the donut and instead, take the time to have a healthy breakfast at your hotel. Eat a good mix of whole grains and protein and you'll ingest fewer calories while staying full later into the afternoon.

Get some exercise.

Spending eight hours or more sitting in the car means that your body is burning a lot fewer calories than normal. Reduce your intake accordingly and try to get a nominal amount of exercise. Even if all you do is take a 15-minute walk in the morning and then do a few bonus laps every time you stop along your route, you will feel good having stretched your legs. Even better: Plan your stops around scenic walks or hikes so you can do a little sightseeing while keeping your body moving.

Pack healthy snacks.

It's easy and tempting to swing through the drive-thru or grab some chips from the gas station, but that won't do your waistline any favors. Pack healthy snacks like raw almonds, granola or trail mix (choose low fat, low sodium, high fiber varieties), fruit and peanut butter, or power bars.

Depending on the length of your drive, pack a cooler with items like string cheese sticks or hummus and pita. Just refill the ice each day at your hotel. And don't forget to drink lots of water throughout the day and to avoid coffee and soda.

Choose your meal stops wisely.

It is harder to make healthy choices at a place where the daily special is a triple cheeseburger or a chicken-fried steak. If you can, take an hour to stop and have a proper meal once a day.

Sit down, eat slowly, and follow the same healthy rules you normally use for eating out. For example, choose grilled or broiled over fried, get dressings on the side, opt for tomato-based instead of creamy sauce. If you don't feel like dining out, try to seek out a grocery store where you are and pick up healthy prepared foods to go. Look for salad bars or premade salads, along with cut fruit.

Special Dietary Requirements

In addition to the above-mentioned ways on how to eat healthier on the road, many travelers have food allergies, intolerances to certain foods or special dietary needs. These are easy to handle in your own kitchen, but they become much more of a challenge when traveling. Add in international travel, where a different language is spoken, and this could be a show-stopper for wanting to travel at all.

Planning ahead, looking at options for grocery stores and restaurants, and learning key words in foreign languages for where you'll be traveling will all make it easier to meet your special dietary requirements while away from home.

As I write this, I am planning a 22-day trip to five different cities in three countries with one country where English is not the primary language. I am on a gluten-free, dairy-free regimen.

Here is my plan:

- List all meals for each day I'll be gone. Some days might only have two meals due to long flights.

- Mark which meals I will have full control over (such as breakfasts where I can make an in-room smoothie).

- Prepare a bag or container of protein powder for the number of smoothies I will have.

- List which meals will be in-flight. For international flights, and some long-haul domestic flights, it may be possible to request a special meal for the flight. Set this up online or call the airline a minimum of 24 hours in advance of the flight.

- Anticipate times where I might need supplemental foods (flight delays, long business meetings) and bring along foods that will keep me from starving. When I get to the "starving" stage, that's when my feet find themselves moving towards the unhealthier food choices for a quick injection of food.

- Request special meals at any conferences or meetings (or bring my own meals).

- Ask the hotel's chef to prepare meals to my requirements.

- Keep snacks with me at all times (fruit, almonds, apricots, energy bars) along with a bottle of water.

If you have allergies or dietary restrictions, there are handy services that will translate your particular needs into the language spoken where you'll be traveling. See the ***Business Travel Success Ultimate Travel Resource*** for such services.

Exercising While on the Road

Fitness Equipment to Pack

It is possible to get a workout in on most travel days, even if it's for just a few minutes. The trick is to have the right equipment with you to ban all excuses. Even a few minutes of stretching in your hotel room to shake out the tight muscles from sitting on a long flight is beneficial.

When it comes to the "right" equipment, what does this mean? How much room in your luggage does it take? These items take up little or no space in your bag and don't weigh that much:

- Exercise bands

- Jump rope

- Exercise DVDs

- Exercise apps for your smartphone

Having any of these with you allows you to get a great workout without even leaving your hotel room. Okay, it is not a good idea to jump rope in a hotel room. Do this in the hotel's parking lot or grassy areas.

A pedometer is also great to wear every day. It can be placed discreetly under our clothes.

To be safe and avoid wasted time in x-ray lines, remove the pedometer and toss it into your shoe when going through airport TSA security. This way, no chance you will forget it. Once you begin tracking your walking, it is interesting to learn that most treks through airport terminals are good for a few thousand steps or more!

Remember to pack your running shoes. Stuff the shoes with underwear and socks - use the space wisely. Pack one pair of shorts or exercise pants, a lightweight wicking top and a sports bra and wash them in the room after your workout. Clothes identified as "wicking" help pull away moisture, keeping you dry when sweating. This helps you stay cooler in hot weather and warmer in cold weather.

Why not download an exercise program or podcast to your iPhone or laptop? There are so many available that you can work out to a different program each day of the year!

Research Before You Travel

Call ahead to your hotel and ask about their fitness center (or to find out if they even have one!). Some property websites will have online photos of their gyms.

Those hotels without their own fitness centers often make arrangements for discounted or free day passes at local centers. Ask about the distance between the hotel and the local fitness center. It may be more than you want to walk, especially when the weather is bad or when it's dark outside.

Inquire at your hotel about nearby fitness clubs that might offer classes you'd like, or research local running routes. Some hotels even offer escorted guided runs, so ask about this if it's of interest. Private trainers also can be found who will make an appointment and come to your hotel room or have in-studio sessions.

If you will be traveling to the same city routinely, look for trainers or classes where you can arrange for a certain number of visits. I have had private trainers in a few cities and have also arranged for Pilates sessions. Private sessions seem to work best when your travel schedule is a bit erratic as these can more easily be set to fit your schedule.

Take advantage of your own gym membership

Many fitness center chains participate in what's called a passport program, which allows you to work out at hundreds of clubs at no cost or for a nominal fee. Go to www.healthclubs.com to find fitness clubs within a short distance of your destination that participate in this program.

In-Room Fitness Equipment

Some of the larger chain hotels have exercise equipment that can be brought to your hotel room. Ask if a treadmill or other equipment is available. Other fitness amenities, such as a 24-hour yoga channel, are offered by Kimpton Hotel's "Women In Touch" program. The more this service is requested, the more hotels will accommodate travelers, so ask!

Hotel Fitness Rooms

Hotel fitness centers are usually quite complete and allow you to get in both aerobic and weight training. Sure, many smaller hotels and motels have one rickety treadmill in a room off the side of the front desk, but major hotel chains usually offer decent fitness centers.

The cost of most hotel fitness centers is included in your room rate. There are, however, hotels and resorts that charge a daily fee for use of their fitness centers. Some include it in a daily resort fee, which you pay whether you use the fitness center or not. Others charge for each day of fitness center usage.

When traveling for business, receiving reimbursement for the fitness center when it's a separate line item on the invoice may not be permissible. Neither may it be deductible for tax purposes if self-employed. Check with your corporate office or tax accountant.

Many hotels and resorts also have a swimming pool. Getting in several laps is a great workout and really relieves the stress after a long business day. While sitting in a hot tub or sauna is also great for relieving stress, it may burn off only a few calories in sweat (but oh, it feels so good!).

Work out in the morning or later in the day? Health experts that I read say it is better to get the metabolism going in the morning. Most travelers must obviously adhere to this advice because a hotel's fitness center is usually busier in the early morning hours than it is in the evening.

The longer you put off your workout, the more likely you are to skip it. Avoid this common downfall by giving yourself enough time in the morning to comfortably fit in your workout.

If necessary, set your alarm for an earlier wakeup. Beginning your day with exercise will increase your blood flow, warm up your muscles, rev your metabolism and increase your energy level for the entire day.

An excellent time to begin a workout in a fitness center is often 5-5:30 am, when the crowds are smaller. Expect the most crowding around 6:30-7:00 am and again around early evening. Yes, I know it can be difficult getting up early, shaking off the cobwebs, and heading down to the fitness center. No one said this was easy, only that it was a healthier choice.

In-Flight Workout

A full workout it isn't, but just walking up and down the aisle a few times gets the blood moving and keeps you from getting stiff.

On the plane, a simple exercise is pushing your heels into the floor while contracting your glute muscles, great for in-your-seat firming. If you are in a seat with extra legroom, do some leg lifts and ankle rotations, anything to keep the blood flowing through the legs.

Even visits to the toilet should involve a few stretches. Lean up against the wall and do wall squats. These are amazing stretches for the legs.

When you are in between flights and have an extended layover, there are many airports with in-house spas or fitness centers either in the terminal or nearby. See the *Business Travel Success Ultimate Travel Resource* for fitness centers in or near airports.

Sleep

To stay healthy, it is crucial to get enough sleep. Most people need seven to eight hours a night, which is a challenge for many busy business travelers. The best way to stay healthy is to pace yourself, know your limits and strive for sufficient sleep.

Some of the challenges of getting and staying asleep when traveling include noises heard in your hotel room and in the hallways, beds and pillows that are different from what you have at home, varying temperatures and climates, and a host of other things that can interrupt your zzzzz's.

A few tips for getting a good night's sleep in your hotel:

- Bring earplugs. Pick up foam earplugs at a travel goods store or local pharmacy, or even at a home improvement store. They block out the worst of the ambient noise without blocking out the alarm clock so you will still wake up on time.

- Generate some white noise. Don't have earplugs? Play soft classical music on your laptop or mp3 player or the radio in the room.

- Avoid hotels near major highways or those likely to be tourist and vacation magnets. Avoid hotels with a lot of commercial vehicles out front, too. If your hotel is being used as a home base for a nearby construction project, expect to be roused at 5 or 6 am when they begin their workday.

- Request a secluded room. If you have any control over where your room is located, try to avoid areas near the lobby, dining room, elevator, or vending and ice machines.

- Post the Do Not Disturb sign. Remember to put the Do Not Disturb sign on your door before you go to bed — this will avoid any unwelcome surprises at 8 am if you are still sleeping.

- Keep the curtains completely closed so the room is dark. Use a clip, clothespin, or duct tape, if needed, to keep the curtains closed. Alternatively, pack a sleep mask in your luggage and don this at bedtime.

 TIP: If your hotel room curtains will not stay closed and there is nothing in your suitcase to remedy the situation, use this simple solution that works in most hotel rooms:

Use a slacks hanger from the closet. Assuming the hotel hangers are not permanently affixed to the closet rod, a slacks hanger, hung vertically to clip the two sections of curtains together, does the trick!.

Stay Healthy

Accidents happen, as do surprise illnesses when you least expect them. Traveling does not make you immune to these unfortunate events. With this in mind, the following are some preventative health tips and safety ideas for all travelers:

- Pack a supply of your normal medications in their original containers.

- Wear a medical information bracelet if needed, especially if you are diabetic or have severe allergies.

- Drink water from sealed bottles.

- Wash hands often with soap and water.

- Pack a small first-aid kit that includes diarrhea and upset stomach medicines, cough and cold medicines, pain medicines, decongestants, bandages, scissors, tweezers and a thermometer.

- Check with your health insurer regarding international coverage. Look at purchasing add-on health insurance to fill the gaps that your own insurance may not cover.

- Take along your health-insurance card with your passport and other important documents such as immunization records and a list of allergies.

- For help with travel emergencies abroad, contact the U.S. State Department.

The simplest way to prevent illness is to pay close attention to hand hygiene. Regular hand-washing and the use of antibacterial wash or wipes are effective measures to help stop the spread of infection. If you are particularly concerned about catching a bug in-flight, paper surgical masks can be purchased in pharmacies or at travel stores.

If you do get sick, be proactive. Get help to get better quickly. For minor ailments, a good first stop is the neighborhood pharmacy. Overall, don't let the fear of getting sick paralyze your travels.

Tips on Avoiding Germs on Planes

One of the most persistent myths is that everybody on the plane is breathing the same air and that germs endlessly recirculate within the cabin. In fact, air on the airplane is no worse than what you'd encounter in your average office building.

Airplanes take about 50% of the air collected in the outtake valves of the passenger compartment and mix it with fresh air from outside that is heated by the engines. That air is then passed through HEPA filters that sterilize it before it's reintroduced into the passenger cabin.

Yet passengers are still confined to an enclosed space where contagious diseases can spread. Contaminants, such as the small droplets emitted by a cough, do move to other areas of the cabin.

When someone coughs or sneezes, 20- to 30,000 particles fly out about three feet and settle on nearby surfaces. Those microorganisms can live from several minutes up to 24 hours. The good news, you don't have much to fear because microorganisms won't propel beyond possibly up to six feet.

Instead of worrying about the cabin air, make an effort to avoid touching objects such as airplane toilet seats, soap dispensers, seatbacks, armrests and especially tray tables, all of which can harbor infectious germs. These are surfaces that everyone touches, and you have no idea if someone with a cold has walked down the aisle touching the seats and armrests as they go.

When you go to the lavatory, use tissues or a paper towel to put down the toilet seat and when opening the door on your way out. Observe flight attendants and you'll see that most of them use a paper towel even when touching the lavatory door handle.

Although exposure does not mean you will get sick, some passengers aren't taking any chances. Many travel with a small bottle or sprayer of hand sanitizer. This can be handy to wipe down a tray or the seat's armrest buttons for sound, volume and reclining the seat.

Here are five tips on how to cut down on germ exposure and help keep you and your family healthy while traveling:

1. If the person next to you is coughing or sneezing, ask to switch seats. Since this is not always be possible, try turning the air vent above your seat to medium flow and pointing the air current just slightly in front of your face so that germs from those coughing or sneezing nearby are deflected away from you.

2. Bring along a face mask. (This has an added benefit of keeping your neighbor's chatting with you down to nothing!)

3. Bring alcohol-based hand sanitizer and anti-bacterial wipes.

4. Constantly wash your hands (and keep your hands away from your eyes, nose and mouth until your hands have been washed).

5. Bring your own pillow and blanket.

Also, bring along bottled water to hydrate yourself. The overall relative humidity aboard an airplane is low — around 6% — and people become dehydrated on long flights if they don't drink water regularly. Staying hydrated will make you less susceptible to viral infections in general.

Nasal passages, eyes, and the mucous membranes in lips and mouths have enzymes to fight bacteria. If you're dehydrated, those enzymes won't work well. Drink at least eight ounces of water every two hours.

When you travel, and after you have put your bag in the overhead bin, take out your hand sanitizer, put some drops on the tray table and clean it with a tissue. Then clean the seat belt, the armrests and your hands. Then you'll know your seat area is sanitized.

If you're the one who is feeling under the weather, do your fellow travelers a favor and stay home.

Preventing DVT

Air travelers have a much higher risk of developing a circulatory problem called Deep Vein Thrombosis (DVT) than non-flyers. DVT is the formation of a blood clot in a deep vein that can develop after sitting on long flights.

Passengers sitting in coach class are particularly vulnerable because of the limited amount of space in which to move their legs, though this affects business and first-class travelers as well. Each year in the United States, some 600,000 new cases of DVT are diagnosed, with 1% of these people dying.[12]

It's important to take steps to prevent DVT, particularly when doing a lot of flying. DVT does not necessarily strike while you're up in the air. The riskiest time to develop DVT is in the two weeks following a flight, according to Veins1.com.

Before Your Flight

Ask your doctor if he or she recommends the use of compression stockings. These can help increase circulation, particularly if you're at high risk of developing DVT. Get properly measured for these stockings so that they provide a comfortable fit. Try on the stockings with the shoes you intend to wear during flights, or wear footless compression stockings.

Many passengers prefer to wear compression stockings on international flights, but they are also popular for those long days working or visiting trade shows. Most wearers are convinced their legs feel more energized.

To help prevent DVT, some passengers use self-injections of a blood-thinning agent such as Heparin. Of course, speak with your doctor about this option.

During Your Flight

Move around! Sitting scrunched up with your knees to your chest for long periods of time is not only uncomfortable, but it can be dangerous, especially if you're at risk for DVT.

Do what you can in the narrow airplane aisles. Walk back and forth, do some toe-lifts against a back wall, and try to do a few stationary lunges from the back of the plane. Try to move around every hour or so during a long flight.

Engage in exercise at your seat. Point your toes up and then down to a flat position. You can also try flexing your leg muscles and lifting your knees periodically throughout the flight. Rotating your ankles is another good way to keep the blood flowing. Don't cross your legs or ankles; this restricts blood flow.

Stay well-hydrated by drinking plenty of fluids such as water and juice. Dehydration can result in thickening of the blood and the narrowing of vessels. Avoid alcoholic and caffeinated drinks because of their dehydrating effect.

After Your Flight

See your doctor immediately following a trip if you have any signs of DVT. These may include swelling in one or both legs, leg pain or tenderness, red or discolored skin or warmth in the leg that's affected. If you feel a bump in your leg, do not try to massage it out. See your doctor first.

Half of all DVT patients show no symptoms. As with any other medical issue, check with your doctor to get their expert advice on DVT.

Health Concerns for International Travel

The "D" Word

The number one health fear for most travelers is probably diarrhea (also called "Turista"), especially when traveling to some foreign countries. Yes, it can be a common and unpleasant experience when traveling. It can also be very dangerous. With a few precautions, however, the discomfort and pain – and the peril of – diarrhea can be dodged.

The cause of traveler's diarrhea is typically from contaminants in food and water, though it can also be caused by the stress of travel itself. Travelers from industrialized countries who travel to developing or less industrialized countries are most prone to getting diarrhea, though it can happen to any traveler when different foods or beverages are introduced into the body.

People taking acid blockers for their stomachs may be more susceptible to stomach issues because there is less stomach acid to give protection against the bacteria that can cause diarrhea. Here are some helpful tips to keep your travels from going down the toilet:

- Avoid drinking tap water. Instead, bottled water (with a sealed cap) is the safest bet. Local water, even when free of contaminants, may be different to your bodily systems than your water at home, so keep to bottled water to reduce the effects of foreign foods and drink on your gut.

- Avoid having ice in your drinks. Since ice is usually made from local tap water, it can also have the contaminants from the local water supply.

- Brush your teeth with bottled water. This is yet another way to refrain from using local tap water.

- Stick with known beverages. Drinks in cans are safer than screw-top caps because screw-top bottles have been known to be refilled by unscrupulous vendors in some countries.

- Eat foods native to the country you are visiting, not foods added to the menu to be attractive to tourists. My daughter got extremely sick from eating a hamburger in Mexico, had to make several visits to a doctor and delay her return home by several days.

- Eat cooked vegetables rather than fresh, bananas over thin-skinned fruits. While it is great to eat salads and fruits for health reasons, fresh vegetables or fruits, such as apples, grapes and berries, can be more prone to contaminants than cooked vegetables or fruits where the skin is not eaten.

- Refrain from eating very spicy foods. It is often the extra spices that cause diarrhea, not the food itself.

- Use non-dairy creamer in your coffee or tea. Hot coffee and tea is usually okay to drink.

- Avoid eating foods from street vendors as their food preparation methods may be questionable.

- Over-the-counter antacids may help. Many come in travel-friendly chewable tablets. Activated charcoal is an inexpensive, natural remedy as well. It absorbs excess gas, relieves symptoms of diarrhea, and even helps to eliminate bad breath. The powder form is available from health food stores. Capsules are more widely available but might be less effective than powder.

- Frequent hand-washing with soap can decrease the spread of bacteria.

Always seek immediate medical attention for serious diarrhea, especially if there is accompanying blood.

Sometimes diarrhea is caused by the stress of travel itself. For some travelers, it may be the stress of a new business setting or of meeting new people. For others, stomach problems can result over having to speak in front of a large group of people or to make a big sales presentation.

For this type of stomach upset, it helps to:

- Be prepared for the upcoming event. Not being ready for a big event is a sure way to have your stomach rumbling!

- Consider the worst case scenario. For example, before a big sales presentation, think about the worst possible outcome ever – that of not making a sale. You didn't have the sale before the meeting and you might not have it after. Are you any worse off? Usually, no.

- Meditate or listen to calming music to quiet your mind.

- Get plenty of sleep. A night with only a few hours of sleep is already stressful on the body, and having to give an early morning presentation makes it worse.

You may find yourself with the opposite problem, that of constipation, when you travel. This is a common malady of many travelers that I have spoken with (though we try to refrain from talking about this topic over dinner conversation!).

When I spoke with a nutritionist about this issue, she suggested taking a daily dose of magnesium. This helps to relax the intestines and reduce the cycle of constipation. Definitely speak with your doctor or nutritionist if you experience this clogged-up problem.

Vaccinations

Preparing your travel checklist for an upcoming international trip? Remember to include a pre-trip travel health checkup. Whether it's vaccinations you need or medications to take along with you, it is smart planning to begin looking into your travel health about 6 to 8 weeks ahead of your trip.

The most authoritative site for what vaccinations you might need, health issues abroad and more is the Center for Disease Control's (CDC) Travelers' Health resource at **http://wwwnc.cdc.gov/travel**. The CDC offers health information on more than 200 international destinations, vaccinations, diseases, ways to stay healthy and safe, links to find a local clinic, travel health warnings and more.

Whether your travels have you going to factories in China for your business, into the jungles of Africa for a bucket-list trip, or the beaches of Cancun for a little R&R, check out the health issues at the CDC well before your trip. Take care of yourself first so that you can have safe and enjoyable travels.

Miscellaneous

European pharmacists typically diagnose and prescribe remedies for the more simpler problems. They are usually friendly and speak English, and some medications that are by prescription only in the United States are available over the counter (surprisingly cheap) in Europe.

Summary

To make your travels healthier, start simple. First, begin with the belief that your health and well-being is your number one priority. Then, increase the pace to incorporate the healthful eating and personal care tips included in this chapter.

Put together your own Stay Healthy and Travel Health kits. Prepare a few healthy snacks for your journey.

You are now on your way to a healthier you *even with business travel!*

10

PERSONAL MATTERS

Long before our time, prior generations talked about how they relied on the Pony Express for mail delivery, and it used to take weeks. Then came telegrams and more recently, the most common ways to stay in touch with loved ones and business associates were postcards and maybe long distance telephone calls if the budget allowed for it. As the old Virginia Slim's cigarette commercial used to say: "You've come a long way, baby!"

Early in my career there was no Skype to speak with my children back home, much less any internet. Geez, even digital cameras didn't exist back then. All I had was my AT&T calling card. For those who are curious, I am not *that* old. We did have electricity.

Fortunately it is so much easier for business travelers today. I receive digital messages all the time from my family members. All of them know work comes first but if it is truly an emergency, they know how to contact me.

It is wonderful that technology now allows us access to so much that never existed before. So many tools, so many ways to stay in touch with our family, friends, and work, not only back home but even on the other side of the planet.

The most common method is the mobile phone. In many locations across America, the sound quality is as good as being next door to someone. Usually the most challenging adjustment is for time zones. Remember that whomever you are calling may be 2-3 hours ahead of or behind you or more.

Another tool many travelers use is their camera. Digital cameras today make it possible to send photos via email or right through your phone. Pushing the envelope further, certain digital cameras have cards that send photos wirelessly to a printer or a computer directly from the camera.

Laptop computers and tablets are very popular for business travel. Nearly all have built-in webcams so you can not only speak with someone but also see them.

Indeed, many business travelers have taken to carrying both a laptop for work along with a tablet for personal use. This is an excellent option for those who work with company-issued laptops, because all your personal data can, well, stay personal this way.

Most everyone today uses email. For techno-savvy folks, text messaging is another way to feel like you are right there with the ones you left at home. Those with smartphones can find applications to help communicate with loved ones.

For those who remember the postcard days, there is an application that allows you to take a photo, then send it as a postcard.

Last but not least, there is social media (see Chapter 11). Keep family, friends, and business associates up-to-date about your travels using Facebook, Twitter and other social media tools.

A word of caution: If your home is empty while you are away, telling the world about a current absence from home is an invitation to burglars. I certainly understand the temptation to share your adventures with everyone but you do so with risk.

Prepare Your Family for Your Business Trip

If you have a family, there are a number of things to consider before heading out the door on a business trip. Some of the most important are the following:

- Fill out consents for medical treatment and leave copies of insurance cards at home.

- Go over your itinerary, including hotel phone number and other ways to reach you.

- Write down all important telephone numbers and addresses:
  - Regular and back up contact numbers for you
  - Doctor
  - Pharmacy
  - School/daycare
  - After school activities
  - Friends/neighbors who are helpful
  - Alarm company.

- Outline the schedule. Write out your children's schedule for each day you are away. Include addresses and phone numbers for each activity. Try to re-arrange doctor appointments and any optional activities until you are back at home.

- Talk with your kids. Let them know your itinerary and when you will be returning home. Tell them how to contact you and when they can expect you to call. With text messaging and emails, it is much easier for you to stay in contact with your family, though help them understand that you will be working while you're away.

- Plan activities for the kids. Journal writing, having them draw "postcards" for you on postcard-sized paper or helping in the meal planning keeps them occupied and is fun for them.

- Leave cash for groceries or emergencies (for the "oh by the way I need money for a school field trip" or for when the Girl Scouts show up with boxes of cookies).

Be realistic on what will get done at home while you are away. Sure you want your kids to keep up with their chores, but will they? Probably not.

Instead of stressing about it from hundreds or thousands of miles away and getting upset when talking with them, focus on the chores that are most important (like doing their homework, walking the dog or feeding the cat) and address the other tasks when you are at home.

The Nanny

You need to go off on a business trip and there is no one to watch your children. Asking family or friends to temporarily house your kids may work for a day or two, but frequent travel usually needs a long-term solution.

Having a nanny at your home while you are away is a solution that works for many business people, travelers or otherwise. I know what that is like because I had to deal with it for some years when my children were growing up.

For many families, there is a spouse available to take on the responsibility of caring for the children in your absence. In some cases, both parents may be traveling. For other families, there is one lone parent with no spouse or other relatives available to help.

This was much more painful during the years when there was no way to connect other than by long-distance telephone. Today, video adds a wonderful dimension but the reality is the same: Who will take care of the children when you are gone?

When there are no other relatives or friends available to fill the parenting role in your absence, hiring a nanny for the children is the next best option. Where do you find a nanny to hire? Look for a local nanny placement service. You will be able to interview nannies who are experienced, security screened, background checked, and maybe even CPR certified.

You may need a nanny to live in, or be at your home only during the day. If you travel a lot, you may have a full time nanny, or an on-call nanny for the occasional trip.

When you do hire a nanny, select a person who looks like an adult! One of my children's nannies, Elizabeth, looked like she was 14 years old. She was actually in her mid-20s, but was very short with a young-looking face.

A concerned (or nosey!) neighbor must have thought there were no adults in the house and called the police.

"Is your mother home?" "No." "Is your father home?" "No."

"Is there an adult in the house?" "Yes, me," answered Elizabeth.

When I heard about this later that day, I was very relieved to learn that the police and the Department of Children and Families hadn't taken away my kids.

You may also want to take your children with you on your travels so you should hire a nanny who is willing to travel with you. If this is the case, give your nanny plenty of notice and ensure they have a passport and vaccinations, if necessary.

If your nanny does travel with you, it is standard to pay for their airfare, food (a meal allowance works), and lodging. Do not ask them to pay for their own way. Secure private accommodations for your nanny so that they may have their own private time as they would at home when not on duty as a nanny.

Communication

Communication is one of the most important things to sustaining healthy relationships. Regardless of whether you are home or on the road, it is essential to maintain good contact with your loved ones. For ease and consistency, I will refer to them as families.

Good communication is more challenging when traveling because you lose the benefit of certain senses. Think about this: In a normal conversation at home, we at least indirectly apply all our sensory factors. We not only hear and see the person we are with but we also touch them. We may smell the perfume or flowers and of course we taste that meal together.

When we travel, most of these senses are sacrificed when communicating with loved ones back home. While not always obviously noticeable, it can cause misconnections in thoughts. So how do people today communicate with loved ones while traveling? Oh, let me count the ways.

The most common methods of staying in touch with family and friends are via email and text messaging. The benefit is quick communication lines but the disadvantages here include occasional delays in sending/receiving messages and no immediate two-way communication. Nevertheless, it serves its purpose of staying in touch.

Next on the list would be telephone contact. Nearly every mobile phone has coverage throughout most of the U.S. so it costs no more to call across the country than it does to call across the street.

Phone contact is often preferable to email/texting because it adds the benefit of two-way communication. Alas, other than hearing, none of the other senses is employed in the conversation.

VoIP services such as Skype add another level of enjoyment by including a video option. Now you can not only hear the other person but see them as well. This can make a world of difference communicating with someone, especially children.

As with everything else, Skype is not perfect either. It requires an internet connection from the person initiating the call and while it can be connected to a landline telephone, the video option requires another computer with internet connection and a webcam on the other end.

Admittedly, sometimes the connection is not great, especially with video. The image may be a bit choppy – and sometimes drops altogether – but for many, this is the preferred way of communicating.

Note that there is no mobility if you are using a desktop-type computer so you must remain at the desk until the call is completed. For that matter, even with a laptop computer there may be limited movement possibilities. Nevertheless, many business travelers swear by this, including me.

Also notice that all these common communication methods lack something. We do our best to adapt but there is still a feeling that something is missing. Well, it is.

Unlike face-to-face contact, business travelers have to sacrifice the use of their other senses. Most travelers are not aware of it but subconsciously it takes a toll when trying to communicate.

One way to ease through this is what I call *touches*. These are frequent occurrences that allow you to communicate more often, especially useful if you are traveling for a week or more. For example, one way to add a *touch* would be to send postcards.

I know some of you are wondering why bother sending postcards when you will be speaking with your family anyway? The reason is to increase the frequency of the contact and remember, it is a different form of contact. Postcards allow families to see the surrounding area where you are, adding another dimension to the connection that they would otherwise miss.

Another nice touch is to send small items back home. It is a thoughtful way to let your loved ones know you are thinking about them. I usually save this for longer business trips.

Personal photos are a simple thing to send back home. They are easy to attach to an email and again give the family a little more sense of where you are, what you see and who you are with.

Much of what I have discussed so far may appear to be one-sided. After all, I keep talking about the traveler initiating the communication. As we shall see, there is much the family back home can do as well.

Spouses and mates can be more sensitive to the reality that you are traveling because it is part of your employment. While many business travelers enjoy their life on the road, others accept it only as necessary, and some don't enjoy it at all.

Even if you feel that business travel is a necessary evil, often it comes down to either accepting this as a way to earn your living or seeking employment elsewhere. In other words, it is an economic-driven reality that is best accepted in order to focus your energy on more positive things.

If that is how you feel, then communicate it. On the other hand, don't be afraid to explain that you actually enjoy traveling for business. While there are certainly some downsides to frequent travel, there are also huge upsides. This is discussed more in Chapter 13.

If your spouse/mate is uncomfortable with the amount of your business travel, it is always wise to discuss it. Perhaps there is a way to make some adjustments in your schedule that are more acceptable. Even if not, it is ever so important that each side be heard.

A word to the wise: When your spouse/mate speaks, really listen to them. I know, sometimes this is difficult but it is critical to a relationship that each person really focus on exactly what the other is saying.

Jack Canfield, international author of the renowned *Chicken Soup for the Soul*® series, suggests that spouses periodically (preferably weekly) rate their relationship. He uses a 1-10 scale with 10 being the best. Each person who rates the relationship less than 10 explains what it would take to get them to feel like it was a 10. For example, you may rate the relationship as an 8. Your partner asks what it will take to get it to a 10. You respond with honest feedback such as "I only rate things as 8 because I felt like I had all the responsibility with the kids' homework and would have liked you to tackle the science homework" or "I would have liked time alone with you this week so can we schedule a date night for next week?"

At first this looks like just another way of asking each spouse what could be done to improve a relationship but it does add another dimension. By using a rating, it forces each spouse to not only defend their position but offers ways to improve it.

When I return home from a business trip, often late at night, my husband always has a treat waiting for me. Well, he does as long as he is also not traveling.

He makes sure the sheets are freshly washed and gives the bed a turndown service. My side of the bed is always turned down very neatly, just like at a hotel. While he jokes that he is "competing for my business," his gesture is very much appreciated. When I return from a multi-week business trip, I frequently find flowers in vases around the house along with a beautiful greeting card on my pillow. Yes, I'm married to a really great guy!

The most difficult part for me when traveling was leaving the children behind. Years ago when they were young – and long before mobile phones and computers – the opportunity to communicate with them was limited to the land line.

Today a whole new world of communication is open for those who wish to take advantage of it. The parent at home can encourage children to share their days and experiences with the traveling parent, making the children feel like both parents are there.

It's also easy to share in the homework discussions. Assignments or report cards can be scanned and emailed to you easily, and online homework discussions can occur with your child. It will seem like you are together in the same room. Many schools also have online parental websites for you to follow along with your child's progress.

When children are infants, they physically change at a rapid pace. Thanks to modern technology, it is very easy for the parent at home to record the child's activities on an inexpensive digital video recorder and send them to the traveling parent. Oh how I wish this were available when my children were young.

As your children grow, they can create their own videos. Older children can express their creativity and talent by making videos for the traveling parent.

Employing these techniques, a traveling parent doesn't have to miss out on school plays or recitals. As you travel, you might even be introduced to your children's new friends. The parent also can benefit from audio recorded meetings with teachers as a way of keeping up with your children's progress at school.

Speaking of meeting with teachers, how would you like to attend the meeting even though you are traveling out of town? Well, it actually can be done today if certain things fall in place. Here's how...

The easiest is to appear by telephone. Calling in with your mobile phone is great when possible. Indeed, a simple phone conversation between parent and teacher is quite easy to do as long as the time zone differences can be worked out.

If the teacher has online video available and you do as well, use it to have your meeting. Both of you can use the internet, and while it's not the same as being in the school office, it is a pretty nice video alternative.

Okay, some of you are thinking about what if the teacher does not have an internet connection. Ah ha, I have a solution for that, too.

Let's say your spouse or significant other can arrange a meeting with the teacher at school and both of you have internet access. Using Wi-Fi or an air card, you can also be at the meeting via laptop computer.

This sounds a little strange, but your mate can take you along as a laptop. In the meeting room, when the laptop is opened and turned on, you are there via video.

This last tip was similar to something my husband did for Halloween a couple of years ago. I was out of town and missed seeing the kids come to the door in their costumes. My husband had a great idea when he opened Skype on his laptop and plopped me down on a chair near the front door.

It was a thrill to be part of the evening and share in the kids' excitement, though in hindsight I suppose it might have scared some of the younger children when the door opened and they saw a disembodied woman's head sitting on the chair!

That brings me to the next issue. I hate to mention it but the fact is, it is a reality for many couples. I am talking about the matter of trust.

Trust

While I am blessed that my husband and I have never felt the need to address this concern, trust is a major issue for many couples. There are entire books written about this, unfortunately for good reason. By all means, read them if necessary to maintain your relationships, but in this section I will share a few good tips I have learned over the years.

Some mates believe that when you are traveling, you are actually sitting in a bar every evening. Of course, their minds begin to wander and... well, if you think about this from their perspective, you can imagine what they are thinking.

Remember, they are missing many cues. They can't see you, perhaps can't speak with you, and the other senses are also unavailable to them. That leaves only that scary sixth sense, something that leads to premature destruction in far too many couples.

As a consultant traveling for more than 25 years, I say with all sincerity that very few married travelers I know actually seek out bars and other nightlife while traveling for business. Most are simply tired after a 12-14 hour day and know the next day will not be any easier. Those who enjoy evening activity like this are usually young or single, or both.

Again, imagine what someone at home may be wondering when they have no idea what you are doing, even more so if you fail to maintain contact with them.

By the way, this cuts both ways. While you are working, your spouse or mate may be out with others and...

See what I mean about trust?

Trust is a feeling. Like all feelings, it is owned by the person who feels it. Painful as it may be to some relationships, there is no way to make a person feel different than they do. It is their feeling, they own it, and even though we may not agree with it, it is their right to, well, feel as they wish.

What can you do about enhancing trust in your relationship? If travel is within the continental U.S., the time zones are relatively close to each other. If you are communicating in the evening, chances are you are not out gallivanting, adding credibility to your relationship.

On the other hand, if you fail to contact your family even one time, at least without prior notice, their minds can begin to imagine all kinds of things.

When I was traveling and my husband was home with the kids, I would call every evening as long as it fit within a reasonable time frame with the home time zone. My husband appreciated it, and I liked connecting with the kids. That daily contact was a win for everyone.

Today my children are older and living on their own but I still maintain frequent contact with them. I speak with my husband nearly every day regardless of where either of us may be. Yes, sometimes it's difficult because of extreme time zone differences, but we almost never fail to speak on a daily basis.

Here's an example. I was recently in Houston while my husband was in Hong Kong, a 13-hour time difference. Despite that extreme, my husband would get up early every morning to ensure we spoke before he went off to work. He enjoyed turning his laptop around and using the built-in webcam to show me the early morning view of Victoria Harbor.

The next time we communicated was the evening for him, which was the morning for me. And yes, this time he showed me the stunning harbor view in the evening. We talked every day for the entire month he was there.

Empathy

Communication and trust are critical to a strong relationship but do not overlook empathy. Empathy is the ability to place yourself in someone else's position, to understand their situation, feelings, and concerns.

For empathy to work, you need to step outside yourself and imagine you are the other person. Think about how they might see something differently than you, and certainly feel different about it. Sometimes it is difficult to remember this but when a spouse or significant other has issues with your traveling, they are not thinking about your needs at that moment. Take a deep breath, listen to what they are saying, respond to their needs, and the communication will go a lot further.

Here's how I relate empathy to business travel. Let's say your partner is jealous about your travel, maybe even insecure that you might engage in… ahem… partner-like activities with someone else. You know what I mean.

I know it is tempting for some to say that if a significant other feels jealousy, that's their problem. In part, I agree. This is the other person's concern, not yours. After all, they own those feelings, not you. In other words, it is not your responsibility – indeed not even within your power – to control someone else's feelings.

While perhaps true, it is also somewhat shortsighted. Remember, we are speaking about a relationship here. By definition it requires more than one person. Whether married or not, you are a team.

Applying empathy, you would place yourself in their position and try to understand what they are feeling and why they may be feeling that way. Let's go back to our example.

Your mate is jealous that you have this ability to travel and they don't. Also, they are concerned that when the two of you are apart, you may use that as an opportunity to seek attention – or more – from others. I am being kind with words here but you get the idea.

After so many years of business travel, I know it is far less glamorous than portrayed. Looking at this from someone else's perspective, however, I also understand how they may believe otherwise.

So what's the best way to address this with a jealous spouse? First, I would approach it by acknowledging and understanding why someone feels jealous. Movies and television shows portray business travelers as going off to exotic locations. In fact, the majority of business travels are anything but exotic.

When we have more time, I will talk about my "exotic" trips to Gun Barrel City, Texas. Nevertheless, any travel may seem exotic to those who do little if any traveling. [Note to friends in Gun Barrel City, it really is a great town even if most wouldn't call it exotic.]

TIP: Using a small digital camera (or the one in your phone), take photos throughout the day and send these to loved ones. Perhaps show some from an airport or train station. Others might be of the hotel where you are staying. And definitely include some from around the area where you will be working. If possible, include photos of co-workers. Also take photos of where and what you eat. Unless you are truly one of the fortunates who works in an exotic location, it won't take long to see that your business city is really just like any other.

When my husband or I travel to different cities, we often communicate via video. That's a good time to show the other partner – indeed, the whole family – what the new hotel room looks like. We actually do a walking tour, though some rooms are so small that the tour takes only seconds.

Also, you might suggest that your mate look into a new career where they also have the opportunity to travel for work. That might reduce any jealousy that you travel and they don't, and they will quickly realize how unglamorous traveling for business can be.

Probably the best way to address these concerns is to have your mate join you. This is not always possible for many reasons but the invitation alone may be enough to quell some of the fears.

Another option is to use vacation time for the two of you to travel to your business location. Alternatively, have them meet you there for a long weekend together. Then you could be the tour guide and show your partner around. If there is nothing exciting about the city, sometimes your partner may be quite happy that you are doing the traveling and they are not.

Will your partner still be jealous? Perhaps, but at least you have taken an active role in trying to understand their feelings and looked for ways to help them feel better.

Fears, by definition, are frequently irrational. FEAR = False Evidence Appearing Real. Real or imagined, they cannot be ignored.

If your partner is concerned you may be out on the town engaging in non-exclusive activities, you might minimize this fear by always calling home at an agreed upon time in the evening. Or tell your partner that you will be in your room after dinner and they can call any time after that.

If that is impossible due to work commitments, let your partner know. Again, the point here is to recognize and understand that they feel this way and that no matter how irrational you feel it may be, you are still trying to do everything possible to address their concerns.

Yes, empathy cuts both ways. Your significant other also needs to be able to imagine and understand your point of view. Business travel is usually a condition of employment. Whether you always enjoy it or not, to stop might mean seeking another job or even another occupation. Certainly in the near term, this can be damaging from both a financial and career perspective.

As for the insecure fear about engaging in extracurricular activities with others, it goes both ways as well. While you are traveling, it might just be your mate who becomes active with someone else. This is not intended to make both of you imagine fears that don't exist, only to point out that merely traveling to another location for business does not provide more opportunity for the traveler than it does for the one who stays home if your relationship is open and strong.

We have talked about communication, trust, and empathy but some maintain there is nothing more important to a relationship than time. I realize that time together with a mate is difficult when one is traveling but I have already given you some ideas on how to use that time to communicate. Now let's talk about time when you are together.

Does anyone know the most important time of the day when you are together? I always thought it was that moment when couples got into bed at night. My husband's guess was dinner time with the family. Both of us were wrong.

According to researchers Les and Leslie Parrott, that most important moment is when couples connect after being apart.[13] For most people, that would be when they meet up after a day's work.

For business travelers, that moment may be days or weeks later. Regardless of the amount of time apart, that moment is critical to set the proper tone when reconnecting.

This is why it is so important to turn off the work switch before you walk in your front door. Unwind on the plane or in the car and start thinking about how you'll spend your time with your family now that you're home.

The authors of the study also stress the importance of doing things together. The emphasis needs to be on quality over quantity. If necessary, make a date with each other. Use that time to make the relationship work for both of you.

A note here: I am not a family or marriage therapist. My suggestions are meant to be general in nature and may not apply to your specific situation.

There are many dozens of books on the topic of relationships so if you want more help, look for those that focus on your particular needs. If you feel the need for personal assistance with your issues, by all means seek out professionals who are accredited in this area.

A final thought: Don't be hard on your family for not thinking of these things. After all, they may see you as the one who "left the family," making their thinking patterns different than yours. Instead, use your new knowledge and work with them to maximize the relationship as a two-way street. That way everyone wins.

No Relationship? No Problem

I realize this chapter may seem focused on relationships and family. Of course, not all business travelers have relationships with others, much less a family.

There are many traveling for business who want to engage in social relationships as an integral part of their lives. So where do you go to socialize when you are traveling?

Opportunities abound. In addition to local lounges, bars, and clubs, here are some that may interest you:

- Colleges/lectures
- Film events
- Museums
- Singles groups
- Church groups
- Professional organizations

You also may find that you don't know many people even in the city or town where you live. If you travel extensively, it may be difficult to get involved in local activities. Use these tips for social opportunities in both your home city and your destination cities.

This is discussed much more in Chapter 6, Traveling Alone.

- There are several takeaways from this chapter. For those with families, design your own best ways to communicate with them when you travel, listen to their feelings and needs, and always place a priority on trust in your relationships. Good preparation in the beginning makes traveling much easier.

- For those concerned about friends or need to communicate with business associates while traveling, these tips will serve you well, too. Remember, good communication is essential in all types of relationships.

11

SOCIAL MEDIA AND TRAVEL

Your business travel can begin long before you get in a car or board your flight. By making the most of social media networking tools, you can get the most out of each business trip – discovering places to visit, hotels and restaurants to experience, finding new business opportunities and building your network.

Travel is inherently social. With today's social media tools, it's even easier to keep in touch with family and friends while out of town – or even when you are in town.

Social media tools are constantly changing and evolving. Here are today's most popular ways to connect online:

Friend Me with Facebook

Facebook is one of the most popular social media services for networking. Visit any airport, bus station or coffee shop and you will see Facebook users reading and sending updates on their laptops and other mobile devices.

Facebook isn't just for the younger generations nor is it just for social media. While you can send gifts, poke friends, play games and add widgets and tools for countless other applications, the most value to a business traveler is in feeling connected to family and friends even when you are thousands of miles away. Notifications of which family members or friends are celebrating a birthday is reason enough for me to use Facebook as it is a quick and easy way to post a birthday greeting.

Besides being a valuable connection to family and friends, there are also travel-related reasons to use Facebook. You can:

- Ask friends for hotel and restaurant recommendations and then share your impressions afterwards.

- Book a hotel room, note a complaint, share a review or request help from hotel, airline, car rental or other travel-related companies' fan pages.

- Learn about the city you are traveling to by visiting their fan page or pages of major attractions.

- Meet other business travelers and use Facebook email to send messages.

- Get travel advice and connect with other travelers at pages such as Smart Women Travelers and Business Travel Success.

Travel companies are rapidly moving to Facebook because they have recently realized that it is a great method for communicating with their customers. Take advantage of this and be connected with your primary airline, hotel and car rental Facebook pages in ways that were much more difficult before the advent of social media.

According to PhoCusWright, a travel research firm, the volume of direct hotel referrals from Facebook is growing, with better conversion rates from referral to actual booking than from TripAdvisor and other review sites.[14] And while web traffic to travel brand sites fell 8% in the March annual comparisons, visits to Facebook increased 20% during the same period.[15]

On Facebook pages for hotels, reviews and opinions can be posted by travelers, which is especially valuable when it comes to researching where to stay and what to do. Though with any reviews, travel or otherwise, it is more likely that the unhappy customers are posting comments.

I have found, however, that both the positive and negative reviews are worth reading for valuable nuggets. Comments such as "noisy rooms along the highway" or "pool closed for renovation" can help you in determining which property to select or specific room requirements to ask for.

 You can also "meet" and become connected with travelers who are customers of the same travel companies, perhaps visit the same city or have similar travel interests or challenges. Facebook members are generally open to connecting. You can easily begin a dialog with others who have a similar travel lifestyle and learn and share ways to travel smarter.

In addition to meeting new travelers, Facebook also allows you to see which of your friends are nearby. Never miss a chance to connect when you happen to be in the same place at the same time.

You can browse the status of friends who are checked in nearby and select "Here Now" to see who else is checked in where you are or view a map of places where your friends have checked in. A nice feature is receiving a push notification from friends who are checked in at nearby places (if this is set up on your mobile device). And if you want to stay incognito and remove a Places entry – or not allow anyone to see where you are at all – you can opt for that, too.

If you like the Places feature, check in with your mobile phone to search for local deals at restaurants, get retailer discounts in the local area, share savings with friends, earn rewards for repeat visits or secure donations for good causes. I have seen incentives such as a free drink in a restaurant bar, a money-off voucher for a certain number of hotel check-ins, free late checkout... even a free night at a hotel.

A growing number of hotels offer a direct booking feature through Facebook. You can check rates and book special packages, with the chance of getting a special rate or offers available only through a company's Facebook page.

Applications for travelers are available on Facebook, with some of the popular apps being "Cities I've Visited." This app is used to track cities throughout the world where you have traveled.

The "Bing Wish List" is where you can create a wish list of where you want to travel or be connected with Bing "Places" pages, which provide information about a city. You can then be linked to flight data, hotel bookings and to other areas within the Bing Travel site.

The Bing Wish List also has a social element with friends having the ability to suggest new locations, add comments and share their own wish lists. Because the list of traveler apps for Facebook is ever-changing, use Google to search for "Facebook apps for travel" to see the most up-to-date offerings.

Twitter for Travel

Twitter is a form of social media where you communicate with people using up to 140 characters. It is wildly popular, not only among young people but with us seasoned folks as well.

Some tweeters use Twitter for personal use, detailing events in their daily lives. Others use it for business purposes like staying in touch with customers or clients or promoting their business.

Today there are thousands of tweeters in the travel field. These include travel vendors such as airlines, hotels, cruise lines, car rental companies, travel agencies, and tour operators.

To look for travel providers, simply go to Twitter and use the Find People link. Type in the name and they may come up. However, some who use Twitter use a different name. For example, mine is *smartwomentrav*. You might have some difficulty finding me unless you do a search under my real name and see that I tweet under *smartwomentrav* instead of Carol Margolis.

Among the best known travel industry tweeters are JetBlue and Southwest Airlines. They each tweet frequently about discount flights. Yes, sometimes the best deals are first announced on Twitter.

One example, this past summer JetBlue offered $9 tickets on Twitter. Needless to say, they sold out very fast. If you are interested in flight discounts where you need to decide quickly, follow JetBlue on Twitter.

Other airlines, as well as many more travel providers, offer special deals periodically. Most of them are available either for a limited time or for a limited number of people. The only way to know about them is to follow them on Twitter.

But the travel arena is much larger. Also on the list are tweeters for many travel deals, special promotions, or hotel packages. Then there are those who tweet about travel news. Some are familiar names, like *USA Today* and the *LA Times*, while others are individual journalists who work for these publications. Look for some of the many outstanding freelance travel journalists who tweet.

Employees of the travel industry are frequent tweeters. For example, there are pilots and flight attendants tweeting about the airline business from their perspectives. Some airports as well as airport lounges also tweet on occasion.

Many businesses or local organizations use Twitter to promote a specific destination. If you are interested only in a certain geographical area, find out who these tweeters are and follow them.

Other Twitter sources are local tourism boards and convention centers. There are even some chambers of commerce tweeting. They can be very helpful if you have a specific destination in mind.

In addition, there are many who tweet about their personal travels. It can be quite interesting to follow their journeys around the world.

Whenever there is a trade show or conference, there is generally an accompanying hashtag (a keyword preceded by a # sign) to help people at the conference, and even those not in attendance, connect. At a Google conference in 2010, for example, they used this hashtag: #io2010.

#TravelTuesday (or #TT) is a very popular travel-related hashtag. Every Tuesday is Travel Tuesday, and anyone who shares travel-related info may use the hashtag on that day. It is a perfect opportunity to connect with other travel aficionados and give a "shout-out" to some of your travel favorites.

Many travel tweeters are more like me. They pass along interesting travel news, mention travel-related events or articles written, or perhaps add a quick comment about something interesting that happened while traveling.

Very often, tweets include links to various website articles or stories. Reviewing this in Twitter offers an opportunity to scan many tweets and see if the subject matter link is something that interests you. It is much faster than trying to see each web page individually.

There are some travel tweeters who are quite prolific, posting 100 or more messages a day. Others show more restraint by posting only a few each day.

It is very common that these tweeters' followers will re-tweet the information to their own followers. This way it gets out to hundreds or even thousands of others very quickly.

The whole point here is that there are many thousands of people and businesses posting messages about travel around the clock. It is impossible to follow everyone's comments but it is manageable once you decide on the type of information that you are seeking or the people you want to follow.

If you are unfamiliar with Twitter, there are many books about the subject as well as lots of information online. Even if you don't want to tweet about anything, there is much to learn about travel just by following other tweeters.

After creating an account, people or businesses can begin following others who have accounts. Over time, tweeters learn about you and begin to follow you as well. In the extreme, a few tweeters have over a million followers.

Another nice Twitter feature is lists. You can create lists for virtually anything, such as a list of travel tweeters.

Alternatively, you can create multiple travel lists. One might be just for travel news, another for those who tweet about personal travels, and still another is maintained only for those offering travel promotion deals. Lists are a great way to be efficient with your time since it is virtually impossible to follow all tweets all day long.

Tweet About It

Many people today are getting issues resolved with companies by tweeting about their problems. I am not suggesting you use Twitter solely to complain about poor service or flight cancellations with airlines, but there might be a good reason to bring certain matters to your travel provider's attention immediately.

The best examples are those that they can remedy quickly. To cite but one example: if you are trying to have something fixed in your hotel room and it has been hours since you reported it, try sending a tweet to the hotel. You might get quicker service.

There are many examples of people using Twitter to resolve issues, but not all providers have a Twitter account yet. I am, however, noticing more and more individual hotel properties setting up their own accounts.

If you don't know if a hotel has a Twitter account, just ask when you arrive. Most hotels are proud to tell you their Twitter name and would be happy to have you follow them.

While on the subject, if you are pleased with your travel provider, it is nice to tweet about their services. While many may not respond directly to you, the gesture is nevertheless appreciated.

I see that more and more people are using Twitter to ask travel questions. Examples might range from the best places to stay in a certain destination to which airport is best to use. People also ask about others' experiences with different travel providers. Really, the possibilities are limitless.

At its best, Twitter allows users to actually have conversations with others. While it is operationally a bit different than an instant message, the result is communication with a focused audience.

It is possible to connect with people who share your interest in, say, a specific location. Once you find these people, it is quite easy to share knowledge and experiences. Older folks may think of it as pen pals on steroids.

At its worst, Twitter can breed danger. I don't mean to sound alarmist but reasonable caution is necessary. Here's a story that will explain it better.

Not long ago, a young man began communicating with some people he had met via Twitter. At some point, he told them he would be traveling to a destination near them. So far, so good.

Eventually he met up with them and, by all accounts, had a great time. They finished the evening back at his hostel room. When he awoke the next morning, all his money and papers were gone. Oh, and his new friends were gone, too.

Or consider the man who tweeted that he was traveling. Nice to tell friends that you'll be out of town, but these are public messages that can be seen by everyone. When he returned home, he found his home had been burglarized.

While Twitter is excellent at bringing people with similar interests together, you need to exercise reasonable caution when traveling no matter how well you feel you know someone. It is easy to develop an online relationship. It is something else to really get to know and trust that person. Meeting in person is a great opportunity but again, please exercise some caution.

Many people include personal addresses on their websites, Facebook pages, or elsewhere on the internet. Don't tell the world that you are out of town if your home will be vacant. Remind traveling children about this as well.

Twitter is great for staying in touch with family and friends. Another nice feature: You can add photos to your tweets. This is a great way to give those back home a quick look at your surroundings.

Tweeting might be the tech equivalent of sending postcards but the best part is it's instant. No postage, no waiting. Send a message with a photo and others can see it immediately.

LinkedIn

Most people create LinkedIn accounts to expand their networks, both professional and personal. Do you know that LinkedIn also can help with your travels?

- Get answers to questions. Ask a question and get answers from the connections and experts on your network. If you have no immediate questions to ask, check out the answers to questions that others in your network have asked. Recent questions included:

    How could business travel be improved and what matters most to you when traveling?

    Any recommendations for wireless carriers for a 2-week visit to the UK?

- Follow companies or join groups that interest you.

- Browse events that your connections are attending and that may be of interest to you also.

- See what your connections are reading and get their reviews.

- Use advanced search to set the location you're traveling to, then browse search results for current or prospective contacts.

Applications can be added to further enhance your use of LinkedIn. For example, Google Presentation allows you to present yourself and your work. Just upload a PowerPoint document or use Google's online application to embed a presentation on your profile.

Another application, My Travel by TripIt, allows users to see where their LinkedIn connections are traveling and when they will be in the same cities as colleagues. Sharing upcoming trips, current location, and travel stats with your network can be fun as well as informative.

A gentle reminder: Heed my earlier advice about what can happen if you disclose that you are traveling and your house is vacant.

Other Social Media Tools

Another social media tool that may become a success is Google+. It was just becoming active as this book went to print so I can't comment yet on its usefulness as a tool for travelers. I am on Google+ so connect with me!

Other great travel tools include **TripIt.com** or **Dopplr.com** to track travel details and share them with friends and colleagues. Another site worth checking out is the business traveler social network **whenthemeetingsover.com**. When you are traveling to the same city as fellow contacts, these services alert you to opportunities to connect or meet up.

Check for upcoming events in the city you will be visiting. **Eventful.com** and **upcoming.org** list conferences and professional gatherings in many cities.

For reviews and advice on hotels, resorts, flights, restaurants and lots more, check out **TripAdvisor.com.** You stand to gain a wealth of information using this tool to learn about which hotels are most popular by reading reviews written by guests.

Note there may be more negative than positive comments written about a property. Before deciding against a property entirely, look for frequent themes in the comments. For example, you may learn the property is undergoing remodeling or perhaps there is nearby road construction.

Rooms near any construction will be most impacted because of the loud noise. If that is the only problem with a property, consider requesting a room away from the noise. After your trip, post your thoughts about the property to help future travelers make their decisions.

Social Media in 15 Minutes a Day

A common complaint among social media users (and social media avoiders) is that participating in social media can be a full-time commitment or a major time waster. If you are active with social media at all, I am sure you have had occasions where the hours in a hotel room have flown by while reading status updates of people you hardly know and tweeting pointless comments to faceless followers.

TIP: When you meet new colleagues or other contacts on the road, ask them how they prefer to connect and stay in touch... Connect on LinkedIn? Become friends on Facebook? Follow each other on Twitter?

Follow up by adding them to your networks when you return home and send them a thank-you via their preferred social media method. .

Here are ways to make great use of these tools without watching hours vanish into thin air:

In Facebook:

- Create lists of:

    Family and closest friends

    Colleagues

    Influencers and people you want to know further

    Connections from events you've attended.

- Send birthday greetings each day by reviewing Events.

- Check recent news from family and close friends and post a few comments.

- Update your status with a newsworthy item or unique experience of your travels.

- Scan the newsfeeds of favorite pages or groups.

- Send out one or two friend requests and respond to those sent to you.

In Twitter:

- Set up lists similar to those in Facebook, including lists for the hashtags you'd like to follow.

- Scan the recent updates on your favorite lists. Retweet or reply to items of interest.

- Post an update of something interesting in your day or a question you'd like answered.

- Send follow-ups or thank-you's to those who mentioned you in updates.

- Follow back interesting Twitter users and follow people you would like to have in your network.

In LinkedIn:

- Respond to invites for connections.

- Review your most important groups for recent activity.

- Post an update (what you're doing, what you're reading, for example).

For quick and easy posting, spread your messages across multiple social media platforms such as Facebook, Twitter and LinkedIn. Hootsuite.com is an example of a tool to use. You type an update and then select which platform(s) to post to.

Phew, so many ways to stay in touch! You could probably fill an entire evening in your room staying busy with phone calls and social media. That is one reason why this book includes the next chapter on Time Management.

12

TIME MANAGEMENT

Conversation with my dentist's office:

> Me: *"I'd like to make an appointment for Friday."*

> Dentist's office: *"We're all booked then. How about Thursday?"*

> Me: *"No, it must be on a Friday. I travel out of town every Monday through Thursday."*

> Dentist's office: *"Okay, then how about next Tuesday?"*

What part of *"No, it must be on a Friday. I travel out of town every Monday through Thursday"* do they not understand?

This has not just happened to me once. . . it has happened numerous times. The life of a perpetual traveler is so foreign to doctors, dentists and other customer service people that they just cannot comprehend it.

Thus the issue of managing your time, even for something as simple as getting your teeth cleaned, is accentuated in a business traveler's life. Adding up the time spent traveling, the hours working in another city, sales and expense reporting, emails and phone calls, it is easy to put personal care last on the list.

Many road warrior business travelers choose to have doctors, dentists, hair stylists, and more in various cities where they travel. With so few days at home each week, this is an alternative for those with a traveling lifestyle.

The surprises, inconveniences, and delays can be interesting and part of the fun when vacation traveling. However, traveling for work is often not quite the adventure that some may believe.

With business travel, the primary focus is on being productive. Thus it is not unusual that typical travel discomforts often seem worse because of additional business pressures.

How often do you travel for business? Do you make occasional trips to conferences, regularly visit clients in other cities, or fly two or three times a week (or more)? If you travel frequently, a high tolerance for accepting the stress of constantly moving around is a job requirement.

For many, the demands of frequent traveling for business cause anxiety, frustration, exhaustion, and often low level physical illness. Things like delayed flights, flat tires, and long working days are to be expected.

Does the following sound familiar....?

Business travel was great for the first year of my career. Now it's a hindrance in maintaining a healthy work/life balance. I eat terrible, rarely make it into the gym with the long hours on the road, and have a hard time keeping up with friends. The worst part is keeping up with my home since I'm gone so often.

Business travelers are often expected to cram more work into less time. The good news is that there are several ways to ensure that your travel will go as smoothly as possible, allowing you to concentrate on your business goals.

The ideas and techniques in this chapter offer ways to manage the time between your two lives of traveling and home. Also, they will help improve your business performance and quality of life. While much of this chapter offers tips for those who travel frequently, even those who are occasional business travelers will benefit here.

At Home

Many a traveler's pet peeve is coming home to an unclean or disorganized home. Whether it was the other spouse who was in charge or a caregiver, the tasks of getting the dishes out of the sink, the laundry folded, or the floor vacuumed just never made it to the top of their list while you were away.

My husband well remembers the first thing I used to do when I got home from a business trip. Before anything else, I would make a beeline into the kitchen to see if it was cleaned up.

Dishes in the sink were a sure way to get my ire up and put all thoughts of gratitude for being home out of my mind. Now that the teenagers have grown up and moved out, my ire has calmed down. The worst part, it all seems very silly and insignificant in retrospect.

So what are some ideas to help you better manage your precious time at home? Start by having realistic expectations. If a few glasses are in the sink, is that so bad? Focus on the big issues and don't sweat the small stuff. Also, think about some outside help. If nagging the family or roommate at home isn't your idea of fun, perhaps bringing in extra hands will ensure the work gets done before you get home.

Even if you live alone, the assistance of a cleaning service makes the coming-home experience more enjoyable. The benefits include a sense of calm and tolerance you might otherwise miss, not to mention hours of cleaning that you no longer need to do. Of course, this needs to be weighed against the cost.

- If this makes sense to you, first come up with your list of cleaning tasks. It is also helpful to write down how you like them done. Next, determine the frequency. Is once a week necessary or is once a month sufficient? Finally, interview cleaning services to learn about their fees, insurance bonding, and availability.

- If you have a family at home while you are away and the service's only available cleaning day is the first day you are away, you will be very sorry when you get home later in the week. The house will be full of dust balls and crumbs again.

- Best option if available: Have the house cleaned on the day of your return if you are comfortable having someone in the house (bonded, of course) while you're away. Alternatively, consider having the cleaning done on your first full day back.

Besides the never-ending cleaning tasks, make a list of all the other things you typically do when you are home. Many of these tasks are just as easily accomplished while still traveling. Examples include paying the bills, balancing the checkbook, and updating your financial accounts. This will relieve you of some of the mundane tasks and give you more quality time at home.

Also look for tasks that you can outsource, such as:

- Online ordering of groceries for delivery once you're back at home
- Pick up and drop off dry-cleaning service
- Bookkeeping
- Closet and cabinet organizing
- Furniture rearranging
- Plumbing and electrical work
- Pool cleaning
- Landscaping
- Watering indoor and outdoor plants
- Car washing and vacuuming
- Cleaning the gutters

Check with your local chamber of commerce for errand service providers that can do some of these chores for you as well as for those once-in-awhile time-consuming errands (such as hauling old clothes to Goodwill).

Before you ask "Hey, what's with this big list of hiring someone else? Does Carol think money grows on trees?" – look at how often each of these is needed. Most are seldom needed, some are monthly and yes, a few may be weekly. What they all have in common is saving your time for other matters.

The years go fast. And they go even faster when your home life is just a few days a week. *Believe me, I know.*

Picture yourself sitting in the backyard on a Saturday afternoon, surrounded by family, relaxing and having fun, a glass of wine or a cold beer in your hand, sharing events of the past week. This is much more fun than vacuuming up dust balls, cleaning out the fridge of green, moldy stuff, and scrubbing toilets.

Family and Friends

A rule of mine is to stay in close touch with my family while I'm gone. When I'm on the west coast, everyone knows that I walk out of meetings every day at 4 pm so I can talk to my kids as they're starting their homework on the east coast. I guard that time slot jealously, for their sake and for mine.

Having quality time with family and friends is your most important travel de-stressor and gets you re-grounded with your home life. Once you walk in the front door from your travels, leave your stories of flight delays, noisy hotel neighbors, and work matters at the door. This is a moment best served by reconnecting with family.

Take turns with your spouse on planning a night out, just the two of you. Whether it is a candlelight dinner while a babysitter oversees the children or just coffee at the local Starbucks, make time to get away from the normal household routine and spend time focusing on each other.

Same for friends. Months may go by before you realize you haven't seen your best friend. Put appointments in your calendar to keep in contact with friends near and far, and catch up with local friends in person whenever you can.

These are most likely the friends you have had the longest. They remember you before your travel lifestyle ever began, and it is always a great time with lots of laughs.

Take time to do the things at home you otherwise wouldn't have time for. There is nothing wrong with taking advantage of a child-free and interruption-free evening, and it helps make the long business days while on the road more manageable.

Social Media

Twitter and Facebook are great for keeping in contact with friends and family while you're on the road. However, they can also be the most distracting and time-consuming things ever invented! When faced with a full list of other tasks to do, it is better to shut them off after a certain amount of time.

Failing to heed this advice may mean spending an inordinate amount of time chatting with friends on Facebook or reading tweets. The hours will disappear and you'll wonder how. To manage your time better here, think about setting a timer to limit yourself to a certain number of minutes.

Business

Many travelers feel that they have to be "on" the entire time they're on the road. Fly in the early morning, meetings all day, then prepare for tomorrow's events until late in the evening. Been there, done that.

My colleagues and I were routinely chased out of a hotel concierge lounge at 10 pm each night because the employees wanted to close and go home. This was in stark contrast to our need to put finishing touches on our PowerPoint presentation for the following morning.

Some business meetings can go well into the very late evening hours. It is common for many events to go until 9 or 10 at night, with an 8 am start the next day. It is total exhaustion by the end of the week. This is one reason the business traveler might be a bit cranky walking in the front door once back home.

A consultant, who routinely travels to the same city week after week, asked about her personal time in the evenings: "Is it okay to attend fitness classes at 7 pm when I'm on the road, or do I need to be answering my boss's emails and phone calls?"

Read on . . .

Whether it's by your own habits and practices or those of your management, the personal time boundaries when traveling are squeezed into near non-existence. It is time to rein in the ropes and put some limits to your work time.

This might mean skipping the last speaker of the evening, taking a pass at a group dinner, or realizing that the PowerPoint slides are not going to be drastically improved between 7 and 10 pm (so you might as well stop at 7). Be more cognizant of opportunities to draw those personal boundary times.

This includes answering your boss's emails all evening. Business travelers often use the available evening time to catch up on email. Indeed, this is sometimes necessary because of time zone differences. When these time zones stretch across the globe, responding to them can be an all-night event.

Instead, a good compromise might be suggesting to your boss that he or she leaves you a voicemail if something is truly urgent. Otherwise, you will respond in the morning. Then turn off the sound on your phone that alerts you to every new email.

Everybody needs time to unwind. When something remains way out of balance for too long, it eventually tips over and crashes to the ground. Don't let this be you.

Here are some tips for being more time efficient in your work:

- Focus on the purpose of the meeting (*what's in it for them*) and not on all the fancy PowerPoint charts and doodles. Get the point across and move on.

- Set meetings for 45 minutes vs. an hour, and start every meeting on time. This leaves several minutes between meetings to make notes, book future travel and check email. This frees up time later back at the hotel.

- Ask a colleague to take notes from the last speaker of the day (or even a mid-day speaker so you can take a couple of hours away from an event). Alternatively, make a recording if it is allowed.

- Go through a convention booth map before you start walking the aisles. Highlight the areas you want to visit and skip the rest, even if they might be giving away some freebies.

- Connect with speakers and meeting attendees via LinkedIn and Facebook prior to an event. Use this initial connection to become familiar with their photos, making it easier to spot them among the masses.

- If you need printed copies, consider sending them to a local store for printing in the city you're traveling to, such as FedEx Kinko's.

- Ask your hotel for the nearest printing office, then go online and use their service to have any documents printed at this location. A hotel may even offer a service to pick up your order for you. This saves you time in printing, collating, and binding the documents, and it means no lugging the documents through an airport, possibly saving the need to check luggage as well as paying a baggage fee.

- Arrange meetings with jet lag in mind. If you are flying from New York to Los Angeles, then mornings are going to be better for you. Spend the "lower quality" time on administrative tasks such as e-mail.

- Spend each leg of your flights relaxing rather than working (if you can only do this one way, relax on your way home).

- Do get-togethers over coffee or drinks rather than lengthy meals.

- Take advantage of conference meet-and-greets but do not get stuck in one place too long. Circulate and keep watch for the people you'd like to meet. Have an initial discussion rather than a long conversation about how you can do business together. Meet them, be interested, make yourself memorable, promise to follow up--and then do. Contact them with a handwritten notecard or via LinkedIn within the next day or two, mentioning something memorable from their conversation.

- At conferences or large meetings, arrive early to increase your chances of engaging with many people while the crowd is still thin; then leave when the official end of the meeting occurs. There will always be several people who will carry a social event on through the evening. Rarely does this kind of activity result in anything business-worthy. The evening time might be better spent on personal matters or getting a good night's sleep.

- Take advantage of social networking tools to increase the number of people you meet at an event. Ask for the Twitter hashtag designated for the event, not only to post your own conference coverage, but to connect with other attendees and to follow their tweets and meet them on breaks.

Look for several business opportunities from the same trip. For example, you might travel to a city for a sales presentation. Look into the possibility of more opportunities with others in the same city. Leads for contacts in other cities might come from your own address book, maybe a referral, or even LinkedIn. Whatever the source, this offers another face-to-face opportunity even if it wasn't planned.

The inverse of the last tip is also important. It is common for business travelers to set up way too many meetings in order to maximize their time in a city. The problem here is overreaching. Attempting too much almost always leads to burn out with the time at home focused on relaxing, meaning other activities won't be finished.

It is not uncommon that over the course of a business trip, there is one major meeting that requires the utmost attention and productivity. Creating too many meetings during a trip means limited resources for all of them. The end result may be a less than productive important event. This is all about balance.

Booking Your Travel

You may think you can book your travel online faster than providing all the details for someone else to do it, but is this the best use of your time?

Whether you have a company-provided travel service or not, it helps to first lay out the plans for the trip.

A simple travel template will work:

- Where are you going?
- When?
- Objective of the trip
- Hours of business event or convention
- Traveling with colleagues?
- Hotel options (list two or three in case your primary hotel is fully booked)
- Car rental?

- Other transportation?
- Address of hotel and business
- Dress code

A handy online source to see all your travel plans at a glance is TripIt. Everything is organized by trip and is easily shared with family and colleagues, as well as printed for your own use. In addition, the information can be accessed from your smartphone.

You can receive TripIt updates via SMS text messaging or use the smartphone applications for more features. It will even notify you of flight delays and the like. TripIt has a free version as well as a paid version with more features.

TripIt also is helpful to see what parts of your travel plans have not yet been booked. For example, maybe you booked an airline ticket and a car rental but forgot about a hotel. Reviewing your itinerary in TripIt makes it easy to see what is missing.

Packing Time-Savers

While we talked about travel checklists in Chapter 2, it is brought up again here to stress how much of a time-saver such a tool can be. Whether you're a seasoned traveler who packs almost every week or a once-in-awhile conference attendee, it is so easy to forget necessary items.

The best way to make the process easier and less stressful is to make it repeatable. Without a list, it is way too easy to forget things. True, some may be purchased at the destination but really, do you want to buy another phone charger or pair of reading glasses that you won't need after this trip just because you forgot to pack them?

Of course, some items can't be replaced. The first one that comes to mind is prescription medications. Failing to include this in your packed items may have serious consequences.

If you forget small items like toothpaste, toothbrush, deodorant or shaving cream, ask at your hotel's front desk for a replacement. Often they have these items and they are complimentary. Other times you can buy them from the hotel gift store.

Another big time-saver that will really decrease your packing time is having your bedroom closet and dresser drawers arranged by type of clothing, then by color. Have your slacks hanging together, then arranged by black, gray, blue, tan, etc. Same for shirts, blouses, sweaters, jackets, socks, hose and shoes, even accessories and jewelry.

When you then choose one or two "colors of the week," it is very simple to go right to that spot in your wardrobe and select a few items. When I did this, my packing time went down drastically.

On the Way to and from the Airport

Driving to and from the airport in your home city, along with commuting to your hotel or business, can easily take up several hours each week. Many of these hours are early in the morning or late in the evening and not as conducive to making phone calls as mid-day hours are. With a little pre-planning, these drives can be very productive.

First, determine if it makes economic sense for someone else to do the driving. I have not driven myself to my home airport in years. When I added up the time spent, along with the dollars, it made more sense to hire a driver to take me to the airport and pick me up on my return.

Here was my logic. For me, it is nearly an hour's drive to the airport. In addition, the time spent parking at the airport and getting inside added another 30 minutes each way. Total time: Almost 3 hours each week.

And then there were the out-of-pocket costs. Using a mileage rate of .50/mile, that totaled $30. Then there were tolls on the way plus parking at the airport garage. That's another $90, making the total cost $120 each week.

I found a car service that charges just a bit more than the $120 that I was spending each week. Suddenly I was picked up and dropped off at the door with three extra hours of productive time.

What can you do with three extra productive hours each week?

- Respond to emails
- Do online research
- Make phone calls
- Make a to-do list for the day or week
- Listen to an audio book or today's news
- Read
- Close your eyes for some relaxation or sleep

Most importantly, you will arrive at the airport and back home again relaxed and without the stress from doing your own driving.

 TIP: How do you find a great car service? Call a few local hotels and ask their concierge or front desk who they recommend. Within minutes you will have several names to call. Don't forget to check out each service yourself. After all, your life may be in their hands.

At the Airport

You can arrive at the airport within an hour of your flight, race through security and arrive at your gate huffing and puffing without a minute to spare;

Or

You can arrive early, head to your airline's lounge, get a beverage and relax while reading a few emails that need attention before heading to your gate.

I personally find the latter method works better for my time management as well as peace of mind.

It used to be that arriving for your flight an hour beforehand was plenty of time to get to the gate in a relaxed fashion. That changed with 9/11, the shoe bomber incident, and terrorist plots using liquid explosives. The airlines usually tell you to arrive two hours before a domestic flight and three hours before an international flight.

Note that these arrival times vary widely based on the airport. For example, flights out of smaller suburban airports often don't require much time to check in and clear security. On the other hand, major airports like JFK, LAX, and all the major airline hubs often require much more time. It is always better to be safe and arrive early rather than late.

Does this extra time at an airport need to be downtime? Not at all. In fact, you might like to have time before boarding a flight to check in with the office before you go silent during your flight.

Here are a few more ideas for making the best use of airport time while waiting for your flight:

- Always have some work with you. With laptops and smartphones, it is almost like taking an office with you. Of course, the downsides include noise and difficulty finding a place to sit, as well as power outlets for today's electronic appliances.

- If you do not normally have access to an airline lounge, consider buying a day pass to one of them. The quieter, more relaxing environment is enough to make it worthwhile but the real benefits are having a near-office ability to complete some work. Even better if the work is billable time.

- Record your expenses and time for the day as well as any other daily reporting you need to do.

- Charge up your mobile phone and laptop and any other electronics.

- Pick up a healthy meal to eat in-flight. Most airport restaurants will prepare meals to go.

- Get your shoes or boots shined.

- Have your nails done.

- Enjoy a massage.

- Get your annual flu shot.

- Withdraw cash from your ATM sufficient for your trip.

- Write and mail a few thank-you or note cards.

If you can arrive two hours or more before your flight, enjoy a meal at a restaurant rather than carrying on food for your flight. Try to find a table away from the entrance or bar area so that you can have a bit of quiet while you eat. As a perpetual multi-tasker, I will read a book or magazine or go through a few time-consuming emails while I'm eating.

 TIP: When you are in an airport restaurant and in a hurry, ask to have the check delivered to at the same time your meal is brought to the table.

On a Plane, Train or Bus

We spend valuable hours on a plane or a train or a bus that we will never get back. Here are a few ideas for productive transportation time:

- Read a few magazines that you've been collecting at home. Toss the magazines into a bag with the goal of leaving them behind at the end of the journey.

- Scan the magazine pages and read the articles most important to you (you don't need to read every article). Rip out any articles, recipes, tips, etc., that you want to follow up with later.

- When you are finished, hand the magazines over to the flight attendants or others. Chances are they will be grateful for something to read or they will recycle any magazines they're not interested in.

- Write thank-you notes or other greeting cards. Finding the time to write a thank-you note after an important meeting, interview or event is a challenge, so do it on the trip home. Bring along stamps so that the note cards are ready to be mailed once you've disembarked.

- Pay bills. Bring along the checkbook and get your bills paid. Get the envelopes stamped and ready for mailing. Look for a mail slot in the terminal or ask your hotel desk to mail them for you.

- Write up your to-do list and day-by-day agenda for the upcoming days. The transiting time is very valuable for giving thought to tasks, business ideas, scheduling, etc., when you are not interrupted by emails and phone calls.

- Clean up email. You can access email through Outlook or Lotus Notes even when there is no Wi-Fi connection. Take advantage of the time to respond to current emails, clear out some clutter, prepare a few quick hellos to contacts you've been meaning to keep in touch with.

- Meditate. With some meditative music on your iPod, let your mind and conscious breathing take over for 20 or 30 minutes. When you rouse yourself, write down any feelings, ideas or other thoughts that came up because these can be very inspirational.

- Take a nap. You are either beginning several days of meetings or conferences or just wrapping up from busy days. Take some time to relax and let your eyes close. Even a 15-minute cat-nap does wonders for the productivity of many travelers.

- Meet your neighbor. Some of your seatmates may seem like people you might want to meet, so say hello. If you're both interested in talking, then relax and enjoy the conversation. I have met some amazing people sitting right next to me and have even done business with some of them. Always have business cards handy if you want to share your contact information.

I may be crazy, but I really look forward to international flights. I have enough to-dos in my laptop tote, along with a book reader stocked with great books, neck pillow for napping, and media player loaded with podcasts and music. I keep myself busy, the flight time goes fast, and I get off the plane feeling wonderful about what I've accomplished as well as refreshed from a nap.

In Your Car

Get out your mobile phone and start texting as you drive. Just kidding! That is the worst thing you should be doing while driving!

Instead, here are better tips for being productive while you're behind the wheel:

- Send text messages safely with the use of applications for your mobile device. These apps convert speech to text and can be done hands-free when using a headset or speakerphone. Instead of providing a list of apps here, which will change before I finish this sentence, check online for apps that will work for you.

- Create reminders of things you think of while driving. Each time a light bulb goes off in your head with another great thought, use your mobile device's voice recorder or a digital recorder to create an audio note. Your mobile device's voice recorder may include a feature to email the voice file to yourself or to someone else.

- Many people do some of their best thinking as they are driving along the highway. Since you will want to remember those brilliant ideas, be sure to have the right tools. Only use the paper and pen method when your car is stopped and not while you're in the fast lane going 75 mph.

- Set your goals and prepare for the day. Take a few minutes to go over what you want to accomplish before the day is over. Record these in the same manner as mentioned above for reminders. It may be the only time of the day when you feel refreshed and relaxed, not pressured.

- Listen to audiobooks or podcasts via your car's CD player or your mobile device. I have enough audiobooks on my phone to get me through a round trip coast-to-coast drive on a lawnmower. Or use the voice option on your eBook reader to have a book read to you.

- Catch up on the day's news. Most cities have an affiliate of National Public Radio at the low end of the FM dial.

- Do breathing exercises. An easy way to help you reduce any anxiety or stress is to practice deep breathing. There are a number of other benefits — like helping you to feel more awake, and helping you to think more clearly. It's a perfect way to spend your commute. Well, as long as you do it safely.

- Make phone calls with a hands-free headset or speaker. Many cities require use of a headset or speaker when making phone calls while driving. While not all cities mandate this, it just makes safe sense. Besides, it's better than looking like you're eating a taco with your head tilted to the side and the phone glued to your ear.

- Use a power inverter to charge your electronics on the go. This handy device lets you plug items like laptops, cell phones, DVD players, MP3s, and camcorders into the car's cigarette lighter using their own power cords. While car adapters also work, inverters have an advantage of not requiring special adapters. A 75-watt/115V power inverter costs about $30 at many retailers.

- Many cars now include a USB charger for easy charging of your mobile phone, bluetooth headset, camera and other items that charge with USB.

Ways to Be Productive in Your Hotel Room

I remember packing my laptop tote for business trips, always including several personal things to get done at night in the hotel room in the evenings. Oh, such an optimist was I!

My real world was almost always different. Dinner took longer than planned, I got back to the hotel later than planned, a conference call with the west coast or overseas was scheduled, and my online fix captured my attention for hours. Seems like before I knew it, poof, it was midnight!

Then I brought everything back home again because I didn't complete my planned tasks.

I know I wasn't alone. Many travelers I speak with are workaholics when it comes to out-of-town trips. They start off on the right track by getting back to their hotel rooms at a normal time, but then it all goes downhill.

Whether it is a dinner with colleagues that goes on for hours, room service brought in while a must-attend conference call takes place, or a quick dinner in the restaurant, then back to your room to finish up tomorrow's presentation – sometimes it ends up being more "work" than "life" in the supposed off-hours.

You justify it. *"Well, if I do the work while I'm away, I can enjoy my time at home,"* or *"I'll just do a little work while listening to TV."*

Trouble is the work and the online activity never seem to end! Meanwhile, one television show bleeds into another and you never noticed!

You finally fall into bed when your eyes can't stay open any longer, right after setting the alarm for a 6 am wake-up call (if you're lucky to sleep in that late). The following morning, a new day dawns with similar results. Think of it as the business traveler's version of the movie, *Groundhog Day.*

Here are some ideas to help balance out the work and still have time for yourself:

- Call ahead to the hotel's restaurant and place your order. Arrive 10 minutes later and your meal will soon be ready for delivery to your table. This saves on the waiting time between order placing and eating. And don't eat in your room with your food tray perched on top of your laptop.

- If you like to get in a workout in during the evening, do it before dinner and before you get online or turn on the television. Better alternative: Get up early in the morning for workouts.

- If you have a conference call in the evening where it's more listen-only, throw on some comfortable clothes and do yoga while listening to the call. At least you'll be relaxing and getting a workout in while you do double-duty with your call.

- Get online and have a long video talk with a family member or friend, maybe someone you haven't spoken with in awhile. This is better than non-stop work and will help clear your mind of business.

- Set a calendar appointment for relaxation time. We adhere to everything else on our calendar, why not commit some time to you? Enjoy a long soak in the tub, play your favorite music, get into a good book.

- To help set the boundaries of your online or television time, call the hotel's wake-up service and ask for a shut-down call instead. They will think you are crazy, but ask them to call you when you want to stop working, say 8 pm. This is just the opposite of a wake-up call.

Here is a tip that deserves its own paragraph. Indeed, it may be the most important tip in time management. While this might sound strange at first, **learn to say, "No."**

I know it sounds counterintuitive but this is how you learn to set firmer boundaries around your time. For example, say no to an occasional evening dinner with colleagues or friends. Use that time instead to connect with family and friends.

Maybe you say no to catching up on the latest television shows or email, instead enjoying an evening turning your hotel room into a spa. Or you may say no to online forums or social media you frequent every evening, replacing them with a relaxing evening in a hot tub.

It's truly amazing how a couple hours or more of true downtime can get you recharged for the next day and help you feel that you've had time for YOU!

When not enough time is taken to shut down from work and relax, the workdays just run together. The inevitable result is feeling exhausted by the time you get home. This is another been there, done that for me.

On the other hand, when you have some time for yourself outside of work, you will feel more grounded, better balanced and much happier. When the time is used productively, that means more family time when you get back home.

Technology

Savvy travelers take advantage of the latest technology to make the most of precious time in the air and on the ground.

Use your smartphone's voice recording device to capture conversations that can be replayed at the end of the day, avoiding the time and hassle of note-taking. I have been using Dragon Dictation on my iPhone and it transcribes my thoughts into words and then sends the transcription to my email. Very handy and decently accurate.

Many travelers use apps on their mobile phones (for example, Evernote) to take pictures of business cards, creating something similar to an online Rolodex. Match these cards with pictures of the person and the recorded conversation – what a great way to remember what you talked about with each person you met!

For system backups (because I know you don't have time to manually recover files and programs if your hard drive goes bad), online backups are great for effortless backups. An automated backup will run on a schedule in the background and magically back up your important files to the "cloud."

Daily Reporting (Expenses, Sales, Time)

After a long day of flights and business meetings, the last thing you want to do is to start updating daily reports. I have yet to meet one person who says they love doing expense reports! They do, however, love getting reimbursed.

It takes only minutes to update your reports if done each day; it can take hours if you wait until the deadline looms or the boss is hounding you. The longer you procrastinate on these daily reports, the more fictitious they become (and not usually in your favor), because it's virtually impossible to remember the day-to-day details.

Remember the saying, *"Inch by inch, it's a cinch. Yard by yard, it's hard?"* Same goes for daily reporting.

The bottom line is that you need to respect your life and be wise with your time. Your personal life does not stop when you travel for business. The values you hold for family and friends, your health, and your spiritual and personal self continue to exist even though you are many miles away from home.

Business travel is part of your life so use as many of these time management tips – along with others you pick up along the way – to make business travel just one aspect of your life rather than having it take over your life when you travel.

13

LOYALTY PROGRAMS:
YOUR REWARD

Μ*y husband and I have countless hotel frequent stayer cards. And now our dog, Toby, can toss his frequent stayer card into the family collection.*

For every five nights at our local pet boarding facility (sorry, I meant to say "Suites"), he gets a free night. These are marked as paw prints on his frequent stayer card upon his checkout. What a great reward program!

Toby's stays include free bowled water, free Wi-Fi and an upgraded room (okay, so it's just a bigger cage where he can stretch out). The Wi-Fi is really more for us. We can watch him from anywhere in the world, via indoor and outdoor cameras, as he interacts with friends, takes a nap in the playroom, and earns his next paw print.

Best yet – he even earns a paw print toward his next award on his free night, too. That's a better award program than what my husband and I receive!

Toby isn't as ecstatic about the free nights as we are since he would much rather be at home than staying in the "Suites." He'd better hope they don't start offering double paw prints as we might just leave him there a few days longer. (Just kidding, Toby!)

As a business traveler, you have sacrificed time with family and friends because your workplace is elsewhere. You have missed family events – maybe even children's birthdays or school recitals – but it was necessary because you needed to be in another location.

It may be painful at times but there *is* a reward, one that can be shared with as many family members and friends as you like. Virtually all travelers can take advantage of loyalty programs. They were created for you and serve as your primary benefit for being away from home.

These programs might give you frequent flier miles, award points, loyalty points, or other aptly named rewards. Regardless of what they are called, they are very popular in the travel industry.

How good are they? The accumulation of miles can be huge. According to Randy Petersen of FlyerTalk and *Inside Flyer* magazine, more than 300,000 people have earned at least one million miles in a single program.

Just about all the airlines, hotel chains, and car rental companies offer some type of rewards program for those who use their services. Nevertheless, I often hear people say they don't want to sign up for these programs but I have yet to hear a good reason why other than you might never use them again. Even that is not a good enough reason.

At the very least, most programs allow you to donate accumulated points to qualifying charities. That means even if you have no plans to add points to your account, you can still help out a good cause by giving them your extra points.

Very simply, these loyalty programs are all upside for you. Just having a membership number tells them you are a customer who wants to do business with them.

That alone may get you better rates or even free upgrades, not to mention easier opportunities to resolve any problems. Many of them send out special travel deals and discounts available only to their members.

 TIP: Sign up for the programs *before* you make a reservation. Adding this information later increases the chance for error.

Do these programs really pay off? My answer is always yes.

With these programs, I have been rewarded with many free flights, upgrades to first class, free access to airport lounges, beautiful hotel suites, free car rental upgrades, as well as free weekend travel, and yes, even free cruises. Indeed, there is an entire cottage industry on the internet dedicated to accumulating and using award points as efficiently as possible.

Airline Programs

As mentioned in Chapter 3, discussion about the airlines is the largest in this book because they have far more rules, regulations and nuances that require additional consideration. The same applies to loyalty programs sponsored by airlines.

The loyalty program idea began about 30 years ago when American Airlines took a small incentive company and turned it into a national loyalty program. Since then, virtually all of the U.S. legacy airlines (American, Delta, United, and USAir) have adopted similar programs. Discount airlines like Southwest and JetBlue also offer loyalty programs to their customers.

Due to space constraints and for ease of discussion, this chapter is limited to the legacy airlines and Southwest because combined, they are the largest programs for most business travelers. Except for Southwest, their structures are similar.

This is not intended to disparage the other airlines in any way. Indeed, some of their flights may be less expensive and they may better serve the routes you need. Alas, it is impossible to list all of them because frequent flier rules change, well, frequently. Instead, this chapter focuses on the programs used by most business travelers.

Even with this limitation, note that by the time this book is printed, some of the specific rules for certain airlines might have changed. It is very common for carriers to modify their programs frequently so if any interest you, follow up by reviewing the current rules on their websites.

Legacy airlines offer two benefits much appreciated by business travelers. The first is business and first class seating; the other is private lounges at airports around the country. Indeed, they may even offer lounge access around the world.

It shouldn't take more than a few moments of business or first class seating on an airplane to appreciate the extra width and legroom. In addition, there is the ability to board first (and get off the plane first), free food and beverage service, as well as other amenities and personal service when needed. The longer the flight, the more appreciative you become of sitting in the front.

Lounge access is a wonderful benefit for business travelers. Lounges are more comfortable and less crowded than gate areas, and they offer food and drink, as well as power outlets and Wi-Fi. Many offer business centers as well, where you can print and fax.

Perhaps the best benefit of lounges is assistance with a delayed or canceled flight. The waiting time to speak with an agent is much shorter than at an airline's gate. Also, agents in the lounges are well trained to assist with changing flights when the need arises.

This is a good place to talk about Southwest Airlines. They acknowledge their program for attracting business travelers has not been as successful as hoped for but they do offer a program that appeals to many. Besides, they are too large an airline to ignore.

True, Southwest does not offer the amenities mentioned above; there is no first class seating or lounge access. Also noteworthy, their loyalty program, called Rapid Rewards, is based on qualifying one-way flights. Generally, a flight is from origin to destination regardless of the number of connections in-between.

Southwest has two tiers, A-List and A-List Preferred. The lower tier requires flying 25 one-way qualifying flights (or 35,000 points) while the higher tier doubles those numbers. Benefits include priority with check-in and boarding, bonus points and a priority phone line.

It is important to understand that there are two types of airline miles that can be earned. One type is called qualification miles, the ones that help you earn elite status with the airlines. The other is called award points, those that can be used to purchase airline tickets as well as other goods and services.

Before discussing the two types of airline miles that can be earned, let's talk briefly about airline alliances. These are partnerships among many airlines.

The largest alliances are OneWorld, SkyTeam and Star Alliance. With some airlines aligning with others in a partnership of this type, passengers are offered more choices in earning and redeeming miles and receiving benefits, even when flying another airline in the alliance.

For example, Delta may be your primary airline, but you want a flight to Europe. You can fly Air France or KLM and still have your miles credited to your Delta account because all of these airlines are in the SkyTeam alliance.

Better yet, when you research airfares, you may find that fares on Air France or KLM are lower than buying the ticket from Delta, even though the flight is the same. When booking an award ticket to Paris or Amsterdam, for example, it may be possible that the mileage cost for an Air France ticket is less than the same flight using miles on Delta.

All alliances work in a similar fashion. This is just a basic example in a world of multi-faceted airline strategies.

Okay, now on to the two types of airline miles.

Airline Qualification Miles

First, a look at qualification miles. The legacy airlines award *elite status* (as it is called) as travelers reach certain threshold amounts. As you will see, the programs vary slightly but all have the same basic format.

American Airlines – Program is called AAdvantage. Three tiers: 25,000 miles/30 segments (Gold); 50,000 miles/60 segments (Platinum); 100,000 miles/100 segments (Executive Platinum).

Delta Air Lines – Program is called Medallion. Four tiers: 25,000 miles/30 segments (Silver); 50,000 miles/60 segments (Gold); 75,000 miles/90 segments (Platinum); 125,000 miles/140 segments (Diamond).

United Airlines – Program is called Premier Mileage Plus. Four tiers: 25,000 miles/30 segments (Premier Silver); 50,000 miles/60 segments (Premier Gold); 75,000 miles/90 segments (Premier Platinum); 100,000 miles/120 segments (Premier 1K).

USAir – Program is called Dividend Miles Preferred. Four tiers: 25,000 miles/30 segments (Silver); 50,000 miles/60 segments (Gold); 75,000 miles/90 segments (Platinum); 100,000 miles/120 segments (Chairman).

Note: Continental Airlines, which merged with United in 2011, is supposed to combine their frequent flier programs sometime in 2012. There has been no announcement as of the publishing of this book as to a specific date.

All airline programs work on a calendar year, not a rolling period, so your status will be based on the number of miles or segments flown as of December 31st of each year.

How do you earn these air miles? Well, by flying, of course. Generally, you will receive one status mile for each air mile flown, though some airlines offer bonus miles for certain fares. In addition, most airlines offer a minimum of 500 miles for each segment flown. They are usually referred to as elite qualification miles (EQM's) but Delta uses a more proprietary term, medallion qualification miles (MQM's).

Also, all the legacy airlines recognize that some passengers fly often but only short distances. Accordingly, they offer a way to qualify for elite status by flying a certain number of segments. You usually need at least 30 segments to reach a minimum status level if you haven't reached that level by air miles already. A segment is generally completed when the plane takes off from one location and lands at another, but you will see there are exceptions.

Here's what I mean. Perhaps you fly every week between Chicago and Cleveland, a short-haul flight for sure. Even with a 500-mile minimum credit for each segment, that would be only 1,000 miles credited to your account each week. If you managed to fly this same route for 50 weeks, it would just barely give you enough credit to achieve the second lowest tier in these frequent flier programs.

Look at the same flight a different way. Flying two segments each week for 50 weeks equals 100 segments. That's more than enough to raise you one elite level on most airlines.

Remember, higher elite level equals greater benefits.

A word of caution about segments: It may seem to intuitively make sense that each time you fly from one destination to another it would equal one segment. Ah, but it doesn't always work that way.

An example will make more sense. Let's say you are flying from Atlanta to Los Angeles but your flight requires a stop in San Francisco.

Very important here: Both flights use the same flight number.

Airlines refer to this as a *direct* flight. Notice I did not say it was a *non-stop* flight. The latter requires that a flight actually not stop anywhere between your cities of origin and destination. A direct flight can have multiple stops as long as it continues to the same destination.

By all appearances, this direct flight would be two segments since you are probably required to deplane in San Francisco. Moreover, it is common that you also need to change aircraft.

However, airlines typically don't recognize this interim stop even if you are required to change planes. To them, it is one flight from Atlanta to Los Angeles as long as the flight number remains the same.

The net result for passengers is losing the additional segment, plus the additional miles flown. You receive the qualifying miles only from Atlanta to Los Angeles, not the miles from Atlanta to San Francisco plus the miles from San Francisco to Los Angeles.

Is it really that big a deal? Applying the direct method, you receive credit for one segment and 1,946 miles. If the two flight numbers are different, you would be credited with two segments and about 2,640 miles.

For someone who is very close to the next elite level, this difference can be maddening. It is a chronic source of irritation for those trying to increase their elite levels but it is airline policy nevertheless. To avoid losing out, be aware of your flight numbers but if you are like most of us, it requires getting burned once before you never forget.

Just what do these qualification miles get you? The answer depends on how many you have. Let's begin with the lowest level at 25,000 miles.

At this level you may enjoy perks such as free checked baggage, expedited check-in, faster security line access (some airlines), some bonus non-qualifying miles, and perhaps the most valuable benefit – an opportunity to receive a seat upgrade to first class.

The second level, at 50,000 miles, adds expanded benefits. These may include special reservation lines, more discounted or free services, greater bonus non-qualifying miles, possible access to international lounges, and of course, a better chance for that first class seat upgrade.

The third level (for some airlines), at 75,000 miles, is where the benefits really increase. Some examples include higher priority access and arguably the best benefit: Upgrade chances ahead of most lower tier elite members, meaning an even greater opportunity for getting a coveted first class seat.

At the published top tier, each airline has a different name but the members enjoy the finest of benefits. All receive dedicated phone lines to airline personnel, many fee waivers, and other discounts. Delta includes a 125% bonus for non-qualifying miles as well as membership to their airport lounges (others offer discounts on memberships).

A side note here, American Airlines and United Airlines offer additional invitation-only levels to their highest elite passengers. The requirements for membership are not published so all I can say is you need to fly a great deal and spend a substantial amount of money on airline tickets to qualify for these programs.

Not surprisingly, these uber elites are the first to receive any upgrades for seats, typically at least a few days before their flights. Then the airlines go down the pecking order, allocating seats to their next tiers.

Obviously the higher tiers are the most desired because they bring the greatest benefits. Also note that as the tier level increases, the number of elite members declines. In other words, there are many more times the number of elite members at the lowest level as compared to the highest level.

This is a somewhat simplistic overview of the most common frequent flier programs. While at first glance they may appear similar, that is not the same as identical.

Some of the differences are more subtle than others, some are very obvious. Read the rules and benefits sections carefully for each airline to see which works best for you.

It might appear that those at the lowest elite level have little, if any, chance of receiving those coveted seat upgrades. According to FlyerTalk, a popular online forum dealing with all travel matters, these elites report receiving upgrades on as much as 50% or more of their flights, a stunning number given their comparatively low status.

Though these numbers are impressive, there are three primary factors that affect receiving upgrades:

- The actual airport. Larger airports, especially airline hubs, are generally known to be what is called elite-heavy. This means that there are more passengers eligible for upgrades.
- Time of the day. Generally, flying mid-day is considered off-peak and an easier time to get upgrades.
- Day of the week. Monday mornings at most airports are extremely busy. The least busy days are Tuesday, Wednesday, and Saturday.

Just how hard is it to get this status? The answer is, it depends. Flying little more than one round-trip a month is nearly enough to ensure status at least at the lowest level.

On the other hand, some will attain at least the lowest level if they fly only once a month, because their distance is sufficient. This is not difficult if you fly just over 1,000 qualifying miles each way once a month, not considered long flights by any means.

Most airline passengers achieve their elite status level by accumulating qualifying miles rather than segments. Here's an example of how it may work.

If you are flying from New York to Los Angeles, a non-stop flight would be about 2,470 miles. If your flight required a connection in, say, Denver, the total would be about the same (1,620 plus 860).

As you can see, some connections are not worth the additional time (and maybe cost) unless this is the airline you fly for status. Most travelers would prefer a non-stop flight over a connection in Denver but you don't always have a choice. For example, the connecting itinerary may simply be more convenient to your schedule or perhaps less expensive.

Now we will change your connection to San Francisco. This provides about 600 more qualifying miles, approximately 3,080 (2,580 + 500 minimum). The distance between San Francisco and Los Angeles is about 335 miles, but as mentioned previously, 500 is the minimum number of qualifying miles for most flights.

That will give you an additional 600 miles each way. All things being equal, this is a good choice as long as you are okay with a longer flight to your destination. Here's why...

Say you do this trip once a month. In the non-stop version, that would be almost 60,000 miles a year, more than enough to meet the criteria for the second tier level. If you do the flight plan through San Francisco, it is just short of enough miles to get you to the third level with most airlines. So, is it worth it to fly the extra miles? The answer is, again, it depends. The reason: There are trade-offs.

Clearly the non-stop flight will get you to your destination quicker. Besides, you may find the flight times more friendly on a non-stop route than on a connecting route. Also note that some corporate policies require you to take the shortest route. The connecting route may be less expensive, however, so this may meet a travel policy requirement.

On the other hand, you can see how those additional 600 monthly miles each way add up to nearly 15,000 more qualification miles for the year. That may possibly be enough to achieve the next higher elite level.

It is important to note that these flights must be on a single airline or sometimes on one of its partner airlines. In the first example, you could achieve second tier status only by applying all your miles to the same airline. If you chose to divide them between two different airlines, you might end up with only the lowest level status on each.

Another way airlines make it easier to reach status levels is by offering promotions from time to time. For example, an airline may offer double qualifying miles on certain routes. Sometimes other airlines match that offer, sometimes not.

It should not be hard to see that if you fly enough of these double-miles routes, your status will increase quickly. Also, airlines may offer incentives from time to time through their credit card offerings. By signing up for their credit cards, you may receive bonus qualifying miles, then receive more miles based on actual card usage.

Some travelers resort to something known affectionately as Mileage Runs. These are routes that allow passengers to maximize the number of miles earned while minimizing the cost. This is best explained by an example.

Let's say an airline that you fly frequently offers a special fare of $200 round-trip for a coast-to-coast flight. Depending on cities of origin and destination, this is about 4,500 miles. The cost for this flight is approximately 4.5 cents per mile, usually less than the normal cost for this route.

Alternatively, let's say the airline offers the flight for $300 but this route earns double qualification miles. That would cost less than 3.5 cents per mile.

Typically, these mileage run itineraries are either same day turnarounds or maybe completed over a weekend. Why would anyone want to do this? Because it is a somewhat inexpensive way to either earn status with an airline or perhaps move up to the next level.

For those who don't have families or just enjoy flying, it may be an exciting way to enjoy greater airline benefits. Obviously this is not for everyone. Moreover, don't expect a business to pay for this because after all, it is a benefit that is entirely yours, not theirs.

If this interests you, check out the **Business Travel Success Ultimate Travel Resource** for sources to assist you.

Status Match

Sometimes people relocate or change jobs and find they need to fly with a different airline. Perhaps a project or key client changes and suddenly you are flying off in another direction with a different airline. If that happens, what about the status with the old airline? Glad you asked.

As always, examples are helpful. Imagine that you have elite status with American Airlines and you relocate to a city they don't serve or perhaps offer too few flight options. After reviewing your choices, you conclude that the best airline for you would be USAir.

This would be a good time to ask USAir for a status match. That's where an airline agrees to match the status you have with another airline. If you have Gold with American, USAir might match that with their comparable Silver level.

Of course I use the term *comparable* loosely because as mentioned, they are similar but different. Some benefits with USAir may be better while others were better with American.

Certain airlines no longer offer status matches. Instead, they offer challenges where fliers need to complete a certain number of miles within a time period, usually 90 days.

Here's how that would work if you are a Diamond level with Delta but you want comparable status with United. The new carrier may offer you a challenge to complete, say, 35,000 miles within 90 days. If you do it, United will grant you a match, which in this case would be their 1K status.

As with most things here, this is part art and part science. Timing is very important, whether match or challenge. Generally, if the match/challenge is prior to July 1st, elite status with the new airline is good only until December 31st of that year. That means you need to complete the minimum requirements before year end or you lose status with the new airline.

When possible, some frequent fliers prefer to complete this match/challenge during the second half of the year. The reason is most airlines will allow you to keep the new status throughout the following year without additional flying requirements in the current year.

In the Delta/United example above, completing the challenge before July 1st may give you status only until December 31st (technically until January 31st of the following year) because of their rules.

However, complete the same challenge after July 1st and United may offer 1K status all the way through the following year. When you are talking about flying at least 100,000 miles to achieve United's 1K status, completing that in six months is difficult for many, probably impossible for most. On the other hand, if there is a chance to have a full 12 months to meet the 100,000-mile requirement, this is realistic for many business travelers.

How do you request a status match? Contact the new airline's customer service department and ask for their requirements. Know that if a status match is given, it is usually a once-in-a-lifetime opportunity.

Is the status really worth it? You bet. At each successive higher level, there is an increase in benefits. What's not to like?

Stick with One Airline or Spread It Around?

Some business travelers have elite status on two airlines, even if at the lower tier. Here are some of the reasons:

- Cost. Sometimes you will find another airline offering a similar flight for less money. Question: Do you take the discount or stay with one airline?

- Already maxed out with one airline. Let's say you flew enough throughout the year to achieve top status with an airline. Is it worth it to add miles to this account or better to put the additional miles on another airline, giving you at least some status level with that other airline?

- Limits imposed by employer constraints. In some cases, your employer may limit you to certain airlines for certain destinations. There also may be constraints related to cost or flight length.

- You relocate and find another airline that suits your needs better.

- One airline might not be the most convenient for your travel. Perhaps a different carrier offers a non-stop route while your status airline requires a connecting flight. Is the convenience of a non-stop flight worth more than the status with another airline?

Very frequent travelers who are able to achieve high level status with two airlines may enjoy additional benefits. For example, some may become United 1K members at the same time they reach Executive Platinum level with American.

This obviously requires a great deal of flying each year but for those who do, rewards include:

- Elite status on two alliances, not just two airlines
- Enjoying the advantage of two airlines' promotions
- Choice of more alliance partner airlines
- Easier routing
- Possibly lower award ticket costs

Everyone defines "high level status" differently but most would agree it should be at least the second level, if not the third. Nevertheless, others prefer to avoid the dilution and maintain a single higher elite level with only one airline. No right or wrong in this case, just different approaches.

Airline Award Miles

Award miles are different than qualification miles. Where the latter helps you with airline elite status level, award miles are used for purchases. Most often, the miles are used for airline tickets but in many instances they also can be used for other products or services.

We will look at the most common use first, purchasing airline tickets. Most airlines offer at least some tickets at the lowest award level, usually 25,000 points for a round-trip domestic flight coach ticket within the U.S. (some limited to continental U.S.). However, it is becoming more common to find that airlines want as much as 50,000 points for a round-trip coach ticket.

Why the big difference? There are probably a couple of reasons. First, each airline sets aside a different inventory of lower priced award tickets. When those are gone, they may raise the award price for any other seats on that flight.

Alas, some airlines are simply stingier about low award tickets. No nice way to say this, some airlines do not set aside many seats at low award levels. For some travelers, it is quite frustrating to pay 50,000 miles for a round-trip coach ticket when they see other airlines selling similar seats for only 25,000 miles. Been there, done that, so I do understand.

What's the Best Time to Book an Award Ticket?

For most airlines, you can begin searching for award seats 11 months (330 days) out. There are many people who are online at the stroke of midnight on the very day that tickets become available to try and score an award seat, especially when multiple seats are needed.

There are other travelers who wait until just a few days before departure to book their tickets. Sometimes airlines may release unsold seats for award space within four or five days of departure, more often seen on international flights. This can be a great time to grab seats for an exciting, last-minute flight, especially in first or business class.

Do not expect to find award tickets just a few days out for high traffic times (holidays or major events) or on the most popular routes.

When looking for an award ticket, many airlines have two or three award tiers. Of course, passengers want the lowest award price possible but each airline decides which award tier they will offer. One thing is certain: If you don't mind paying the highest award prices, those tickets are readily available.

Watch for first class "saver" awards that do not require many more miles than a coach "standard" award. These are great finds and are usually seen during low-demand times and when business travel is slow. Also note that some airlines may offer more award seats – and at lower cost – to their higher tier elite status members.

Hotel Loyalty Programs

Airline loyalty programs are the largest and let's face it, many people like the idea of flying for free. But don't overlook hotel programs. There are far more hotel chains than airlines, giving you a variety of choices. This is why hotels make up the second most popular loyalty programs.

Members of hotel loyalty programs may enjoy great benefits such as:

- Free stays
- Upgrades to nicer rooms
- Early check-in
- Late check-out
- Guaranteed rooms even for late bookings
- Executive lounge access
- Free breakfast, Wi-Fi, and parking

Many hotels allow you to use your points for air travel or other uses. They may also offer exclusive hotel discounts that the general public doesn't know about.

Because there are so many hotel programs, it is impossible to list them here. Instead, a few larger programs are mentioned but these are intended to be examples only, not endorsements. Also note that benefits can vary widely among programs.

Like airlines, hotels have elite status membership levels. Different names are used for each, and the rules for qualifying are also different, but the structure is similar to the legacy airlines. Basically the more you stay, the higher your status. However, you need to read the rules carefully for each one.

Most hotels award status based on either number of stays during the year or number of eligible nights. For business travelers who frequently change hotels during the week, the number of stays adds up quickly.

Qualifying on stays varies by program. Most require 3-5 stays before you reach any elite level, though some may require more. Usually 25 is enough to achieve the highest status level.

Likewise, the number of nights required will vary. With some programs you may need only 5 nights for their entry elite level where others might require 10 or more.

Hilton, for example, requires 10 nights to achieve their Silver level while Hyatt requires 15 nights to reach their Platinum level. Top level status also varies. Some, like SPG Hotels, which includes Sheraton and Westin properties, require 50 nights, while others, like Marriott, need 75.

There are a couple of nice benefits to hotel membership levels that are not usually found in airline programs.

- Some hotel chains let you apply your excess nights from one year to the following year. This rewards frequent travelers by ensuring that the excess nights continue into a year when travel may be less frequent. Also, the rollover nights start at the beginning of the year, helping a traveler to achieve a higher status level by the next year. The only airline that currently allows this is Delta.

- There may be some hotels that allow you to maintain your status level for an additional year beyond that in which you qualify. This can be a huge benefit for those who have a year of frequent travel followed by a year of less travel.

Another hotel-only benefit is receiving loyalty points for using hotel services. This offers great value for business travelers. Need to reserve a meeting room? Most hotels allow you to earn points for this as well.

Copying the success of some airlines, hotels also may offer an invitation-only level for their most frequent guests. They are not published so it is impossible to describe them but I can say that they offer very nice services above the listed tiers, including frequent upgrades to larger rooms or suites.

Hotels frequently offer promotions. One of these is a new member sign-up bonus. For example, Priority Club (which includes Holiday Inn) may offer an incentive of perhaps 2,000 points if you create an account and stay with one of their member hotels within a certain period of time. For this reason, it is generally a good idea to wait and sign up for an account when you are ready to use it.

Many hotel chains also allow "double dipping," which means you not only get hotel points but also airline points. These hotels allow you to select an airline and when you stay at their hotel, you accumulate points for both.

Just as airlines offer free flights, hotels offer free rooms. The total points required for a free hotel stay vary widely based on program, hotel location, day of the week, and whether there are ongoing promotions. Another nice benefit is using points for free rooms at many international locations.

Previously I discussed Mileage Runs. Well, there is a hotel equivalent known as Mattress Runs. Here, travelers will book hotel rooms with the primary purpose of either achieving a higher status level or maybe to receive a bonus of free nights.

Remember, higher elite levels mean more benefits. In this case, it could include free Wi-Fi and parking, as well as executive lounge access. Best part, these additional bennies may be good all the way through the following year.

Some travelers are only looking for short-term benefits. Here is a real life example. One hotel chain offered a deal where if you stayed at one of their properties for five nights, you could get three nights free in any of their hotels worldwide. At least one person took advantage of this in a big way.

This traveler went to Costco and purchased five $100 hotel gift certificates because they were on sale for $80 each. Then he reserved a room at one of the hotel properties for five consecutive nights. The cost for the room was almost $100 per night, including tax.

Each night after work, this inventive guy went to the hotel to check in. To make it easier, he paid up front with one of the gift cards. After paying, he walked out the door and went home, repeating the process over the next four evenings.

I know, this sounds crazy. Why would anyone throw away $400 to get five nights at a hotel where he never even looked at the room?

Remember, this qualified him to receive three free nights at any of their hotels worldwide. Well, he used airline miles to book an award travel ticket in business class to Singapore, then stayed at the hotel there for three nights free. Each of those hotel nights normally costs around $400.

If he had paid for the entire trip, it would have cost thousands of dollars. Instead, he spent a total of $400 (plus some airline taxes) and took a long weekend trip to Singapore. He flew in luxury and stayed in a luxury hotel the whole time.

Again, this is not for everyone but with some planning, there are quite a few creative ways to take advantage of using miles and points most efficiently.

Car Rental Award Programs

The car rental companies are also in the award-giving game and offer benefits for frequent use of their cars. There is much consolidation in the auto rental business, with Hertz and Avis owning most of the companies, but each of the separate companies maintains its own loyalty program.

Frequent renters might enjoy privileges such as free rentals and upgrades, no blackout dates, and bonus points. Also be on the lookout for rental promotions. Like all the other loyalty programs, car rental programs are based on a calendar year.

Hertz offers a couple of elite levels in their program. One is called Five Star (10 rentals annually) and the other is President's Circle (40 rentals annually). Actually, Hertz has a lower elite level known as Hertz Gold. While it includes some benefits, there is a $60 annual fee, though in some cases it is possible to have that fee waived.

I know what you're thinking. Okay, maybe you aren't thinking this but you would be if you had thought about this for a moment.

Hertz gives credits based on number of rentals, not the number of days the car is rented. If you rent a car one time from Hertz for ten days, your status level is Gold. If you do the same thing but return the car to Hertz and pick up a new car each day for ten days, your status level is President's Circle.

Avis has a similar program, called Avis First, where you enjoy their elite benefits after 12 rentals. However, they also allow you to reach this level with 35 qualifying rental days.

National's program, called Emerald Club, focuses on rental credits. You earn one credit for the lesser of one paid rental or for renting a car for four days. Seven rental credits earns you a free rental day.

Thrifty calls its program Blue Chip but it ignores number of rentals. Instead, they reward you with a free rental day for every 16 paid days.

One of the nice features of most rental companies is their offering a program to bypass the counter and check-in. Since the company already has all the necessary credit card information, it allows you to go directly to your car. This usually comes with their elite membership program, such as Hertz Gold, Avis First or National Emerald Isle.

The annual cost for such a program may be covered by your credit card or by your employer, so ask. Also, some of the car rental companies may offer "double dipping," where you can receive airline or hotel points as well.

There are many other car rental companies out there, at least a dozen, along with many that are local to a destination area. At the very least, sign up for their program if they offer one. It certainly can't hurt and it might even give you a discount benefit.

Other Programs

One program is very popular in the eastern U.S. but unknown almost everywhere else. Amtrak has a very loyal following with their points-based Guest Rewards program.

Their top tiers (called Select and Select Plus) require serious commitment to train travel but the rewards are nice. They include bonus points, train lounge access, award travel, and many deals with travel partners.

Even Greyhound offers a program for loyal travelers. Theirs is a little different in that they use a rolling 12-month period for qualifying while the others usually apply your travel to a calendar year.

Nevertheless, they are worth checking out. For example, merely signing up for the Greyhound programs gets you a 10% discount. Your better benefits begin as soon as you complete three round trips.

Actually, Greyhound says you need what they call six "destination points," which would be more accurate. The reason is you can have more than one destination point in a trip.

As an example, you might have three destination points traveling from one coast to the other. The return trip would be the same, enough for you to meet their next level, with additional benefits, simply by booking one qualifying trip.

Credit Cards and Points, Points, Points

Another way to earn points is through various credit cards. This is how many people achieve some of those great awards. After all, if you are going to use a credit card, why not get a benefit for doing so? Virtually all the airlines, many hotels, and some others offer affinity cards. They work like this:

Say you have a credit card sponsored by United Airlines. For most purchases, you will receive one airline mile for each dollar spent. However, they will give you double that if you use the card to purchase a United airline ticket, and you will still get frequent flier qualification miles credited to your account.

A nice thing about the credit cards: Most of those associated with travel vendors offer incentives for selecting their cards. For example, an airline might give you, say, 25,000 miles or more just for getting the card, or for making a minimal purchase with it.

How much is that? Well, it only takes 25,000 miles to pick up a round-trip domestic ticket from some airlines so you are well on your way. Indeed, some will offer other incentives to get you to that 25,000-mile point quickly. In addition, some of these cards may include bonuses for elite qualifying miles as well.

Of course, these credit cards can be used for all types of purchases. This includes groceries, restaurants, gasoline, and sometimes even mortgage payments. It is pretty much anything that you can pay by credit card. Generally, you receive one mile for each dollar spent.

And there are other ways to earn points. Most airlines partner with different companies from time to time. Typically these are nationally recognized retailers whose products cover most everything. It works like this:

If you were interested in a $3,000 Apple computer, you could order it from Apple's website or simply buy it from one of their retail outlets.

Alternatively, you might go to the United Airlines website and find out one of their partners is Apple. If you use the United site link, you pay the same price to Apple but airlines often sponsor deals with companies. In this case, let's say United will give you four MileagePlus points for every dollar spent on a computer.

Here are your options:

- Buy a computer from the Apple website for $3,000; or

- Buy a computer from an Apple retail outlet for $3,000; or

- Buy a computer through the United program where you pay $3,000 and receive an Apple computer plus 12,000 MileagePlus Points with a 4:1 promotion.

All three options cost $3,000 but two of them give you only a computer. The third choice gives you a computer and leaves you only a few points short of a free one-way airline ticket. Which way looks better to you?

 QUICK TIP: If you use a United-sponsored credit card to pay for your purchase, you will actually receive one additional point for each dollar spent. Again using the Apple example, that would be more than enough for a free one-way ticket on the airline.

 ANOTHER QUICKIE: Using this purchase method also keeps your points from expiring. See below for more about this.

 A FINAL QUICKIE: Check the credit card benefits as there may be warranty protection available for your purchases in the event of loss or damage. This may be a benefit not available if you pay by cash, check or other method.

Each vendor has a slightly different program, and special promotions like the Apple example come and go. The bottom line is still the same: It is easy to rack up lots of mileage points. Like I keep saying, there just isn't any downside to this.

Well, I take that back. For some there is a downside but it is not because of the programs. The problem instead is with credit card usage.

As good as these credit card programs may appear, look at all of them with jaded eyes if you are unable to pay off your bill in full each month. Like all credit cards, the interest rates may be extremely high. What I am saying here is that while the benefits may be terrific, the cost may not be worth it. Lastly, note that most of these cards charge an annual fee, though it may be waived the first year. Make sure the benefits to you justify the cost.

What Do I Do with These Points?

I have offered many ways to earn travel points but now that you have them, what do you do with them? Most people use them for travel though some credit cards, like American Express, allow you to use your accumulated points to acquire gift cards for other purchases.

These points accumulate faster than you probably think. If you consider all the purchases you make during the year, including maybe a few flights, you may have easily earned at least one free flight if not two. And don't forget those free hotel rooms either.

Other times, travelers give the points as gifts to friends or relatives, or maybe take a special vacation. In many cases, you can use your points to move up from coach class on an airline to first class. Note that the amount of points varies among airlines.

But there's another use for your accumulated points. Consider giving them to a charity. Nearly all the programs offer you this opportunity, and non-profit organizations appreciate the gift very much.

Very important: Points can expire. Each vendor has their own rules but most have a system where all your accumulated points may expire. Some award points may drop off after a specified period of time while others may disappear due to inactivity. If your account is inactive for a period of time – maybe a year or two – all those accumulated points disappear. Don't let that happen to you.

Always follow up with the loyalty program providers because the rules for accumulating points may change. For an inactive account, you may not even know your award points have already disappeared.

Here's my own boo-hoo story about losing points. For 13 years I predominantly traveled on an airline out of Chicago. Then I moved to Orlando, where a different carrier became my primary airline. I was so busy up in the air that I didn't realize I hadn't seen a statement from the Chicago airline in a year ... or two ... maybe three. By then, not only had my address changed but so had my last name.

I contacted that airline repeatedly but they could not locate my dormant account. Years of mileage and history with them was poof! gone. I wish I had known then about expiring mileage and how easy it would have been to keep the account active with a credit card purchase.

Regardless of the type of loyalty or rewards program, the best time to sign up is before you want to use it. Note that quite a few offer some benefits or a discount to first-time members. If you sign up after making a purchase, you may lose that benefit.

As I mentioned above, there is an entire industry out there of people who share their tips and tricks to maximize obtaining elite status and searching out the best travel deals to get the most points possible. They are also quite generous about sharing the best ways to use points for traveling. Perhaps some of their ideas won't apply to you but to their credit, nearly all of them work quite well.

14

CONCLUSIONS

This book is full of tips on how to be a successful business traveler. It would have been wonderful to include even more strategies on how to maximize some of the travel benefits but time and space limitations make that impossible. Perhaps there will be another book in the future.

However, this is far from the end. My SmartWomenTravelers website (**http://www.SmartWomenTravelers.com**) and my blogging site (**http://www.PearlsOfTravelWisdom.com**) have hundreds of articles with many tips not presented in this book, and most of the articles apply to men as well as women.

BusinessTravelSuccess.com offers live events where even more information is delivered to business travelers to help them integrate business travel successfully into their lives.

Regardless of how much you travel for business, you have learned that there are many ways to define a business traveler. The book began with tips about attending conventions and seminars and always tried to save you money when possible.

From there, we discussed packing, one of the greatest concerns of business travelers. Hopefully the tips about selecting the right clothing and bags will help you to prepare a carry-on bag if that is all you want to take.

Next, we covered just about every possible way to get to work. While most of them are pretty straightforward, the rules for flying are nevertheless quite complex. Unfortunately, flying will always include some issues but if you follow these tips, your flights will be much more relaxing and enjoyable.

Then there were tips and strategies about transportation at your destination. Not only are there many choices but you learned some important questions to ask, along with tips on saving money.

This was followed by an entire chapter on all the things to consider when staying at a hotel. Now you know many more options, the right questions to ask, and some ideas you probably didn't think about before.

Traveling alone and travel safety go hand in hand for many business travelers. You learned some secrets if you desire to be alone, as well as many more when you want to be with others. Most importantly, you know that safety should never be sacrificed. These tips are for you, so please take advantage of them.

International travel is becoming more common. Now you have some great ideas to implement before you travel, as well as when you arrive at your destination. And don't forget the tips about jet lag. It is a chronic problem for many business travelers but following this guide, its effects can be minimized.

You also learned some great strategies for staying healthy and fit on the road. You now have many additional ways to eat healthy on the road, as well as tips for staying fit.

The book then included chapters dealing with relationships and social media. Sometimes these seem to be intertwined but the important takeaway here is that there are all kinds of relationships. These include family, friends, and business associates. Good communication is at the core of all of them but honestly, social media is so woven into our lives today that it is impossible to dismiss outright.

Next was a chapter on time management because this is the single thing most business travelers say they have difficulty, well, managing. That is understandable since time is finite. You now have lots of ways to manage your time better, giving you even more time for other important things in your life.

The book concludes with your rewards, what you earned for the sacrifices made with business travel. There are so many ways to earn free or very inexpensive travel. Learn more about the programs that interest you so you can travel in more comfort and feel "rewarded" for your time on the road.

I hope you learned that business travel is neither a luxury nor a chore. It is simply part of business, sometimes frustrating but more often an important and necessary way to communicate and work with others. At times it is challenging but the rewards can easily make up for any deficiencies.

With this knowledge, you enter the world of business travel knowing that most of what you may encounter in the future has been addressed right here. You are more knowledgeable, and ready to be more productive, as you travel with less stress and more confidence.

We end this book where we began, by reminding you that there are tens of millions of business travelers out there. You are an important one of them with a distinct advantage: You now understand Business Travel Success!

You are welcome to a free copy of our *Business Travel Success Ultimate Travel Resource.* **It is a guide with hundreds of resources to help business travelers. Simply go to BusinessTravelSuccess.com and you'll be directed to how to get a copy.**

If you use any of the social media sites, please stop by and say hello. You can find me on...

- Facebook: **https://www.facebook.com/SmartWomenTravelers**
- Twitter: **http://www.twitter.com/smartwomentrav**
- LinkedIn: **http://www.linkedin.com/in/carolmargolis**

If you have any questions or comments, please feel free to contact me at **book@ BusinessTravelSuccess.com**. As you know from reading this book, I am not on email every minute but I promise you a response.

Welcome aboard, fellow business travelers. I hope our paths connect one day.

Safe and enjoyable travels to you!

Carol

FOOTNOTES

Introduction

1   Travel study by the Travel Industry Association of American, reported by Frequent Flyer Services.

2   Oxford Economics study, reported by the U.S. Travel Association (ustravel.org).

3   U.S. Bureau of Transportation Statistics, 2001-02 NHTS survey of 60,000 people.

4   *Harvard Business Review*, September, 2009.

5   Wakefield Research (wakefieldresearch.com). Email survey of 584 business travelers and 501 significant others, conducted September 24 – October 1, 2009.

6   National Business Travel Association, 2004 Business Travelers Survey.

Chapter 2

7   Reported at **ABCNews.go.com** online August 24, 2010

Chapter 3

8   Bureau of Transportation reported statistics, 2008-10.

Chapter 4

9   NAIC news release November 14, 2007.

Chapter 6

10 Survey by website, Women Traveling Together.

Chapter 8

11 British Airways poll in July 2005, reported by *Entrepreneur* magazine online December 20, 2005.

Chapter 9

12 Reported by the Society of Interventional Radiology.

Chapter 10

13 Interview with Darren Hardy of *Success Magazine*, November 2010.

Chapter 11

14 Reported by USAToday online March 25, 2011.

15 Reported by USAToday online May 4, 2011.

ABOUT THE AUTHOR

Carol Margolis is a 25-year road warrior veteran, traveling the globe over six continents for business. She is the CEO of an international consulting firm as well as founder of SmartWomenTravelers.com, an online community dedicated to women who travel, and author of "70 Secrets to Safe Travel."

In addition, Carol is the creator of Business Travel Success, a program assisting individuals with improving their business travel experiences or making the transition to business travel. She also writes the popular online blog, Pearls of Travel Wisdom. You will find her online appearing on Reuters.com as well as USAToday.com.

Carol is a frequent guest of radio and television, including Good Morning America and Fox News. She is often quoted by such newspapers as USA Today, LA Times, New York Times, and the Wall Street Journal. Carol has been invited to speak to many organizations across the U.S. as well as internationally.

Carol also is active in social media. You can find her on Facebook (SmartWomenTravelers fan page), Twitter (@smartwomentrav), and LinkedIn (Carol Margolis).

HAVE A FUNNY TRAVEL STORY?

While following the tips and advice in *Business Travel Success* should help to reduce the agonies of travel, bizarre and funny experiences happen despite our best laid plans. What can result is the type of story you can't wait to share with fellow travelers as you know they will laugh along with you when you relay the funny things that happened along the way.

If you would like to share your bizarre or funny travel story with a wider audience of travelers, you may just have the opportunity to do so! A collection of funny travel stories, great for sharing over a beer or a glass of wine with fellow travelers, is underway and here is how you can be a part of it:

What can my story be about?

Stories can be about air travel, driving, or luggage. The story might be about renting a car, something that happened at a hotel, or a strange travel event in a city. It might even be a story of what happened at home while you were away or how your child explained your absence at a school event.

In other words, it could be about anything that has to do with travel, either for business or pleasure.

How long will each story be?

We need enough information to be able to complete a story around it. However, the length of each story submitted will vary depending on content. Without trying to be too specific, we estimate most stories received will be in the 500-2000 word range though some might be longer. More detail is generally better than less.

Where can I get more details?

See Submit Your Funny Travel Story at our companion site,

www.smartwomentravelers.com

ABOUT THE FREE ULTIMATE TRAVEL RESOURCE:

Claim your

FREE! Ultimate Travel Resource at

www.businesstravelsuccess.com/resources.

Business Travel Success Ultimate Travel Resource

Sources for productivity, health and fitness, packing, safety, networking, international travel, language help, airport parking, loyalty programs, flight delays ... and lots, lots more!

CPSIA information can be obtained at www.ICGtesting.com
Printed in the USA
BVOW030059010512

289074BV00003B/2/P